STUDENT BEHAVIOUR

STUDENT BEHAVIOUR

THEORY AND PRACTICE FOR TEACHERS

Louise Porter

ALLEN & UNWIN

For Gerard
who tolerated my actual and
mental absences while I wrote this text

First published in 1996

Allen & Unwin Pty Ltd
9 Atchison Street, St Leonards, NSW 2065 Australia

Phone: (61 2) 9901 4088
Fax: (61 2) 9906 2218
E-mail: 100252.103@compuserve.com

National Library of Australia
Cataloguing-in-Publication entry:

Porter, Louise, 1958– .
    Student behaviour: theory and practice for teachers.

    Bibliography.
    Includes index.
    ISBN 1 86373 956 4.

    1. Educational psychology. 2. Students—Psychology.
    3. Behavior modification. 4. School discipline. I. Title.

370.15

Cover design by Liz Seymour
Set in 10/12 pt Garamond by DOCUPRO, Sydney
Printed by Southwood Press Pty Ltd, Sydney

10 9 8 7 6 5 4 3 2 1

CONTENTS

FIGURES AND TABLES

FIGURES

TABLES

ACKNOWLEDGMENTS

I am indebted to the following people for their contributions and support in producing this book.

Colin MacMullin gave inspiration and guidance on the structure of the degree topic that formed the basis of this text, and in particular guided the review of his specialty area of children's social skills.

My colleagues—Colin MacMullin, Brian Matthews and Caroline Storry—plus Gaye McAllister, private practising psychologist, gave detailed and helpful reviews of some chapters.

Stephen Cornellisen guided my review of the literature on systems theory and Phillip Slee did likewise on the issue of bullying.

Finally, I thank all my graduate students who travelled the road of producing this text with me and whose willingness to be enthused and challenged has supported and strengthened my commitment to rigorous theory and practice.

GENDER NEUTRAL LANGUAGE

In the interests of using language that is nonsexist and yet not cumbersome, odd-numbered chapters use female pronouns (she, her, hers) for teachers and male pronouns (he, him, his) to refer to students of either sex. Even-numbered chapters use the reverse gender. In either case, the pronoun used is intended to refer and apply to individuals of either sex.

PART 1

THE THEORIES

1

INTRODUCTION

At this point in your personal and professional life, you have solved many problems and have developed numerous skills. You have a personal and professional style that provides you with a useful foundation for finding solutions to chronic problems. (Molnar & Lindquist, 1989, pp. 164–5)

KEY POINTS

- *While teachers have many skills for responding to disruptive behaviour, they also need to be familiar with theory so that they can explain why they use the approaches they do.*

- *Teachers have two functions: instructional and managerial.*

- *Discipline has several functions: the managerial function of maintaining order so that learning can occur, plus the three educational functions of: teaching children self-discipline, promoting group cooperation, and educating students to participate in a democracy.*

- *Classrooms have certain characteristics that challenge the maintenance of order.*

- *Difficult behaviour is any act that disrupts order and thereby interrupts teaching and learning.*

- *A discipline plan improves a teacher's effectiveness and provides for accountability.*

- *A plan has three parts: the teacher's beliefs, guiding theories and practice.*

- *The theories to be discussed in this text differ in their philosophical beliefs, and this yields differences in their recommended practices. A key belief is their view on the relative status of teachers and students.*

- *Criteria for assessing the theories are introduced, based on maintaining a coherent set of beliefs, theories and practices.*
- *While practice can be eclectic, philosophy cannot.*

INTRODUCTION

This text aims to build on the foundation of teachers' personal and professional skills referred to by Molnar and Lindquist (1989). It is based on the premise that while it is important for professionals to have skills, we also need to be able to explain the approaches we use. Explanation begins with clarifying the teacher's role in classroom management and the purpose of discipline itself, identifying the impediments to order in classrooms, and enunciating the teacher's own theory that guides how she approaches the issue of discipline in the class.

THE TEACHER'S FUNCTIONS

Teachers have two functions, the first dealing with the content of instruction and the second focusing on the process of teaching and learning. The instructional function requires teachers to cover the curriculum, to ensure that individual students master the content, and to promote favourable attitudes to the specific subject and to learning in general (Doyle, 1986). The second function is a managerial one that promotes order through procedures, rules and responding to disruptive behaviour (Doyle, 1986).

Doyle (1986) observes that the teacher's instructional and managerial roles are intertwined: if the curriculum is relevant and attractive to students, then they will be motivated to become involved and cooperate in a lesson. In turn, they are less likely to be disruptive and the teacher therefore has fewer management challenges. In short, quality academic work will achieve order. However, the reverse is also true: order is necessary (but not sufficient) to promote high achievement. Some complex activities are difficult to manage if there are disruptions, and so a teacher who lacks confidence that the students can be orderly will assign less complex academic activities (Doyle, 1986). To create the conditions, therefore, in which students can achieve high quality work, order needs to be a priority for the teacher.

THE PURPOSE OF DISCIPLINE

The purpose of maintaining order is to create an environment in which learning is not only possible but probable. This is the managerial function of discipline. Discipline also has a broader educational function, which has three levels. The first level is training students to take responsibility for their own observance of reasonable rules, that is, to acquire self-discipline (Rogers, 1991). A second level refers to socialising students so that they acquire the skills to function cooperatively in groups (that is, respect the rights of others). The third educational purpose of discipline involves preparing students for citizenship by engaging them in democratic processes throughout their school life.

DEMANDS OF THE CLASSROOM

While many writers have attempted to explain why teachers today report so much student disruption in schools, many of these explanations have more to do with ideology than with data. In contrast, Doyle (1986) reviewed research into classrooms and identified some elements of that special environment that present a constant challenge to order. He lists these characteristics as follows:

1. Multidimensionality refers to the fact that many people with different interests and abilities are sharing the same space and are attempting many tasks. Management choices by the teacher that favour one demand—such as encouraging an individual student to learn some content—may be detrimental to achieving another goal—such as maintaining the group's focus and the momentum of the lesson.
2. Simultaneity, as its title implies, refers to the fact that many different things are happening at once in a classroom.
3. Immediacy refers to the rapid pace of events, giving teachers little time to reflect before acting.
4. Unpredictability refers to the fact that teachers cannot always predict how a given group of students will respond to a particular activity.
5. Publicness means that the actions of individual students and the teacher are witnessed by the other students. This means that an individual's disruptive behaviour can become contagious as the group copy him, and that any teacher errors in judgment about discipline inform the group about the teacher's skill.
6. History refers to the fact that the group establishes routines and norms over time. The group is also responsive to changes in its membership, the time of year and other fluctuations. History also acknowledges that students develop reputations that affect how their behaviour is interpreted by teachers and peers.

These characteristics of classrooms mean that teachers continuously have to monitor and protect teaching and learning from distractions, intrusions and unpredictable events (Doyle, 1986). Management, therefore, is not something that teachers do once so that learning can occur; rather it is an ongoing process of first establishing and then maintaining order.

DEFINITION OF DIFFICULT BEHAVIOUR

This emphasis on order brings us to a definition of difficult behaviour as being any student act that disrupts teaching and learning. The disruptiveness, and therefore inappropriateness, of a particular behaviour will depend on its circumstances—for instance, the activity being done (namely, direct instruction, individual seatwork or group work), its aims, who is involved and the time of day (Doyle, 1986). For instance, clapping wildly when your team wins is appropriate from the sidelines but is disruptive and therefore less suitable during school assembly.

Rogers (1991) draws a distinction between primary and secondary behaviours. Primary behaviours can be classified as behavioural excesses, deficits or behaviour combinations which by themselves would not cause difficulties, but when present together make management difficult (Herbert, 1987). Specifically, these may include unsafe acts, property damage, aggression, immoral behaviour (such as cheating or lying), defiance of the teacher, active off-task behaviour that disrupts others and its more passive equivalent (such as day-dreaming or not beginning work), and violations of a behavioural agreement (Charles, 1996; Doyle, 1986; Grossman, 1995; Rogers, 1991). The humanists describe these or other acts as inappropriate when they violate an individual's rights (Gordon, 1970, 1974, 1991). The individual affected may be the student himself (such as when his behaviour causes ostracism by peers), the teacher or other students in the class.

Rogers' second class of behaviours is secondary acts (1991), which are students' responses to the teacher's correction. These can include defensiveness, arguing, answering back, baiting the teacher, anger, demeaning the activity, and so on. These are typical responses to an assertive message (see chapter 6). The teacher's skill in responding to the primary behaviours can avoid provoking many of these secondary responses.

Doyle (1986) distinguishes between behaviours that minimise a student's learning, such as disengagement, and those that disrupt the flow of the activity for the whole group (disruptive behaviours). He concludes that for the preservation of order in a classroom (but not necessarily the promotion of learning), the minimum requirement is that students cooperate with reasonable requests aimed at preserving the flow of the activity. Failure to do so constitutes inappropriate behaviour.

THE IMPORTANCE OF A DISCIPLINE PLAN

Even though inappropriate behaviours can be annoying, usually a teacher's frustration is directed at herself for not knowing how to respond, rather than at the student himself. Teachers are also under pressure to make decisions on the run: if they lack a rationale or plan, their decisions can be based more on emotion than reason (Canter & Canter, 1992; Rogers, 1991).

Therefore, to reduce teachers' frustration and to improve the quality of their decisions, they need a discipline plan. Having a plan allows teachers to decide what to do with their own behaviour, rather than having their reactions dictated by their students. As well as informing teachers' actions, a discipline plan also provides consumers (students, parents and the wider community) with professional accountability.

A plan will comprise a clear statement of beliefs, a statement of a theory that describes and predicts most eventualities, and a repertoire of practical responses that are congruent with the philosophy and theory.

1. PHILOSOPHY

A philosophical statement will comprise beliefs on issues such as those described later in this chapter. Awareness of her principles or philosophy gives the teacher confidence in her practice and allows her to form a commitment to her approach, which is essential for success (Edwards, 1993; Young, 1992). It also avoids hypocrisy and inconsistencies in practice which will make the teacher less effective and also less respected by students.

2. THEORY

A theory is an orderly set of beliefs, concepts and models (links between ideas) that is used to describe, explain and predict behaviour. Having an underlying theory or rationale for her approach allows a teacher to observe closely the effects of her work and to make changes when necessary. Practice needs to be guided by a coherent theory, for if the teacher relies simply on what works, she has no system for understanding what to do and when (Young, 1992). She may respond to a new behaviour in a way that worked in the past, when instead a new solution is necessary (Fisch, Weakland & Segal, 1982).

3. PRACTICAL RESPONSES

These will focus on ways to establish, maintain and repair order in the classroom.

THE LIMITATIONS OF THEORY

Having described the benefits of theory, it is worth stating that we must also be cautious about theories, for at least two reasons. First, theory is useless without the skill needed to perform the techniques (Young, 1992). Second, while theory is crucial for practice, it can be taken too literally and can be regarded as a higher form of truth rather than just one possible interpretation of reality (Fisch et al., 1982). Theory allows the observer to simplify what she observes and to direct energies towards change on the most central problem. In this way, it provides both focus and direction (Young, 1992). However, an inflexible belief system based on a reified theory biases our observations. We become subject to the theory, instead of using it as a tool for understanding our subject.

A useful theory, then, is one that provides focus and direction without blinding the observer to other issues and to the individuality of each case (Young, 1992). By presenting a range of theories, this text has two aims: to empower the teacher by confirming and expanding her repertoire of responses to student behaviour and, second, to enable a comparison of the various theories so that the reader is able to evaluate rather than adopt uncritically the theories and their recommendations for practice. Criticism rests, first, on an understanding of the philosophical assumptions of the theories.

PHILOSOPHICAL ASSUMPTIONS OF THEORIES OF STUDENT BEHAVIOUR

This text details seven theories about the behaviour of school students, each with its own philosophical assumptions. Given the research diffi-culties, there is little empirical evidence for the superiority of any of the theories in promoting student learning and avoiding student disruptiveness (Doyle, 1986). Instead, the theories differ mainly in their philosophical beliefs about the nature of childhood itself, how learning occurs, the purpose of discipline, what causes inappropriate student behaviour, and the relative status of teachers and students. These assumptions in turn lead to an explication of the teacher's role. It is important to make these assumptions explicit, because that enables them to be evaluated (Fisch et al., 1982).

NATURE OF CHILDHOOD

Theorists either believe that children are deficient in moral reasoning or cognitive skills and therefore need constant guidance and supervision, or they believe children are inherently moral and rational human beings who will behave accordingly when given the chance. A third view is that children are born with both capacities, and that a child's environment will influence which characteristics are expressed.

CONDITIONS NECESSARY FOR LEARNING TO OCCUR

Edwards (1993) summarises three different views about how children learn and develop. The first view is that children grow as a result of external stimulation over which they have little control. This view implies that children and their environments need *managing*. A second view is that children develop from an inner unfolding, driven by biological maturation and curiosity. This implies that children need to be free to direct themselves. The assumption is that if children are permitted to make choices, those choices will be appropriate. Edwards calls this approach the *nondirective* approach, and attributes it mainly to Carl Rogers. The third view is the *leadership* approach which holds that children develop from an interaction between inner and outer influences. Therefore, teachers are advised to take a leadership role with students, showing students how to control their own lives responsibly by monitoring and changing their behaviour when it disrupts others or hinders their own development. The main proponent of the leadership approach is William Glasser (Edwards, 1993).

PURPOSE OF DISCIPLINE

All theories aim to enhance student success in schools by promoting an orderly learning environment. However, some see this managerial role as an end in itself, while others add an educational role with various purposes, including: teaching self-discipline (level 1), fostering group cooperation skills (level 2), and preparing students for democratic citizenship (level 3).

REASONS FOR INAPPROPRIATE BEHAVIOUR

Most of the theories to be covered in this text advocate that inappropriate student behaviour occurs when the internal needs of the student are not being met. They list these needs differently, however, and also highlight either emotional, cognitive or relationship needs. A contrasting view of behaviour is presented by systems theory. It advocates that chronic misbehaviour comes about when a normal behavioural difficulty is unintentionally mishandled, leading to both the behaviour and the response it provokes becoming part of a repetitive problematical pattern.

ADULT–CHILD STATUS

Some theories advocate that to achieve order, teachers must exercise ultimate control of students, while other theories advocate that students and teachers need to be equal partners in managing group processes and developing individual self-discipline. The question of ultimate or shared power rests on the ideological question of whether age (or any other human characteristic) limits one's rights (Walker & Shea, 1995). A second key question is whether it is necessary for adults to have power over children, or whether children can learn self-discipline and still ensure the common good without sacrificing individual autonomy.

Figure 1.1 places the theories of student behaviour on a continuum defined by the relative power of the teacher and students. The theorists on the left of the figure place the power in the hands of the teacher and endorse the use of that power to control children and teach obedience. For instance, James Dobson (1970) believes that unless we punish children, they will not learn appropriate moral (by which he means sexual) standards of behaviour, and will be 'damned in hell'.

In contrast, the democrats argue that not only does no one have the *right* to force someone else to comply, but also that coercion does not *work.* They state that the individual himself must decide that his behaviour is not working for him. The teacher's role is an authoritative one whereby she discusses her standards and teaches students how to meet them (McCaslin & Good, 1992), ensuring that they have the necessary information to make an informed choice about their actions. This is the basis of self-discipline. But while democracy means that the teacher and students have equal rights to having their needs met, they still have different roles. They are equal but are not the same. The teacher has authority to decide *that there will be* expectations for students' learning and behaviour, while the students and teacher collaborate to determine what those expectations will comprise.

ROLE OF THE TEACHER

On the basis of these five philosophical assumptions, each theory then draws some conclusions about the role of the teacher, both in preventing and intervening with disruptive behaviour. The focus of prevention will be the dynamics of the class group, while intervention is likely to focus on an individual student's behaviour, thoughts, feelings or relationships, depending on the theory's underlying philosophy. Doyle (1986) contends that intervention only repairs order in the classroom, while the preventive approaches create that order in the first place. This makes prevention more powerful than intervention.

Figure 1.1   The balance of power proposed by theories of student behaviour management

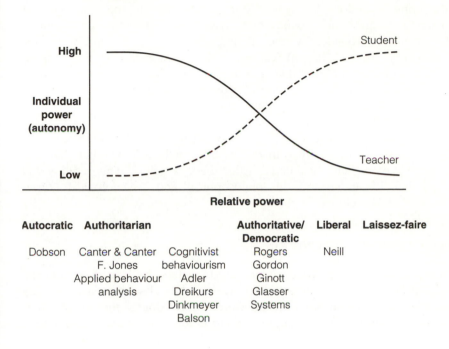

Autocratic	Authoritarian		Authoritative/ Democratic	Liberal	Laissez-faire
Dobson	Canter & Canter	Cognitivist	Rogers	Neill	
	F. Jones	behaviourism	Gordon		
	Applied behaviour	Adler	Ginott		
	analysis	Dreikurs	Glasser		
		Dinkmeyer	Systems		
		Balson			

THEORIES NOT INCLUDED IN THIS TEXT

The theories at either end of the continuum in figure 1.1 are not included in this text. At the autocratic pole, Dobson's approach draws on biblical support rather than on evidence from the social sciences or education. This renders it a philosophy rather than a theory and, for this reason, it is not covered here. The opposite pole on the continuum, which is also not covered by this text, comprises the liberal or laissez-faire positions that suggest adults make little or no effort to discipline children (McCaslin & Good, 1992). These positions have no adherents in the area of student behaviour management.

ASSESSING THE THEORIES

To adapt the theories to arrive at a coherent discipline plan that will work for each teacher, she will need to evaluate each theory as it is presented. The criteria for the reader's judgments might encompass the following dimensions (adapted from Edwards, 1993).

PHILOSOPHICAL BASE

Measuring a philosophy against our own values is the only way of ensuring integrity and avoiding hypocrisy in our classroom management. The teacher can identify the assumptions that each theory makes, particularly on the philosophical issues described earlier in this chapter, and then choose a theory that is consistent with her own beliefs. Central to her choice will be the issue of students' autonomy versus teachers' control, and how this affects children's learning.

The teacher can test the validity of a theory's assumptions through her own personal experience, by reviewing the empirical evidence, and by comparing one theory with others. She might ask whether the bulk of other writers share or contradict this theory's beliefs. This scrutiny will allow her to understand the philosophical and psychological consequences of her choice of theory.

COMPREHENSIVE DESCRIPTION

Next, the teacher can decide which theory offers the best description of student behaviour, allowing her to organise her observations coherently so that she understands the behaviour. In so doing, the theory must agree with her own understanding of the motives for students' behaviour.

PREVENTIVE FUNCTION

Next, she might ask which theory best equips the teacher to prevent inappropriate behaviour?

IMPLICATIONS FOR INTERVENTION

A further question is which theory offers the best cause-and-effect explanations that suggest how the teacher can apply the theory to improve student behaviour? Which theory best allows her to predict and so anticipate the effect that her preventive and interventive approaches will have on student behaviour?

In selecting a theory that describes student behaviour and suggests interventions, the teacher could employ the systems theorists' criteria for a useful theory. These writers believe that there are many ways of describing a behaviour, each equally true but not all equally useful (Fisch et al., 1982). When we are trying to change student behaviour, a *useful* theory would tell us how to promote change. To do this, the theory would have the following capacities (Haley, 1980; Molnar & Lindquist, 1989):

1.   On the grounds that a positive explanation is just as likely to be

true as a negative explanation, the theory would be positive because blaming teachers, students or parents reduces their openness to change.

2. It would allow the teacher to focus directly on ways to change the problem, rather than on diagnosing (or blaming) the individuals involved in it.

3. The theory would suggest what to do, rather than what to think. It would indicate how problematic behaviour can be changed.

4. Therefore, it would focus on the present (which is changeable), not on the past (which cannot be altered).

5. It would generate hope in teacher, student and parent. A positive perspective is essential to this; another tool is to encourage light-heartedness (humour) and open-mindedness when confronted by chronic problems.

6. The theory would embrace the rights of all individuals.

7. A theory of student behaviour would be simple, so that it can be mastered without specialised background knowledge; on the other hand, it should explain most eventualities so that teachers can anticipate the effects of their interventions and so can act in a reasoned way.

CONGRUENCE WITH TEACHING GOALS

Next, the teacher may ask which theory has approaches (processes) that are most consistent with the instructional program (content) being taught? Which approach fulfils her own purpose for discipline (managerial or educational—levels 1 to 3)?

USER REQUIREMENTS

A final question may be which theory can be most easily learnt and implemented? Which theory can be applied by the whole school? Which has practical recommendations that can be employed easily without disruption to teaching?

ECLECTICISM

There is debate in counselling and related fields about the value of adhering to one theory versus adopting a range of approaches in an eclectic manner. To be eclectic means to select what seems best from various theories (Corey, 1991). Eclecticism takes three forms (Young, 1992). The highest form, *synthetic* eclecticism, is an attempt to synthesise or draw together two or more theories and to find common themes in their practices. This creates a new, higher form of theory that blends the originals. The resulting approaches are integrated systematically, which implies that the practitioner must thoroughly understand the principles and philosophy on which the theories are based (Corey, 1991). A second form, *technical* eclecticism, utilises one organising theory but borrows a number of practices that originated in other theories. These practices, however, are still compatible with the over-riding theory. Both the synthetic and technical approaches require that the user understand the philosophy that underpins the theories. A third form of eclecticism is *atheoretical*, whereby practitioners use any approaches without an organising theory. Corey calls this sloppy and labels it the worst form of eclecticism, saying that it represents a haphazard picking of elements of theories without any overall rationale. He says that this type of undisciplined approach can be an excuse for failing to understand the theories adequately, and that it allows the user to pick and choose elements of theories that merely support her preconceived notions and biases.

Synthetic eclecticism, in contrast, has many advantages. The practitioner is not restricted by a specific theory, but still has a personal theory that organises and directs her practice. The theory can be applied and adapted to a range of individual difficulties and can be sensitive to the needs of those involved. An integrated synthesis preserves the integrity of the original theories' philosophy, while leaving the teacher free to employ a range of useful approaches rather than just those contained in the original theories. This makes practice more effective (Corey, 1991).

However, while practice can be eclectic in this way, philosophy cannot be. When blending together a number of theories, the teacher cannot blend contradictory philosophies. For instance, the fundamental philosophical difference between the theories of student behaviour management is their view on the power of teachers versus students. Because this belief is fundamental, the teacher cannot hold the view that students have the same rights as adults to have their needs met (that is, adopt a democratic philosophy) and at the same time use approaches that compel students to behave in prescribed ways (use authoritarian practices).

My conclusion on the issue of eclecticism is that the philosophy behind an eclectic theory must be consistent, even though its practices may have originated from a number of theories. The hybrid will not create contradiction and confusion as long as the original philosophical principles have been preserved.

SUMMARY

The teacher's discipline plan will depend on her beliefs about children and how they learn, about the purpose of discipline, the reasons students behave inappropriately, and the autonomy afforded to students versus the power of teachers to control them. These beliefs will yield a view of the teacher's role. Once the teacher is aware of her beliefs and is familiar with a range of theories of student behaviour, she can generate a repertoire of congruent responses. Now she is empowered: she not only knows what to do, but why.

DISCUSSION QUESTIONS

1. Think about your own goals for maintaining discipline in a class. Are your goals managerial or educative or, if both, which do you emphasise most?

2. If one of your goals for discipline is educative, which level do you believe you promote—self-discipline, group cooperation, or training for citizenship?

3. With which of the theories mentioned in this chapter are you already familiar? Which do you use, and which have you (so far) found unattractive? What beliefs of yours (perhaps on the issues mentioned here) influence your preferences?

4. Think about the approaches you presently use or are familiar with for responding to students' disruptive behaviour. Where and when did you learn these approaches—from study of theory, from other teachers, from your own beliefs, or from somewhere else altogether? Which source was the most useful? Why?

5. What classes of difficult behaviour do you believe are most important for a teacher to address? Are there behaviours that you would include in a list of difficult behaviours but which are not mentioned in this chapter?

6. What effective responses do you presently use for these behaviours?

7. Are there any types of difficult behaviour that your present approaches are less successful at managing?

8. If you are already teaching, do you have either a formal or informal discipline plan to guide you in responding to students' behaviour? If you have been teaching for some years, how has this plan, your beliefs, ideas, and practices evolved over time?

2

THE LIMIT-SETTING APPROACHES: CANTER AND CANTER, FREDRIC JONES

An assertive teacher [is] one who clearly and firmly communicates her expectations to her students, and is prepared to reinforce her words with appropriate actions. She responds to students in a manner that maximizes her potential to get her own needs to teach met, but in no way violates the best interest of the students. (Canter & Canter, 1992, p. 14)

KEY POINTS

- *The teacher has a right and a duty to enforce order so that teaching and learning can be accomplished.*

- *The teacher establishes order and prevents disruptions by being assertive in word and manner.*

- *Warm relationships are established with students to encourage their cooperation.*

- *Rules are taught to maximise the students' ability to observe appropriate expectations.*

- *Positive recognition and incentives build cooperation.*

- *Graded consequences are applied for serious or repeated disruptions.*

- *Teachers need the support of parents and school administration when handling intractable disruptive behaviour.*

INTRODUCTION

Lee and Marlene Canter (1992) and Fredric Jones (1987a, 1987b) emphasise that teachers have both a right and a responsibility to establish order in classrooms so that they can teach and students can learn. Jones's suggestions were derived from systematic observations and comparisons of classrooms being managed successfully and less effectively, while Canter and Canter's approach was born from an attempt to answer the practical problems that they encountered in their own work and, later, in the classrooms of teachers to whom they consulted (Canter & Canter, 1976). Both approaches are skills-based, requiring the teacher to practise the techniques to become skilful at using them (Jones, 1987a).

PHILOSOPHICAL ASSUMPTIONS

NATURE OF CHILDHOOD

The question of the particular needs of children is not addressed by either theory. Canter and Canter (1992) assume that children want and need clear limits on their behaviour so that they know what they have to do to be successful (Charles, 1996), and that they have a right to encouragement when they do achieve the teacher's standards.

CONDITIONS NECESSARY FOR LEARNING TO OCCUR

Learning requires order. Aside from this statement, Canter and Canter detail no other conditions required for learning. This lack of an underlying philosophy about childhood and how learning occurs leads to a unitary purpose of discipline.

PURPOSE OF DISCIPLINE

The purpose of discipline is a purely managerial one of creating order, that is, to maintain an effective and efficient learning environment (Jones, 1987a) through teaching obedience to authority. The goal of order is to provide psychological safety, to protect children from performing behaviour that they would regret later, and to allow individuals to build on their positive skills (Charles, 1996).

REASONS FOR INAPPROPRIATE BEHAVIOUR

Canter and Canter (1992) assert that students no longer respect teachers and education, that their homes lack stability, support and discipline, and consequently children lack the self-esteem and self-control needed to choose responsible behaviour. Resulting behaviour problems in school continue because teachers lack the confidence to be clear about their expectations and consequences for infractions of rules.

ADULT–CHILD STATUS

The classroom belongs to the teacher. The teacher has an unquestioned right to determine expectations and consequences for students. This external control is intended to teach students how to exercise control over themselves, although no specific management approaches are recommended for enabling control to be transferred back to students.

ROLE OF THE TEACHER

The teacher's job is to establish order by defining rules and delivering positive consequences for compliant behaviour and negative consequences for rule violations. These management procedures must always be positive and gentle, developing cooperation without coercion (Jones, 1987a).

PREVENTION

Prevention of classroom behaviour problems rests on establishing and maintaining order. The limit-setting teacher will have regard to the quality of his instruction, his body language, verbal response style (non-assertive, assertive or aggressive), and his relationships with students. These interaction processes are backed up with a discipline plan that details the procedures for promoting order in the classroom.

QUALITY INSTRUCTION

A good curriculum is necessary for maintaining order. Lesson design and presentation, giving corrective feedback, and incentives for diligence and excellence will maintain order, while the teacher's demeanour will establish that order in the first place (Canter & Canter, 1992; Jones, 1987b).

A crucial ingredient of quality instruction is momentum. If the teacher provides lengthy help to individuals, then others are free to be disruptive, while those being helped can become dependent on the teacher's personal support (Charles, 1996). Jones suggests that the teacher giving help should comment on something the student has achieved, give a straightforward suggestion or hint, and then leave, communicating the teacher's confidence that the student will be able to carry on independently. In short, the teacher should 'be positive, be brief, and be gone' (Charles, 1996, p. 139).

BODY LANGUAGE

To establish order, the limit-setting teacher uses assertive body language. It conveys more powerfully than any other medium that the teacher 'means business' (Jones, 1987a). His self-assurance will convey the expectation that students will respect his limits. This does not mean that the teacher is overbearing but instead is calmly confident and supportive. Effective body language can also restore order by giving a non-confrontational reminder to the student about the teacher's expectations, while interrupting the teaching process only minimally.

Eye contact

Even if a disruptive student does not return eye contact, the teacher's gaze communicates that he has noted the behaviour and disapproves of it.

Physical proximity

When one or two students are being disruptive, the teacher can step in close without necessarily saying anything. Physical proximity alone may bring the behaviour back into line. Room and desk arrangements need to facilitate quick access to students.

Tone of voice

The teacher should avoid sarcasm, abuse and intimidation, but instead should convey firmness (Charles, 1996). Also, the appropriate use of humour is a very powerful way to soften a behaviour plan (Canter & Canter, 1992).

Facial expressions and gestures

More than anything else, facial expressions and gestures can convey humour and confidence in oneself and in the students' cooperation (Charles, 1996). Frowns and other expressions can cue students to stop inappropriate behaviour or can re-engage an uninvolved student, without interrupting the flow of a lesson. Touch can be used cautiously to encourage a student, but should never be used to discourage disruptiveness.

ASSERTIVENESS

To set limits effectively, the teacher needs to be assertive. The assertive teacher chooses how to respond to students' behaviour, rather than simply reacting. The assertive teacher is able to communicate his pleasure clearly to students when they are behaving appropriately and can state what he needs when they are not (Canter & Canter, 1976). Students learn what is expected of them, feel good when their achievements are acknowledged, and respect the fair treatment they receive from an assertive teacher. The teacher benefits by having his needs met and achieving job satisfaction from discharging his professional duties well.

In contrast, the timid teacher does not have his needs met because he does not state what he needs clearly, or does not back up his words with action (Canter & Canter, 1976). Students feel frustrated, manipulated and angry while the teacher feels frustrated, inadequate and hostile towards students he 'cannot handle'.

The hostile or aggressive teacher, on the other hand, has his needs met but at the expense of students' self-esteem—by putting students down, issuing threats, or administering harsh consequences (Canter & Canter, 1976, 1992). Teachers feel guilty about being aggressive, while children comply only because they fear and dislike the hostile teacher.

While acknowledging that no one is assertive all the time, the Canters' program aims to encourage teachers to be assertive more consistently.

WARM RELATIONSHIPS WITH STUDENTS

Warm, positive relationships in the classroom allow teachers to have an influence on students (Jones, 1987a). The respect a student receives translates into respect for the teacher's values, rules and opinions. Teachers will need to get to know students and their interests, encourage them to get to know each other, greet students by name daily, have fun together, give individuals a few special minutes, make home visits by arrangement and always help students to do their work, within the specific guidelines already discussed (Canter & Canter, 1992; Jones, 1987a).

THE CLASSROOM DISCIPLINE PLAN

The purpose of a classroom discipline plan is to avoid hasty, timid or hostile responses to student behaviour, so that the teacher's response can be consistent and therefore predictable for students. It also enables the teacher to get support from parents and school administrators. While the plan is designed to apply to all students, on occasions modifications are made for individuals whose behaviour is not improving under the class-wide plan. The plan consists of rules, positive recognition and consequences that result when students do not follow the rules.

RULES

General rules

General rules are guidelines about good behaviour and good work habits (Jones, 1987a). Canter and Canter (1992) suggest these general rules: follow directions; keep hands, feet and objects to yourself; no teasing or name calling; no swearing. These rules are observable, and they apply throughout all classroom sessions. (Behaviour outside the classroom is dealt with by a school discipline plan and does not affect the classroom plan.) Students can contribute to determining rules (Canter & Canter, 1992; Jones, 1987a), although the teacher will need to guide them in not making their expectations too strict.

Specific rules

These detail the procedures that students need to observe when carrying out specific activities; they also specify standards for students' work (Jones, 1987a).

Teaching the rules

The teacher must thoroughly teach the rules, since he cannot assume that students will know the rules and so cannot simply announce them and expect that students will understand them. Instead he should describe the rules and explain what they mean, why they are in place and what will happen when they are violated. He may direct younger children to rehearse rules and procedures. The positive consequences should be described also. At each teaching step, the teacher should check that the students understand what is expected of them.

POSITIVE RECOGNITION

Positive recognition is 'the sincere and meaningful attention you give a student for behaving according to your expectations' (Canter & Canter, 1992, p. 57). Its aims are to motivate students to repeat appropriate behaviour and so reduce disruptive behaviour, to increase their self-esteem, and to create a positive environment for the class and positive relationships between the teacher and each student. Positive recognition is especially crucial during the first days of working with a class, but remains a high priority all year since it conveys the message that the way to gain teacher attention is to obey rather than to disrupt.

The first form of positive recognition is praise, which must be simple, direct, personal, genuine, specific and descriptive. Calling parents, giving students awards, awarding special privileges and tangible rewards might also be included in the teacher's discipline plan. These more formal forms of recognition can be applied to the whole class as needed rather than being in place permanently, while recognition of individuals' compliance is a permanent feature of the discipline plan. Older students may be embarrassed by public positive recognition, so instead it can be delivered in private. So that the older student learns to feel good about herself, the praise can be followed with a statement such as, 'You should be proud of yourself'. Another way to avoid an individual's public embarrassment is giving the whole group bonus points for individuals' successes.

The criteria for earning a reward need to be reasonable and realistic for the students' ages (Canter & Canter, 1992).

GROUP INCENTIVES

An incentive system is a program for delivering reinforcers for cooperative behaviour.

Informal systems

The student–teacher relationship is 'money in the bank' (Jones, 1987a, p. 148): its quality determines how willing students are to cooperate with their teacher. A warm relationship is necessary but not sufficient for discipline, however, so formal systems for delivering reinforcers will need to be developed as well.

Formal systems

Jones (1987a) contends that incentive systems have to be cost-effective: while a particular plan might work, it may take up too much teacher time to plan and execute, especially when tailored for individuals. Therefore, Jones devised a group incentive system based on 'responsibility training'. A simple incentive involves Premack's principle (see chapter 3) or 'Grandma's rule'—that once you complete something distasteful, you can have something you like. Three elements are in operation here: the task, the reward, and monitoring to check that the reward has been earned.

These simple incentives are difficult to operate for a whole class, because a few individuals will abuse them. For this reason, more complex incentive systems are needed. Two elements are added: bonuses and penalties. A complex system involves rewarding the whole class for orderly behaviour by allocating a certain amount of time for them to do a preferred activity, which is both fun (so that students want to do it) and educationally valuable (so that the teacher can justify the time it takes). Canter and Canter (1992) advise the teacher not to impose fines for misbehaviour, while a central feature of Jones's system is penalties for individual misbehaviour. Jones uses a stopwatch to time any student's infraction of a rule (even one as basic as having to sharpen a pencil because she did not have a sharp one ready ahead of time). The time it takes for the individual to correct her behaviour is subtracted from the time the group is allowed to engage in the preferred activity. The whole class is penalised if a single individual breaks a rule (Edwards, 1993; Jones 1987a, 1987b). The exception is a student who loses self-control altogether, in which case she is removed from the room rather than penalising the whole class.

Jones (1987a) gives detailed advice on fine-tuning the incentive system to suit individual students and particular situations. This is beyond the scope of this text, although the reader is referred to Jones (1987a) for more detail.

INTERVENTION: ENFORCING THE LIMITS

The limit-setting sequence follows an invariant series of steps, which are terminated when the student corrects her behaviour. The process is based on firmness as well as kindness, even when the student is being nasty to the teacher (Jones, 1987a). This demeanour helps students accept responsibility for their own behaviour and models the maturity and self-possession the teacher wishes students to learn.

MONITOR THE CLASSROOM

The teacher needs to stand where he can see most of the students readily, and needs to listen for disturbances that he cannot see.

TERMINATE INSTRUCTION

Disruptive behaviour entertains students so it has its own rewards. Therefore, Jones (1987a) advises teachers not to ignore it because fun, not teacher attention, is maintaining the behaviour. Instead, the teacher should stop teaching, and begin the following steps to quell the behaviour.

1. *Face and name the disrupting student.* First, the teacher faces the most disruptive student squarely and gains eye contact, to convey the expectation that she will cease her disruption.
2. *Move in.* If the ringleading student does not turn her body fully back to her work in response to the teacher's direct gaze, then it is clear that she is not committed to returning to work. In that case, the teacher will move unhurriedly to the student's desk and stand in front of it for the count of two slow breaths. This pause gives both

the teacher and student time to calm down and gives the student time to think about her behaviour.

3.   *Prompt.* The teacher leans with one palm on the student's desk and states exactly what he wants the student to do. He stays in that posture for two breaths.

4.   *Camp out in front.* If this does not provoke a return to work, the teacher slowly moves in closer by leaning on both palms placed on the student's side of the desk. At no time does the teacher offer academic help, since disruption is not the correct procedure for seeking or gaining help.

5.   *Camp out from behind.* If two students continue to talk while the teacher is camping out in front of a student's desk, then he can move around behind the students and place himself physically between them.

6.   *Move out.* At whatever stage the student resumes work, the teacher watches for two breaths (15 seconds) and then thanks her genuinely for cooperating. The teacher will then move in on an accomplice and repeat the moving out sequence, even if the second student is already back on task.

7.   *Return to instruction.* Finally, the teacher returns to the student he was instructing, and pauses to watch the disruptive students for two breaths before resuming his instruction. If a disruptive student issues a cheap shot while the teacher is moving out, the teacher recycles the limit-setting steps, beginning with moving in.

8.   *Responding to back talk.* During the limit-setting steps, a student may back talk by asking for help, denying responsibility for the disruption (which is sometimes paired with blaming someone else), accusing the teacher of causing the problem through his poor teaching, inviting the teacher to leave, insulting the teacher, using profanity, crying, giving compliments, saying something irrelevant, or pushing the teacher aside (Jones, 1987a). Regardless of the content of these plays, they are all attempts to gain control. The teacher must stand his ground impassively without saying anything. To reaffirm his resolve, the teacher may lean on elbows rather than palms, and wait.

CONCLUSION: THE LIMIT-SETTING SEQUENCE

Jones (1987a) details variations on this sequence, such as how to respond when a student says something genuinely funny while the teacher is camped out at her desk, what to do when the teacher is already behind the student when she disrupted, and when not to use the sequence at all.

NEGATIVE SANCTIONS (CONSEQUENCES)

If limit-setting fails, then a backup system of a series of progressive negative sanctions is needed. Negative sanctions suppress severe disruptions and buy time for the teacher to consult parents and the school administration (Jones, 1987a). Any backup system of sanctions will be over-used if it stands alone. It can only repair order, not establish it, and so will be effective only in the context of an overall management plan.

The chosen sanctions cannot add to the teacher's workload and must be cost-effective, since the process of management cannot become more important than teaching. Canter and Canter (1992) contend that consequences are not punishments (which are something teachers *do* to students) but are a natural outcome of students' behavioural choices. They are something that students do not like but they are not physically or psychologically harmful. The students must not be humiliated or embarrassed.

Consequences do not have to be severe, since it is their inevitability, not their severity, that has an impact. They must be delivered in a calm, matter-of-fact manner, when the teacher does not threaten, but only reminds a student about the consequences if she continues to behave inappropriately. A consequence must be followed with positive recognition when the student returns to appropriate behaviour.

In the first instance, the teacher deals with the behaviour himself, but then calls on the school administration and parents as the need arises, and finally invokes social welfare agencies and the criminal justice system if necessary. Canter and Canter (1992) advise teachers to apply consequences in a step-wise manner for repeated infractions on the same day, and to start each new day with a clean slate.

The first infraction is met with a warning, comprising the teacher's assertive message or a request for appropriate behaviour. The limit-setting sequence would constitute this first warning. The second and third infractions earn a consequence such as a brief time-out period, or a 1-minute wait after class. For the fourth infraction on the same day (in primary school) or in the same lesson (in secondary school), the teacher would contact the parents or have the student ring them herself. The final consequence (for the fifth violation) is being sent to the principal, with this having been planned in advance so that the teacher knows what support he will receive from the principal. This sanction is also invoked for dangerous behaviour that needs an immediate intervention. Canter and Canter (1992) call this the 'severe clause'.

To keep track of the infractions of individual students' behaviours and their consequences, the teacher is advised to write these on a clipboard rather than on the blackboard so that students are not publicly humiliated.

Students will need an 'escape mechanism' that allows them to tell their story later, but not while a lesson is in progress. This may mean that a student is allowed to write down what she wants to say, which she and the teacher discuss together later.

CONCLUSION: THE DISCIPLINE PLAN

Canter and Canter (1992) caution the teacher to use the discipline plan as a tool rather than as a law. A counselling approach is built in to help the teacher tailor the plan to suit individual needs. Counselling will occur outside class time and will begin with asking the student if something is the matter, since the teacher cannot assume he knows why the student is misbehaving. The teacher can offer to help in some way such as by moving the student away from a troublesome peer, giving academic help, or renewing his commitment to giving positive recognition. The aim of such a discussion is to gain an agreement to a specific plan for improved behaviour.

OBTAINING SUPPORT

No teacher can work successfully with each and every student. Sometimes, support from parents and the school administration is necessary. The first step for achieving this is for the teacher to advise parents and administrators of his classroom discipline plan and to make routine and positive contact with all parents early in the school year (Canter & Canter, 1992; Jones, 1987a) through phone calls to all parents or only to those whose sons or daughters are most likely to present difficulties, or through form letters to all parents (Jones 1987a). Sending a student's work home can also promote contact with parents.

Once a behaviour problem arises, the teacher will document the steps he has taken to handle it. Canter and Canter (1992) advise a teacher to contact parents at the first sign of a problem that he would like to hear about if he were the child's parent. When calling, the teacher will need to state his specific concerns, describe what action has been taken so far, listen to the parent's view of the problem and suggestions for handling it, agree on what the teacher and parent will each do to solve it, and arrange for a follow-up call. The teacher will express confidence that the behaviour can be mended. School administrators can be supportive by counselling or arranging for counselling of the parent or student, setting up a meeting with the parent and the school, and instituting in-school suspensions.

SUMMARY

Canter and Canter (1992) and Jones (1987a, 1987b) detail a discipline plan that requires the teacher to set limits on students' behaviour so that order is maintained and teaching and learning can occur. The teacher is assertive both in word and manner, while being warm and supportive with students. He teaches rules and rewards compliance with personal and formal recognition and incentives. If disruptive behaviour occurs, the teacher can enforce the limits, and will invoke backup sanctions if this fails. The teacher is empowered to seek support from parents and the school administration when faced with intractable disciplinary problems.

CASE STUDY

Adam is seven. He has difficulty with reading, spelling and writing, although he enjoys and is capable at maths. During non-maths lessons, you have noticed that he spends a considerable amount of time off-task, when he frequently disrupts the other students. This is worse in the afternoon than in the morning.

He is in a composite class of six and seven-year-olds. He spends most of his play time with the younger children. Frequently a pair including Adam is apprehended during play times doing such things as harassing passers-by from an out-of-bounds area of the playground which is close to the street, rifling through rubbish bins for food or cans to swap for other items with students, or engaging in fights in and around the toilets.

He seems bemused by the trouble he gets into, usually saying when challenged that he doesn't know why he behaves in these inappropriate ways, that he couldn't remember a given behaviour was against the rules, or that the other child was at fault for suggesting the activity.

Until a recent assessment, it was believed that Adam behaved as he did because of low academic ability. However, a battery of tests has shown his overall ability (IQ) to be average, with his maths skills in the high-normal range and his reading and spelling skills, while delayed, still within the lower range of normal limits. Teaching staff are now at a loss for a new explanation of his behaviour.

A LIMIT-SETTING APPLICATION

Under a limit-setting approach, a teacher might respond to Adam's behaviour with the following steps:

Step 1: Adopt an assertive demeanour Adam's teacher realises that he has been non-assertive with Adam, sometimes virtually pleading with him to 'pull his socks up', but also at other times, he has expressed some frustration at Adam's behaviour and has been punitive and almost hostile. The teacher practises verbal assertiveness, and resolves to make his body language convey more confidence in his handling of Adam, so that Adam learns his teacher is to be taken seriously.

Step 2: Reduce Adam's dependence on supervision The teacher has been taking responsibility for Adam's behaviour by reminding Adam to bring required equipment to school or to do his homework, and by giving Adam excessive one-to-one guidance in class about his work. To teach Adam to work independently, the teacher resolves to give him only brief instructional help. This will be done in the three steps Jones recommends, namely: 'be positive, be brief and be gone'. The teacher will seek to convey to Adam that he (the teacher) is confident that Adam can work alone successfully.

Step 3: Foster a warm relationship The teacher's frustration and near-hostility towards Adam will have harmed his relationship with Adam. The teacher will therefore make some time to be alone with Adam to get to know him better and take an interest in what Adam enjoys. Until now, when Adam has worked appropriately, the teacher has felt relieved that this has freed him to work with other students; from now on, the teacher will increase his rate of positive recognitions of Adam for his appropriate behaviour.

Step 4: Teach the rules Adam clearly knows about the rules, but not how to observe them. In a class meeting, the teacher will instruct all the students about what the rules are, why they are in place, the positive and negative consequences of infractions and reasons for them, and how to abide by the rules. Adam and all students will be given the opportunity to check their understanding of the rules and to role-play how to observe them.

Step 5: Distinguish between in-class and out-of-class infractions The teacher will stop being responsible for infractions of the rules in the playground. This is the responsibility of the school as a whole, guided by its discipline policy. In class, the teacher will consistently enforce the limits taught to the group in step 4.

Step 6: Use the limit-setting sequence Adam's teacher will respond to Adam's off-task or disruptive behaviour in a sequence of graded steps suggested by Jones (1987a). He will not ignore this type of behaviour and will suspend instruction whenever Adam or any other student is disengaged or disruptive. The steps of facing and naming the student, moving in, giving a prompt, camping out in front (or behind, as required) and moving out will be enacted routinely and calmly.

Step 7: Use incentives If Adam is just one of many disruptive students, the teacher will set up a group incentive program; if Adam is the only student whose behaviour is seriously disruptive, the teacher will establish an individual program with the incentive of time spent on a preferred activity.

Step 8: Invoke negative sanctions (consequences) If Adam disrupts repeatedly in the same day, the teacher will invoke a series of consequences. The limit-setting sequence will be considered as a warning, and later consequences will be time out from the class or staying back briefly at the end of a session.

Step 9: Obtain support Any further infractions on the same day will lead to Adam's parents being called. Also, the teacher and the principal will plan what they will do if Adam needs to be sent to the principal in the future. This final consequence might involve a conference with the principal, perhaps in conjunction with the parents.

Step 10: Devise a plan If earlier steps prove unsuccessful, in consultation with Adam's parents and the principal, the teacher will devise a plan for responding to Adam's behaviour. The plan will refine, adapt and add to the interventions already tried. The plan will be monitored and follow-up meetings will discuss and reach agreement on any changes necessary to increase its effectiveness.

DISCUSSION QUESTIONS

1. Do you agree with Canter and Canter's assertion that children *need* adults to exercise control over them?
2. Do you see any pitfalls in the assumption that external controls will teach children to exercise self-discipline?
3. What do you think your own body language conveys to students? Does it contribute to a picture of a teacher who is assertive, non-assertive or aggressive?
4. What rules would you include in your classroom discipline plan? How would these be established and taught to students?
5. Do your rules highlight order, or do they have a broader educational aim?
6. What forms of positive recognition do you routinely use (or plan to use) when you teach? Are they individual or given to the class as a whole? How effective are they?
7. Would you feel comfortable using Jones's limit-setting sequence? What steps, if any, would you want to modify?
8. What do you think about the use of negative sanctions? Are they necessary? Effective? Practicable? Under what conditions would you apply negative sanctions?
9. At what point do you (or would you) plan to involve a student's parents in their son or daughter's school behaviour problems? What routine communications with parents do you favour prior to advising them of their son or daughter's difficult behaviour?
10. What supports do you have or would you like to receive from your school for any students in your class who have difficult behaviour?
11. Write your own case study. What responses would a limit-setting approach recommend for that student?

SUGGESTIONS FOR FURTHER READING

For a summary of the limit-setting approaches:

Charles, C.M. 1996, *Building classroom discipline: from models to practice*, 5th edn, Longman, New York.

For a detailed description of assertive discipline:

Canter, L. and Canter, M. 1992, *Assertive discipline: positive behavior management for today's classroom*, Lee Canter and Associates, Santa Monica, California. This edition is strictly limited to participants in assertive training courses. Instead, their 1976 volume, *Assertive discipline: a take charge approach for today's educator*, Lee Canter and Associates, Santa Monica, California, covers similar material and may be more widely available.

For a detailed description of Fredric Jones's approach:

Jones, F.H. 1987a, *Positive classroom discipline*, McGraw-Hill, New York.
——1987b, *Positive classroom instruction*, McGraw-Hill, New York.

3

APPLIED BEHAVIOUR ANALYSIS

A major concern within the behavioural approach to teaching is with the identification of things and events which children find rewarding and to structure the teaching environment so as to make access to these rewards dependent upon behaviour which the teacher wants to encourage in his class. (Wheldall & Merrett, 1984, p. 19)

KEY POINTS

- *Behaviour is controlled by the response it receives (its consequence).*

- *The environment (antecedents) can also make behaviours more or less likely to occur.*

- *Behaviours can be increased by delivering a consequence that the actor values (a reinforcer) immediately after the behaviour is displayed. Reinforcers vary in intrusiveness (which is the extent to which they interrupt teaching).*

- *Behaviours can be decreased by delivering a consequence that the actor dislikes (a punishment) immediately after the behaviour is displayed. Punishments vary in their restrictiveness (the extent to which control is external to the actor).*

- *The behaviour to be changed (the target behaviour) must be described in specific terms.*

- *A program's effects must be monitored. Measurement is done by recording the frequency or intensity of the target behaviour before and during intervention.*

- *Behaviours must be manipulated by the least restrictive and intrusive methods that are practicable.*

- *Ethical issues inherent in applying external controls need particular attention when designing an applied behaviour analysis program.*

INTRODUCTION

As its title implies, applied behaviour analysis (ABA) focuses on behaviour rather than thinking or feelings, even though it acknowledges that these exist. This is because behaviourists believe that we cannot change a student's thinking and feelings. Instead ABA aims to change the conditions that surround a behaviour, so that a desirable behaviour is strengthened by receiving a favourable response from others and an undesirable behaviour is either no longer provoked by its circumstances, or is no longer maintained by the positive response it receives.

PHILOSOPHICAL ASSUMPTIONS

NATURE OF CHILDHOOD

Children are behaving beings, and so their actions are governed by the same rules that apply to the behaviour of adults.

CONDITIONS NECESSARY FOR LEARNING TO OCCUR

Skinner (1989) states that learning is not an act: it is changing how we act (acquiring a new behaviour). The individual may begin a new behaviour by imitating another person, and that behaviour is then maintained by its consequences. Therefore, consequences shape learning.

PURPOSE OF DISCIPLINE

Behaviourists would define the main purpose of discipline as a managerial one of maintaining or reinstating order so that students can be successful at learning. Given the complexity of ABA technology, while the theory can be used to *maintain* order, mostly it is used to *restore* order. This makes its prime purpose interventive rather than preventive.

REASONS FOR INAPPROPRIATE BEHAVIOUR

Behaviour, appropriate or otherwise, is more likely to recur when it receives a positive response that is, when the behaviour *works*. Therefore, to change inappropriate behaviour, the adult must change the response it receives.

ADULT–CHILD STATUS

From Wheldall and Merrett's statement (1984) that opened this chapter, it is clear that the teacher remains in control of the students. She manipulates their external environment to alter the probability that they will behave in certain ways. However, latest applications of ABA do consult students about their actions, the conditions that give rise to them, and their effects on others. The more student involvement there is, the less authoritarian ABA becomes in practice.

ROLE OF THE TEACHER

Watson (1913, in Heward & Cooper, 1987, p. 7) wrote that the goal of ABA is 'the prediction and control of behaviour'. This, plus the opening quote, gives a succinct description of the teacher's managerial role: to structure the responses to student behaviour in such a way that desired behaviour is more likely to recur, and undesired behaviour is displayed less often.

BEHAVIOURIST PRINCIPLES

Behaviour is any action the individual does (Axelrod, 1977). It can be of two types: reflexes, such as eye-blinking (which are termed *respondent* behaviours), and all other behaviours (termed *operant* behaviours), which are voluntary. ABA draws on a series of principles to identify the lawful (that is, predictable) relationship between a voluntary behaviour and the events that follow it (consequences).

PRINCIPLE 1: CONSEQUENCES

All voluntary behaviour (as distinct from reflexes) is controlled by its consequences. These consequences will *reinforce* the behaviour (result in its increase), *punish* (result in a decrease in the behaviour) or will be *neutral* in their effects (the behaviour rate will be unchanged).

PRINCIPLE 2: ANTECEDENTS

It is not enough to explain behaviour by describing its consequences only. We must also note the conditions under which the behaviour occurs. These are the *antecedents*. Antecedents can greatly increase the likelihood that a given behaviour will occur, and so these conditions must be understood in detail so that preventive measures can be enacted (Bailey & Pyles, 1989; Horner, 1994).

There are many advantages of altering the antecedents rather than the consequences. It can be easier to change the antecedent, and also more humane and ethical than allowing the student to get into trouble unnecessarily. Changing the antecedent can remove the need for an intervention, and is also more likely to ensure that behaviour improvement is maintained (Bailey & Pyles, 1989).

Thus, addressing antecedents is the first step in a behavioural program, followed by altering the consequences only if the first step is unsuccessful. General antecedents can be addressed by ensuring the students have a comfortable working environment, with adequate space and materials, an effective instructional program that maximises their engagement, and a high level of natural reinforcers (Wolery, Bailey & Sugai, 1988). More specific and individualised manipulation of antecedent conditions may be suggested by affirmative answers to the following questions (adapted from Bailey & Pyles, 1989):

- Are there any circumstances under which the behaviour does *not* occur?
- Are there any circumstances under which the behaviour *always* occurs?
- Does the behaviour occur at certain times of the day?
- Does the behaviour occur only with certain people?
- Could the behaviour be related to any skills deficit?
- Does the behaviour occur during certain seasons of the year?
- Could the behaviour be a result of any form of physical discomfort (including allergies or food sensitivities) or side effects of medication?
- Does the behaviour allow the student to gain attention, which may imply that there is insufficient attention (an antecedent) in the normal teaching situation?
- Does the behaviour allow the student to escape the teaching session, in which case some aspect of the material or teaching process is aversive to the student and acts as an antecedent for the behaviour?
- Does the behaviour occur to offset loneliness or boredom?
- Does the behaviour occur as part of a chain of behaviours?
- Does the behaviour occur as a result of having another ongoing behaviour terminated?

PRINCIPLE 3: DEFINING TARGET BEHAVIOURS

The behaviour that is of concern and becomes the focus of intervention is termed the *target* behaviour. This must be defined precisely in behavioural terms rather than diagnostic ones—that is, in terms of what actually *happens* (for instance, student A hits student B during library session) rather than by labelling the behaviour or the student (for instance, student A is aggressive). The behaviours must be observable and measurable, which means their frequency and duration can be quantified. The definition of the target behaviour must be complete or comprehensive so that the behaviour can be discriminated from others that are not the focus of intervention.

PRINCIPLE 4: OBSERVATION AND RECORDING

Systematic observation and recording of the antecedent conditions and consequences that surround a behaviour are used to establish how often the behaviour occurs, under what conditions, and what response it engenders. This information is used to plan an intervention and to check whether it is having an effect. Data collection is essential to the accuracy and success of any behaviour modification program, because intuitive judgments about improvement or lack of change may be inaccurate and are subject to the observer's discouragement and mood fluctuations.

Observation and recording can focus on:

- the *frequency* of the behaviour, which is the number of times it occurs
- its *rate*, that is, the number of times the behaviour occurs within a specified time period
- the *accuracy* of the behaviour, for instance the number of items the student gets right on a series of tests over time
- the duration of each instance of the behaviour
- its *intensity*
- its *latency*, which refers to the amount of time it takes for a student to begin a task once instructed.

Every instance of the behaviour can be recorded, which is termed *frequency* or *event recording*. Another method is *interval recording* in which the observation period is divided into time intervals, and the observer notes whether the behaviour did or did not occur during, throughout, or at the end of each interval. Intervals need to be short enough that success will be demonstrated by the behaviour occurring in fewer and fewer intervals.

A more descriptive method of data collection, termed descriptive analysis (Lalli et al., 1993) involves observation of the student and teacher in their natural setting and analysing possible reinforcement contingencies maintained between them, rather than observing the student's behaviour alone. This analysis then forms the basis for individualised programs to change the reinforcement contingencies.

The observation method chosen depends on the type of behaviour, the context in which it is occurring, and the time available to the observer. The classroom teacher may not be able to use the more intensive observation and recording procedures because of their heavy demands on her time, and so for accurate observation, she may have to call in an observer.

PRINCIPLE 5: ESTABLISHING BEHAVIOURAL OBJECTIVES

Having observed the target behaviour and the conditions under which it occurs, the teacher then defines her behavioural objective for the student. In positive terms, the objective states what modified form the target behaviour will take as a result of successful intervention—that is, it states what the student will be doing rather than what he won't be doing (Zirpoli & Melloy, 1993). This is called the *terminal* behaviour, which specifies to whom the objective applies, what the person is expected to do, under what conditions, and how well the task is to be performed before the program is deemed to have been successful (Wolery et al., 1988).

PRINCIPLE 6: INCREASING BEHAVIOUR

Behaviour is strengthened by reinforcement, that is, by delivery of a consequence which the behaver values. This is the defining characteristic of reinforcement: that it *increases the rate of behaviour*. This means that reinforcement is defined by its effects, not by what an outsider may assume will be reinforcing.

When an action results in the *presentation* of a stimulus, and as a result the behaviour occurs more often in the future, it has been *positively* reinforced. When the action results in the *termination* of a negative stimulus and the action increases in frequency, then it has been *negatively* reinforced. Something negative has been removed in the hopes of increasing the desirable behaviour. An example of negative reinforcement is allocating no homework if students complete their work in class.

PRINCIPLE 7: DECREASING BEHAVIOUR

Behaviour can be reduced or weakened by *punishment*. Again, what seems to be a punishment may not be so for a given individual. As with reinforcement, punishment is defined simply by its effect, not by any intention on the part of the teacher. To reduce undesirable behaviour, an aversive consequence can be delivered (type 1 punishment) or a positive one can be withdrawn (type 2 punishment).

Behaviour can also be decreased by removing the specific consequence that maintains it. This is termed *extinction*. Extinction is discussed again later in this chapter.

PRINCIPLE 8: CONTINGENCY

The consequence earned must differ for different acts. It must be delivered when the behaviour occurs, and not when the behaviour is not displayed: in short, presentation of the consequence must be *contingent* on the behaviour.

PRINCIPLE 9: LEAST INTRUSIVE METHODS

A key axiom of ABA is that the controller must use the least invasive, intrusive and aversive methods that are available but which will still be successful. Reinforcement must be the first method used and if punishment becomes necessary, the particular form chosen should be the least aversive.

PRINCIPLE 10: INDIVIDUALISATION

Any technique may or may not work for a given student and, therefore, the key to effectiveness is to individualise instruction methods for each student (Wolery et al., 1988). Detailed data collection and accurate analysis are needed to document the effects of every intervention. For this reason, ABA is mainly used for intervening with individual students, rather than a whole class, since it will be impractical to design individual reinforcers and consequences for every student in the class.

DEVELOPING NEW BEHAVIOUR

Consequences can increase the rate of existing behaviours, but if a behaviour is displayed infrequently, then the consequence is delivered too seldom to be effective. In this case, the new behaviour must be developed by reinforcing improvements in appropriate behaviour, while at the same time using the process of extinction (which is described in later sections) to decrease inappropriate acts. This requires judgment and skill on the part of the teacher, often because the inappropriate behaviours allow the student to escape work demands and so are being strongly reinforced (Mace & Wacker, 1994; Zarcone et al., 1994), which can make extinction ineffective.

MODELLING

If another person's behaviour is reinforced, then the student is more likely to display the same behaviour. For modelling to work, the model must be highly respected and must seem similar to the imitator in significant ways. Also, the imitator must observe the model receiving reinforcement and he must be capable of performing the same behaviour. Finally, the imitator must be reinforced when he performs the behaviour for which the model was reinforced (Kerr & Nelson, 1989).

PROMPTS AND FADING

Prompts are given to help the student complete a task, and then are gradually withdrawn (in a process called *fading*) until the student can complete the task alone. Most teachers will be familiar with Axelrod's example of the teacher writing most of a letter of the alphabet, and then writing less and less of it until the child is able to write the letter without any visual prompts at all (Axelrod, 1977).

SHAPING

Shaping is 'the reinforcement of successive approximations' to a target behaviour (Axelrod, 1977, p. 9). It is used when the student does not often perform the target behaviour, and its purpose is to provide reinforcement for small improvements in behaviour (Wolery et al., 1988). Reinforcement is initially delivered for a less than optimal performance, and gradually the standards expected of the student are raised until he is able to produce an acceptable quality of work or standard of behaviour. Each new standard must be only a small improvement on the last and must be within the student's capabilities.

MOMENTUM OF COMPLIANCE

The teacher gives a series of instructions with which the student is likely to comply, followed by an instruction with which the student usually does not comply. This sets up a momentum of compliance (a 'yes set') that increases the student's compliance with the low-probability instruction (Davis et al., 1992; Mace & Wacker, 1994; Zarcone et al., 1994).

CHAINING

When a student cannot complete a task that comprises many steps, it can be broken down or *task analysed* into a series of steps small enough that he can achieve each one in turn. Knowledge of the student's abilities is required so that the steps are manageable for him.

Forward chaining

In this process, the student is reinforced for completing the first step successfully, and then for completing the first two, then three, and so on. In this way, over time he acquires all the steps and so learns the complete task.

Backward chaining

For some tasks, if the student were to do the first step it might seem out of context and irrelevant and so he will not be motivated to complete it. Instead, he can be prompted through the earlier steps but is reinforced only when he completes the *last* of these independently. Next he is required to achieve the final two steps before being reinforced, then the last three, and so on. In this way, the student immediately receives reinforcement for completing the task, which can increase motivation.

CONTRACTING

The teacher and student negotiate, write and evaluate an agreement that when a certain behaviour is displayed to a specified level, the student will earn a specified reinforcer. Likewise, what constitutes failure and its consequences must be specified, with the student given a right to renegotiate and to correct failure. Last, a reliable means of record keeping needs to be instituted (Wolery et al., 1988). All this may take some time to set up, although it has many of the advantages of self-regulation— namely, that the student oversees and is accountable for his own compliance and so is more motivated to adhere to the agreement (Olympia et al., 1994).

INCREASING EXISTING BEHAVIOUR

To increase the rate of a behaviour, the teacher can arrange for the delivery of reinforcers which, by definition, strengthen the behaviour. Reinforcers can be delivered naturally, by the student, or by the teacher, with natural reinforcement and self-reinforcement being less restrictive than adult-delivered reinforcement. Kerr and Nelson (1989) define restrictiveness as the extent to which the intervention restricts the student's freedom to be treated like any other student. However, I use the term to refer to the degree to which the student is subjected to external controls.

METHOD OF REINFORCEMENT DELIVERY

Natural reinforcement

The teacher can remove the need for a behavioural intervention by increasing the rate of natural reinforcers so that they are available to a student at a high enough rate to influence his behaviour positively. For instance, the teacher can structure group learning tasks so that a student whose behaviour has led to peer rejection may participate in positive peer interactions without needing to resort to the disruptive behaviour.

Natural reinforcers are again strengthened at the end of an intervention, so that the activity itself becomes intrinsically rewarding, allowing external rewards to be gradually withdrawn altogether (in a process called fading).

Self-reinforcement

Self-management approaches, which include self-reinforcement, are such a significant part of ABA that they have become a separate approach in their own right. These methods are detailed in chapter 4.

Adult-administered reinforcement

To increase the rate of a student's desirable behaviour, the teacher can deliver a reinforcer. Available reinforcers include (from least to most intrusive): social, activity, tangible, token, edible, and tactile and sensory reinforcers.

TYPES OF REINFORCERS

The types of reinforcers used can be arranged in order from the least to the most intrusive. Intrusiveness is the extent to which interventions interfere with the educational process.

Social reinforcers

These have three aspects: feedback, attention and approval (Kerr & Nelson, 1989). Feedback on its own is a weak reinforcer, although attention and approval can be powerful, as long as the student values the teacher's evaluation of him.

Praise is a common social reinforcer, and can be used alone or paired with other types of reinforcement. To be effective, it must be contingent on the desired behaviour, must be specific, credible, high in quality, not over-used and it should not interrupt student attention (Wolery et al., 1988).

Caring touch can also be a social reinforcer. This of course must be controllable by the student and must be perceived as safe. When choosing to touch students the teacher would need to consider issues of child protection and abuse, and ensure she is not exposed to allegations of improper conduct. School policy may determine whether teachers are permitted to touch students.

Other social reinforcers include: appointing the child as student of the day or leader of an activity, and calling or writing to the student's parent/s about his positive behaviour (Zirpoli & Melloy, 1993).

Activity reinforcers

A student can be encouraged to perform an activity he does not like by rewarding him with the chance to do an activity which he prefers. This is Premack's principle (Kerr & Nelson, 1989), also known as 'Grandma's rule'. Preferred activities may include free time, time with the teacher, an opportunity to hand out materials to the other students, use of the computer, feeding the class pet, bringing a toy to school, listening to music, or reading a story (Zirpoli & Melloy, 1993).

At first it may be necessary to give the student access to the preferred activity after just one instance of the target behaviour, since a reinforcer may be ineffective if there is too long a delay in its delivery.

Tangible reinforcers

Tangible reinforcers are non-food items which the student values for their own sake. They may include stars, stamps, stickers, points, toys or magazines (Zirpoli & Melloy, 1993). Tangible reinforcers differ from tokens in that they are valued in themselves, and are not traded in for any other reinforcer. Determining a reinforcer for each student separately can make using tangible reinforcers intrusive (Kerr & Nelson, 1989).

Token reinforcers

A portable and durable token (such as a poker chip) is given for target behaviours and is later traded in for pre-negotiated backup reinforcers. Setting up a token program is detailed and demanding. The teacher needs to determine how many tokens each desired behaviour earns, plus the costs of the various backup reinforcers and procedures for exchanging tokens for them, and decide on fines for misdemeanours. A reliable recording system will be needed. The token system must seem fair to the students or they will stop working within it. The reinforcers will need fading out once the program has achieved success, which will take skilful handling in case the behaviour deteriorates again. Finally, an ethical issue with using token economies is the claim that students have a right to noncontingent access to many objects and activities, which therefore should not be used as backup reinforcers (Williams, Williams & McLaughlin, 1989). This criticism can be overcome if the backup reinforcer is a special privilege to which the students do not ordinarily have access, although this can be difficult to arrange in schools.

The major advantage of token programs is that the token can be exchanged for a variety of reinforcers, which avoids the problems of deprivation and satiation (Axelrod, 1977). The symbolic reinforcer can be delivered immediately, although the actual reinforcer itself is delayed. This may be sufficient for some students; others may not be able to delay gratification until the backup reinforcer is delivered, however.

Edible reinforcers

Food is a reinforcer for everyone as it satisfies a basic physiological need. However, determining the student's food likes and dislikes makes edible reinforcers difficult to establish. Issues such as nutrition (including issues of obesity and tooth decay), food sensitivities, the ethics of depriving a student of food prior to training sessions, and parental preferences about their child's diet, will affect the decision to employ edible reinforcers.

Tactile and sensory reinforcers

This class of reinforcers has been used mainly with people with severe and profound intellectual disabilities, especially to replace self-stimulation with a less dangerous or more appropriate form of stimulation.

CHOICE OF REINFORCERS

A specific reinforcer for a particular student is selected by knowing which general reinforcers often work for people (Martin & Pear, 1992), such as the ones listed above. Then specific reinforcers for a given student may be selected by having the student make a list of his interests and preferences, although items on the list will be subject to the teacher's veto. Next, the teacher may use any items from the menu, observing their effects and abandoning any reinforcer if it does not increase the frequency of the desired behaviour. The teacher will need to make her chosen reinforcer relatively more attractive than naturally occurring alternatives, for instance when a behaviour allows students to escape the learning task altogether (Zarcone et al., 1994).

GUIDELINES FOR ADMINISTERING REINFORCERS

Having chosen a reinforcer, the teacher will need to consider the following issues about its delivery (Martin & Pear, 1992; Wolery et al., 1988; Zirpoli & Melloy, 1993):

1. The teacher should allow the student to choose from a range of reinforcers, rather than selecting these herself.
2. It can be effective to vary the reinforcer.
3. If a reinforcer is to be effective in increasing behaviour, the student must have been deprived of it initially.
4. Behaviourism accepts that a reinforcer will lose its reinforcing capacity if it is over-used. This process is termed *satiation*.
5. Reinforcers work best when delivered immediately. Students with impulsive behaviour choose the most immediate reinforcer, even when it is less attractive (Neef, Mace & Shade, 1993), which implies that for these students in particular, the teacher will need to deliver reinforcement immediately if her reinforcer is to be more potent than competing reinforcers.
6. Reinforcement must be contingent on the occurrence of the behavi-

our—that is, delivered if the behaviour is displayed, and not when the behaviour does not occur.

7. The teacher should move from a continuous to an intermittent schedule of reinforcement as soon as possible (see below for an explanation of these terms).

8. If the student is told in advance what consequences his actions will attract, then his behaviour will change more quickly than when he does not know the consequences. This also allows for delayed gratification, that is, for the use of less immediate reinforcers.

9. Improvement and generalisation will be most easily assured if the teacher employs reinforcers commonly and readily available in the student's environment.

REINFORCEMENT SCHEDULES

A reinforcement schedule refers to how often the individual has to display the behaviour (or how much time must elapse) before receiving reinforcement. In *ratio* reinforcement regimes, the behaviour is reinforced after either a fixed or an average number of occurrences of the target behaviour (termed *fixed* or *variable* ratio reinforcement, respectively). If reinforcement is delivered *every* time the behaviour occurs, this is termed a fixed ratio of one, or *continuous* reinforcement. Behaviour is acquired more rapidly when it is reinforced every time it is displayed but if the reinforcement stops, the learner can detect this readily and the behaviour may cease altogether. Furthermore, continuous reinforcement is difficult to administer since the teacher will not be available to observe and deliver reinforcement every time the behaviour occurs. Therefore, both in reality and for maintenance of behaviour change, *intermittent* reinforcement is preferred. This means that not every instance of the behaviour is reinforced.

When the behaviour is reinforced after a specified *time* period (rather than *number* of instances of the behaviour) then it is said to be on an *interval* schedule. This is used for continuous behaviours such as a student's in-seat behaviour, when the student is reinforced if he remains in his seat for a specified time span. For discrete acts, it is better for teachers to reinforce a student after a number of behaviours (ratio reinforcement) rather than after a period of time (Axelrod, 1977).

Cyclical behaviour that improves and then deteriorates can be caused by the inconsistency and the leanness (too few reinforcers) of the reinforcement schedule. A schedule must be applied consistently for it to have a consistent effect, with changes introduced gradually to ensure gains are maintained.

METHODS FOR REDUCING BEHAVIOUR RATES

Having examined ways of increasing students' behaviours, next we shall look at ways to reduce their inappropriate actions. The two aspects are considered in this order for two reasons: first, it is more ethical to use the less intrusive methods for increasing student behaviours before reducing behaviours by more intrusive means; second, reinforcement gives a student something else to do in place of an inappropriate behaviour that is being reduced.

In ABA, when a behaviour has been reduced, it is said to have been *punished.* This demonstrates that the term *punishment* has a specific meaning in ABA, one that is different from the lay use of the term. The lay use refers to the administration of some aversive consequence to a misbehaving individual. However, in this lay use, the behaviour may or may not in fact decrease. In the technical ABA definition, punishment is *any* consequence that *decreases* the likelihood that the behaviour will be repeated. It includes a broader range of interventions than that to which the lay use refers.

Nevertheless, whether we are talking about the lay or technical use of the term, Wheldall and Merrett (1984, p. 21) caution that: 'Contrary to popular belief, punishment plays only a minor and infrequent role in the behavioural approach, not least because what we believe to be punishing could, in fact, be reinforcing to the child'.

The strategies for decreasing inappropriate behaviour can be ranked in order from the least to the most restrictive methods, which refers to how much external control is imposed on the student:

1. discrimination training
2. simple correction
3. self-punishment
4. differential reinforcement
5. stimulus satiation
6. extinction
7. withdrawal of positive stimuli (type 2 punishment)
8. overcorrection
9. presentation of aversive stimuli (type 1 punishment)
10. negative practice

1. DISCRIMINATION TRAINING

While a behaviour may be appropriate in one setting, the same act can be inappropriate somewhere else. When the teacher administers the consequences differently in different circumstances, the student will learn to discriminate the difference and will behave accordingly in those differing conditions. The teacher can respond by offering cues that help the student discriminate one circumstance from the other, even if that is only to state, 'That won't work with me'. In this way, the student learns not to display the inappropriate behaviour when the punishing conditions are present. Some measure of self-control (learning) is achieved.

2. SIMPLE CORRECTION

Unlike overcorrection (to be discussed in a later section), simple correction, as the name implies, requires the student simply to undo or correct the results of his behaviour (Wolery et al., 1988). The restrictiveness of this approach depends on the extent to which the student corrects his behaviour willingly when asked. If no other punishment is delivered, then it is one of the least restrictive (and intrusive) methods available.

3. SELF-PUNISHMENT

This is discussed in chapter 4, although two conflicting points can be made here in advance of that discussion. An advantage of self-punishment is that it is less restrictive than adult-administered methods because the student has agreed to it and is in control of it. A disadvantage is that self-punishment can have a negative effect on the student's motivation because it highlights his errors and so may activate a fear of failure.

4. DIFFERENTIAL REINFORCEMENT

Differential reinforcement procedures involve reinforcing a positive behaviour and withholding reinforcement of an undesirable target behaviour (Vollmer et al., 1993; Wolery et al., 1988). They are less restrictive than other reductive methods (Alberto & Troutman, 1995), although the extinction component can make differential reinforcement ineffective (Vollmer et al., 1993) for reasons discussed in a coming section.

There are four types of differential reinforcement. The first is differential reinforcement of lower rates of behaviour (DRL), in which the student is reinforced when his inappropriate behaviour occurs less frequently. A number of permissible instances is specified per time period, and if the student does not exceed this number, then he earns a reinforcer. Gradually, the permitted number of behaviours decreases, or the time period increases, until the behaviour occurs at a tolerable level. This approach relies on careful measurement of the frequency of the behaviour.

In differential reinforcement of other behaviours or of zero rates of behaviour (DRO), the student receives reinforcement for not displaying the target behaviour at all.

Incompatible behaviours such as staying seated when the target behaviour is out-of-seat behaviour, can be reinforced (a process called differential reinforcement of incompatible behaviours (DRI)), or alternative (not opposite) behaviours such as putting your hand up rather than calling out, can be reinforced. This is differential reinforcement of alternative behaviours (DRA).

5. STIMULUS SATIATION

Stimulus satiation involves giving the student so much of the antecedent to the behaviour that he tires of it. An example is giving pencils to the student who frequently steals them from his classmates. The theory predicts that he will eventually become overloaded with pencils and will no longer choose to steal them.

6. EXTINCTION

Extinction is the process of withdrawing the reinforcer that is maintaining the behaviour. This means, first, that the teacher must be able to identify what is reinforcing the behaviour and, second, has control over whether it is delivered or not. An example is when teacher attention is reinforcing student misbehaviour, in which case ignoring the behaviour is intended to result in its reduction (Alberto & Troutman, 1995). Extinction procedures present a number of difficulties for teachers, however, including:

1. It may not be possible for the teacher involved to notice how her own actions are maintaining the student's behaviour. A consultant may be needed to observe the teacher's role in unwittingly reinforcing inappropriate student behaviours.
2. Successful extinction relies on the teacher being able to identify the particular reinforcer for each student. However, this can be difficult to do since the same outward behaviour may have different reinforcers for different students (Iwata et al., 1994).
3. The target behaviour may initially deteriorate, or a new aggressive behaviour may emerge as the student tries to regain the reinforcement he previously received (Alberto & Troutman, 1995). The teacher may become confused about whether the increase in the inappropriate behaviour is a sign that the extinction procedure is ineffective, or a sign that it is working and just needs to be persisted with.
4. If the behaviour is being maintained on an intermittent reinforcement schedule, it will be resistant to extinction, and so improvement may be slow to appear. The teacher may not be able to wait for the predicted improvement, as the behaviour may in the meantime become so intrusive or so dangerous that it must be dealt with. Yet

paying attention to the behaviour after some delay means that the student has been reinforced for persistence.

5. When extinction is tried with groups of individuals—as in a class-room—the teacher cannot control the reinforcement delivered by the student's peers. So, the behaviour may never actually be placed on an extinction schedule.

6. Nor can the teacher control the fact that other students may copy the target behaviour, since they observe that it is not attracting punishment.

7. Extinction will not eliminate behaviours that are self-reinforcing (Axelrod, 1977)—for example, students talking to each other. Their conversation itself is reinforcing and has no additional reinforcer which can be withdrawn.

8. Behaviour that has been extinguished in one setting is still likely to occur elsewhere. That is, gains made with extinction do not generalise readily (Alberto & Troutman, 1995).

These limitations will make extinction inappropriate for certain behaviours, especially if in addition they are dangerous, intolerable or contagious and therefore cannot be allowed to escalate.

7. WITHDRAWAL OF POSITIVE STIMULI (TYPE 2 PUNISHMENT)

As the name implies, withdrawal of positive stimuli means that something the student likes is withdrawn when the undesirable behaviour is displayed, with the expectation that this will decrease the rate of the inappropriate behaviour. The two main types of this form of punishment are *response cost procedures* and *time out*. For each of these, the natural situation must have a high level of reinforcement, so that the punishing condition is noticeably less positive than the natural condition.

Response cost procedures

With these approaches, the student is fined or otherwise penalised if the behaviour occurs. In practice, response cost procedures are used most effectively when combined with token economies because token econ-omies can be flexible (Alberto & Troutman, 1995). However, it can be difficult for the teacher to take tokens away from a student, so a points system may be more manageable since the teacher can withdraw points at her discretion. Another difficulty with response cost approaches is establishing the magnitude of fines: if they are too severe and a day's gains can be wiped out with one misdeed, then the students will resist working for the tokens, points or stickers. Also, the student may soon become bankrupt of points or tokens, meaning that the teacher cannot exact further punishment so has no further influence over the behaviour.

If fines are too lenient, on the other hand, then the punishment will have no effect.

Time out from positive reinforcement

This involves removing the student's access to reinforcement following an unacceptable behaviour (Axelrod, 1977). It is important that the natural setting is very attractive, of course, so that removal from it is indeed a punishment rather than a reinforcer. The corollary of this is that reinforcement cannot be available in the time-out condition.

There are three types of time out (Alberto & Troutman, 1995; Wolery et al., 1988):

- *Nonseclusionary* time-out procedures involve removing reinforcement from the student, who remains where he is but is denied access to reinforcers. Teacher attention is frequently thought to be a reinforcer, so ignoring the student is a form of this type of time out. However, it is not always effective (Wolery et al., 1988). A variation is removal of materials the student is using.
- *Exclusionary* time out involves removing the student from the activity so that he has no access to reinforcement, but not necessarily isolating him. He may be directed to sit in a quiet corner of the room. From there, he may be expected to observe other students behaving appropriately. This method is favoured when the reinforcers cannot be withdrawn from the student, and so instead the student is removed from the reinforcers.
- *Seclusionary* time out involves confining a student to an isolated area for a specified and brief period of time. The room must be a reasonable size with adequate ventilation and lighting, it should be free of objects with which the student could hurt himself, should provide facility to monitor the student continuously, and should not be locked (Gast & Nelson, 1977, cited by Wolery et al., 1988).

Time out has some difficulties: defining an appropriate duration and the criteria for exiting is an issue with all forms. Other disadvantages depend on the type of time out: nonseclusionary and exclusionary time out can cause embarrassment to a student, which may engender defiance. On the other hand, supervision of seclusionary time out so that the student remains safe and is not forgotten places high demands on school staff.

8. OVERCORRECTION

The first form of overcorrection is *positive practice overcorrection*. In this approach, whenever the student misbehaves, he must practise a more appropriate form of the behaviour. Foxx (1982) gives the example of a teacher who required a self-abusive student to hold an ice pack to his head whenever he hit himself. A second and more restrictive form is *restitutional overcorrection*, in which the student repairs the damage done, restoring it to a state that is a vast improvement on what existed before his inappropriate behaviour. An example is requiring a student not only to clean off his own graffiti, but also to remove all graffiti in the school.

Overcorrective procedures need to be delivered with firmness and with an emphasis on their educative nature. The activity itself must not become reinforcing. Overcorrection is accompanied by verbal instruction and, if necessary, force, to make the student repeat the appropriate behaviour. One problem is that a physically strong student may defy the teacher's directive and become unmanageable. Also, the time involved in the procedure and its aversive nature for both student and teacher suggest caution in its use.

9. PRESENTATION OF AVERSIVE STIMULI (TYPE 1 PUNISHMENT)

This form of punishment involves administering an aversive consequence with the aim of reducing the student's inappropriate behaviour. Aversive consequences include verbal and physical aversives.

Verbal aversives

Verbal reprimands can be very effective with mild behaviour difficulties, although they are less successful with more severe behaviour problems (Kerr & Nelson, 1989). Verbal aversives can be more effective when the teacher gains eye contact, stands close to the student, and delivers other aversive consequences at the same time.

Physical aversives

In discussing physical aversives, we must be aware of the reluctance of a significant sector of the community to endorse physical punishment, especially when delivered by professionals rather than parents. Most school and education department policies will not permit administration of physical aversives, so this approach cannot be used by the classroom teacher. Alberto and Troutman (1995) make it clear that they do not advocate the use of physical aversives, although they note their effectiveness as a last resort when dealing with extreme or dangerous behaviours.

10. NEGATIVE PRACTICE

In contrast to overcorrection, negative practice involves repeating the *inappropriate* behaviour on the assumption that fatigue or satiation will result. It may be that because the teacher is now in control of its occurrence, the behaviour is robbed of its power to inconvenience her, and so it is no longer being reinforced. Force may be needed to make the student repeat the negative behaviour over and over again, which provides a strong argument against the use of this procedure.

GUIDELINES FOR ADMINISTRATION OF PUNISHMENTS

Punishment should be delivered immediately after the undesirable behaviour, and every instance of the behaviour must be punished. This advice implies that if a teacher is not able to detect most instances of the undesired behaviour, then she should have serious doubts about attempting to use punishment to decrease the behaviour (Martin & Pear, 1992). Perhaps instead some discrimination training is needed to teach the student that certain behaviours can be performed in one circumstance but not in others.

The punishment should be delivered matter-of-factly, so that high emotion does not reinforce the inappropriate behaviour or interfere with the teacher's judgment about administering the program.

The teacher should be aware that punishment should work quickly and if it does not, then it should be abandoned. Punishment should be faded out as soon as it has produced the desired result and, at the earliest opportunity, it should be replaced with reinforcement.

INSTRUCTION TO PROMOTE GENERALISATION

Behaviourism has had a disappointing record with maintaining behaviour gains over time and generalising these gains to other settings or with other teachers. In most cases, generalisation does not occur naturally and so needs to be taught (Zirpoli & Melloy, 1993). Some approaches for improving the generalisation of new behaviours include: teaching the behaviour in the setting in which it will be used (rather than in the classroom), using a variety of teachers, fading artificial prompts and cues so that naturally occurring cues come to control the behaviour, using natural consequences as reinforcers and, when artificial reinforcers have been used, shifting from continuous to intermittent reinforcement and, finally, developing objectives for and reinforcing generalisation itself.

ETHICAL ISSUES WITH ABA

Martin and Pear (1992, p. 393) contend that 'The history of civilisation is a continuous story of the abuse of power'. Thus, the powerful techniques of behaviour analysis need to be handled with care.

RIGHT TO MANIPULATE OTHERS

Wheldall and Merrett (1984) ask what right does one person have to manipulate the behaviour of another? They answer by observing that if our behaviour is modified by its consequences, then this process is going on continuously and naturally, regardless of whether or not we are aware of it. Teachers have a responsibility to teach students the most adaptive behaviours in the most effective way so, rather than leaving consequences to chance, they should manipulate them deliberately in their students' interests.

NECESSITY FOR EXTERNAL CONTROLS

A second issue is whether control has to be external to the individual, or whether he can exercise judgment. This is the debate between controlling and guiding (Glasser, 1992; Gordon, 1991) that states that people can learn without direct experience of behavioural consequences, and so they can make valid behavioural choices for themselves without being manipulated by others. In rebuttal, Edwards (1993) states that while this may work for most people, students who are discouraged about learning may need some external reinforcers to encourage them to put in effort, especially when the task is difficult.

SYMPTOMS, NOT CAUSES

ABA is accused of addressing the behaviour, not its cause. In ABA's defence, Wheldall and Merrett (1984) argue that labelling students with difficult behaviour does not help them. This is true, but not because causes are irrelevant, but because labels (such as 'hyperactive') only describe and do not explain behaviours. Wheldall and Merrett's second argument is that the problem *is* the behaviour, not its underlying cause and, in any case, inner needs are difficult to identify so should not be of concern. This is an efficiency argument: that it is quicker—and more humane—to deal with what can be changed readily.

COMPLIANCE TRAINING

ABA and other authoritarian approaches may teach children to comply with adult direction without teaching them to judge the merits of what they are being told to do. This may make them vulnerable to abuse by adults who direct them to do something harmful. Some would argue further that the practices of behaviour analysis *in themselves* abuse children's right to self-determination.

REINFORCEMENT

Alberto and Troutman (1995) list four advantages of delivering reinforcement in a structured, contingent manner: first, it improves student behaviour; second, students can easily identify the link between their behaviour and its consequences; third, it demonstrates how reinforcement works in the 'real' world outside school; and fourth, reinforcement teaches students to value naturally occurring reinforcers which ordinarily occur at school, at home and in the community.

However, reinforcement does have disadvantages. The debate on these is usually opened with the question of whether reinforcement is really the same as bribing. Kaplan and Drainville (1991) answer this by saying that while successful students find enough reward in their success, children who are less successful may need extrinsic reinforcers until they can achieve at the task and gain the reinforcers inherent in it. Therefore, extrinsic reinforcers are in students' best interests; bribery is in the adult's interest, argue Kaplan and Drainville. The adult needs to be confident, however, that she can judge what constitutes someone else's 'best interests'.

Edwards (1993) also presents the argument that external reinforcement is no different from adults receiving salary for their work. However, adults choose to undertake their work (albeit from a restricted range of options) and are in control of ceasing the reinforcement by quitting their job, and may even change to lower paying work to gain improved work satisfaction (intrinsic reinforcement). We could conclude, therefore, that while we all work for reinforcement, much of our reward is intrinsic rather than external to us.

Reinforcement is powerful, and when over-used can produce undesirable side effects. It can produce docile, compliant children who lack spontaneity and who produce only reinforced behaviour rather than a wider repertoire of desirable actions. Alternatively, it can excite negative actions such as lying or cheating to earn artificial rewards (Wolery et al., 1988). Praise, a key social reinforcer, may teach children to become dependent on other people's opinions of them. If these opinions are unduly judgmental, children's self-esteem will be lowered.

Reinforcement may also interfere with a student's concentration, especially when he finds the activity difficult (Biederman et al., 1994). It can also reduce generalisation, in that the desirable behaviour may cease when the reinforcement does (Wolery et al., 1988).

Finally, children may copy their teachers' use of systematic rewards to manipulate their peers, which in their hands may become coercive and manipulative, and so will amount to bribery (Wolery et al., 1988).

PUNISHMENT

Aversive consequences work quickly to produce a change in behaviour, they provide unambiguous cues that teach the student to discriminate acceptable from unacceptable behaviour, and punishing one student reduces the likelihood that others in the class will copy his inappropriate behaviour (Alberto & Troutman, 1995). Having recognised these potential gains, however, we need to consider the costs.

Ends and means

The first question is whether the results of punishment justify its use. Axelrod (1977, p. 28) answers in this way:

> . . . the judgment as to whether or not a procedure is humane should be based more on its long-term effects than by the immediate discomfort which results. Few people would consider a surgeon or dentist, whose operation is painful, to be cruel if procedures ultimately improve the health or extend the life of a patient.

The essential difference here, though, is that the recipient has no choice about treatment from the behaviour modifier, but can choose not to be treated by the surgeon.

Ineffectiveness

Punishment is fundamentally ineffective because the teacher cannot respond until the student has behaved inappropriately, causing hurt or inconvenience to someone else. This is like shutting the stable door after the horse has bolted. Aside from the harm to the victim, waiting for the behaviour to occur means that the student misbehaves more often than he otherwise might and his disruptiveness stretches unreasonably the tolerance of those around him. The democratic writers suggest instead that a teacher who uses guidance rather than controlling methods will be able to prevent inappropriate behaviour and also therefore will avoid the need to punish. This will be both more humane and more effective. These arguments will be expanded in later chapters.

Second, punishment has only a limited effect on learning. First, students learn to behave appropriately not because it is the right way to act, but simply to avoid being punished. In short, they do not *learn* standards for their actions. So they then behave well only when someone is present who is likely to punish them (Rolider, Cummings & Van Houten, 1991). Or, they restrict themselves to only the safest of activities, fearing punishment for anything else (Gordon, 1991).

Third, since punishment works best when applied to all infringements, the teacher must be constantly vigilant to detect all instances of misbehaviour. Constant surveillance is of course impossible, so the teacher will not punish consistently, and the punishment will be less effective.

Fourth, punishment can be unfair because the teacher cannot see all the circumstances of a misdeed, and so there is a high risk of:

- misinterpreting these and punishing the wrong person
- not acknowledging that the student did not intend the consequences
- failing to appreciate that the outcome has already frightened (punished) the student
- not understanding the student's perception of events and what he regards as a fair punishment.

Even if the misdeed were detected every time, and if the punishment were perfectly and fairly administered, its effects may be only temporary and may suppress the inappropriate behaviour but not necessarily replace it with a better one. Therefore, punishment will need to be used for a long time.

Finally, Dreikurs and Cassel (1990) state that punishment is effective only for those who do not need it. Most students will respond to lesser methods; for those who do not, punishment seldom works either.

Effects on the recipient

Punishment produces emotional side effects such as fearfulness and frustration from not having one's needs met. Ginott (1972) claims that whereas the purpose of punishment is to convince students to stop unacceptable behaviour, it is more likely to enrage them and make them ineducable. It can also make children sick and emotionally unstable (Gordon, 1991). Some of these effects include accident-proneness, suicidal tendencies, 'neurosis', low self-esteem, shyness, poor peer relationships, increased worry, and poor relationships with adults. Feeling that he has failed will lower a student's self-esteem and perhaps give rise to more infringements because he feels discouraged.

Punishment may provoke retaliation against the punisher, and imitation of the punisher's aggression (the student bullies others as he is being bullied).

The student may learn to avoid the circumstances in which he is punished or to avoid punishment at all costs. This means that he may withdraw at least emotionally, may tell lies rather than own up to a misdeed (Ginott, 1972), or may tell tales on others so that they look bad and in comparison the student himself looks good. None of these behaviours is attractive in children, and they tend to attract further punishment. An opposite way in which individuals avoid punishments is

Table 3.1   Summary of disadvantages of punishment

Limited effectiveness
1.   The student must infringe someone's rights before punishment can be delivered.
2.   Children learn how to behave well only to avoid punishment rather than developing a 'conscience'.
3.   The adult must be constantly vigilant to detect all misbehaviour, and cannot. Failure to identify the full circumstances leads to error in administering punishment.
4.   Its effects may not be permanent.
5.   Punishment may not replace the inappropriate behaviour with a more desirable one.
6.   Punishment only works for those who do not need it.

Effects on the recipient
1.   Punishment can produce negative emotional side effects, including low self-esteem.
2.   It can teach students to imitate the controller.
3.   Students may avoid punishing situations either by withdrawing or by currying favour.
4.   Punishment may provoke inappropriate behaviours that in turn attract more punishment.

Effect on the administrator and society
1.   Punishment can become addictive and can escalate into abuse.
2.   It can teach students to ignore the teacher who threatens but does not deliver punishment.
3.   Students may push a teacher who threatens punishment, to see how far she will go or to force her to back down from an empty threat.
4.   Violence at home or school leads to a violent society.

to become submissive, compliant and a 'goodie-goodie'. These students become the 'teacher's pets', but at the same time they lack self-esteem because they and their peers despise their actions. As Ginott (1972, p. 151) says: 'Punishment does not deter misconduct. It merely makes the offender more cautious in committing his crime, more adroit in concealing his traces, more skillful in escaping detection. When a child is punished he resolves to be more careful, not more honest and responsible'.

Effects on the administrator and society

Because punishment can work quickly at first, it can become addictive, with the adult forgetting to use more positive approaches (Martin & Pear, 1992) or succumbing to increasing brutality (Ginott, in Edwards, 1993). In this way, punishment can escalate into abuse (which is defined as causing physical injury).

Alternatively, the teacher who is aware of the abusive cycle may instead threaten to carry out a more severe punishment, but never does so. This teaches students not to take their teacher seriously and so, not surprisingly, they ignore her in future. Or, says Ginott (in Edwards, 1993), the students push the teacher to see how far she will go, and to force the teacher to back down from a threat she has no power to enact. In the process students are assaulted verbally with blame and shame and teachers are unnecessarily stressed.

Finally, violence at home or at school begets a violent society.

ETHICAL GUIDELINES

It is crucial that practitioners are sensitive to the individual's right to freedom and dignity and, at the same time, give the individual the most effective intervention (Rekers, 1984). However, while a treatment may be effective, it may still be illegal or open to criticism. With these ethical dilemmas in mind, many authors have offered guidelines for administering ABA programs, especially when they involve the delivery of punishments (Alberto & Troutman, 1995; Axelrod, 1977; Martin & Pear, 1992; Wolery et al., 1988).

PARTICIPANT INVOLVEMENT IN THE PROGRAM

The student and teacher will collaborate on determining program goals and methods (Fawcett, 1991).

ANTECEDENTS

The teacher should minimise the causes of inappropriate behaviour. This means changing the antecedents that give rise to the behaviour and making natural conditions highly reinforcing so that students are motivated to behave appropriately.

A THERAPEUTIC ENVIRONMENT

The teacher needs to provide a setting that is safe, humane, responsive to human needs, enjoyable, and which imposes the fewest restrictions necessary (Alberto & Troutman, 1995).

HIGH PRIORITY BEHAVIOUR

The behaviour targeted for change should be a high priority, defined as one that violates someone's rights, rather than an act that is merely inconvenient to others (Alberto & Troutman, 1995). At the same time, however, interventions (or a lack of them) cannot be to the detriment of others (Martin & Pear, 1992).

FUNCTIONAL SKILLS

Students need to learn skills that benefit them and are functional for them and, equally, they do not need to learn skills that are not functional in their lives (Alberto & Troutman, 1995). An intervention aimed at teaching non-functional skills is not ethical. A corollary of this view is that a dysfunctional behaviour (such as hand biting) *must* be replaced by a more functional one.

LEAST RESTRICTIVE TREATMENT

A key axiom of ABA is the use of reinforcement as a first measure, with more restrictive methods employed only when reinforcement has failed. Punishment should be reserved only for those behaviours—such as self-abuse—that cannot be suppressed in other ways and it must always be followed by positive reinforcement to maintain the new desired behaviour.

Advice differs on how severe a punishment should be. In line with the least restrictive principle, some writers say that the teacher should use the gentlest available form of punishment first, and increase its restrictiveness only if the first method has failed (Axelrod, 1977; Kerr & Nelson, 1989). However, other writers advise that the initial punishment should be fairly intense (Foxx, 1982; Martin & Pear, 1992) because if the first punishment is ineffective and then has to be intensified, the student might not notice punishments that only gradually increase in intensity. This would cause the undesirable behaviour to persist unnecessarily (Martin & Pear, 1992).

COMPETENT TREATMENT

The teacher has a responsibility to be competent, which includes knowing the theory guiding an intervention, knowing the range of treatment options, being aware of her own limitations and referring student problems to specialists if the teacher herself is not equipped to deal with them (which also involves knowledge of appropriate services), and collaborating with other professionals working with the student. Intensive training and ongoing supervision are also desirable, especially for the teacher who is addressing complex behaviours (Alberto & Troutman, 1995).

ADVANCE PREPARATION

When planning an intervention that uses punishment, the teacher should be clear about exactly what punishment is to be used, and for what behaviour. The punishment should be individually selected for each case, and must be abandoned if it is not decreasing the behaviour.

ONGOING EVALUATION

Defining the target behaviour in operational (behavioural) terms allows
the teacher to observe the initial behaviour rate (the baseline) and to
evaluate the effect of the intervention. The use of punishment in particular
must be documented to verify its effectiveness and to ensure unwanted
side effects do not result. This makes the entire process visible, under-
standable and open to evaluation by others, which is the basis of
accountability (Alberto & Troutman, 1995). As well as monitoring for
possible negative effects, this accountability allows teachers to demonstrate and document their successes.

CONSENT

If all these criteria are met, then the crucial one of consent is more likely
to be satisfied also. Rekers (1984) identifies four types of consent: legal,
competent, voluntary and informed. The first two are beyond the capacity
of young children and so instead parental consent will be necessary. The
third form, *voluntary* consent, requires that no unfair consequences would
occur if the individual withheld consent to the program (Rekers, 1984).
Parents who refuse to consent to a behavioural program cannot be
threatened with no service for their child or with school suspension, but
neither can they be promised extravagant benefits if they participate
(Alberto & Troutman, 1995). The professional's status may mean that
parents or students are subtly pressured into consenting, so the onus is
on the teacher to ensure that what students or their parents are agreeing
to represents best practice (Rekers, 1984) and that a range of viable
treatment options have been fully considered and discussed with them
(Martin & Pear, 1992).

CONFIDENTIALITY

This is a dilemma in all interpersonal work. Confidentiality involves the
teacher's duty to protect students' privacy: safeguarding their files or other
records; keeping these records accurate, unbiased and fair; avoiding
staffroom gossip about students and their families; and making available
to the students or parents all information in their files. Geldard (1993)
discusses the limits on confidentiality, which include the need to pass
on information to other school staff or other agencies whose work with
the students would be affected by their ignorance of key information.
Staff who team-teach or work in secondary schools may all need to
know information that the students or parents would rather keep
confidential. What information will be disclosed to whom can be agreed

at the outset or renegotiated during the program, so that parents and students are aware of who knows what about them.

CONCLUSION: ETHICS

Each administrator of behaviour analysis will differ on the cut-off point where, for her, the result does not warrant the methods used to achieve it. The use of punishment is clearly an issue; the use of controlling strategies *per se* is a still more fundamental question. Guess and Siegel-Causey (1985, p. 232) ask the final question: 'Does the prevalent behaviourally-based technology used with severely handicapped persons adversely affect the emergence of those human qualities that we are striving so hard to develop in them?'. This question can be applied to people of all ability levels. It can also apply to the administrators as well as the recipients of behaviourism since teachers can be as constrained and unspontaneous as the students on whom they use these methods (Guess & Siegel-Causey, 1985).

SUMMARY

Applied behaviour analysis in schools focuses on defining, observing and recording the outward behaviour of students. Behaviour analysis contends that human behaviour is lawful—that is, it can be predicted by observing the events surrounding it. Behaviour that is followed by a consequence that the recipient values will increase in frequency; behaviour followed by a negative consequence will reduce; the conditions (antecedents) under which either positive or negative consequences occur will themselves acquire the power to change the rate of behaviour (Matthews, personal communication).

When attempting to change the rate of a behaviour, the conditions under which the behaviour occurs (antecedents) are altered to prevent recurrence of the behaviour. Next, the events that follow the behaviour (consequences) are changed.

When administering consequences, the primary focus is on reinforcing appropriate behaviour to increase its occurrence, using a range of reinforcers from natural to edible, and to reinforce fewer instances of a negative behaviour (differential reinforcement). If all else fails, then punishing or reductive procedures are used, under strict conditions. Table 3.2 gives the methods for delivery of consequences in order of how restrictive (or controlling) they are of the individual.

Table 3.2   Methods for delivery of consequences (from least to most restrictive)

Reinforcement procedures
Natural reinforcement
Self-reinforcement
Adult-administered reinforcement

Reductive procedures
Discrimination training
Simple correction
Self-punishment
Differential reinforcement
Stimulus satiation
Extinction
Withdrawal of positive stimuli (type 2 punishment)
Overcorrection
Presentation of aversive stimuli (type 1 punishment)
Negative practice

In addition, the types of reinforcers can be ranked by how much they intrude on the individual, the environment or the process of teaching (see table 3.3).

Table 3.3   Types of reinforcement (from least to most intrusive)

Social reinforcement
Activity reinforcement
Tangible reinforcement
Token economies
Edible reinforcement
Tactile and sensory reinforcement

CASE STUDY

Adam is seven. He has difficulty with reading, spelling and writing, although he enjoys and is capable at maths. During non-maths lessons, you have noticed that he spends a considerable amount of time off-task, when he frequently disrupts the other students. This is worse in the afternoon than in the morning.

He is in a composite class of six and seven-year-olds. He spends most of his play time with the younger children. Frequently a pair including Adam is apprehended during play times doing such things as harassing passers-by from an out-of-bounds area of the playground which is close to the street, rifling through rubbish bins for food or cans to swap for other items with students, or engaging in fights in and around the toilets.

He seems bemused by the trouble he gets into, usually saying when challenged that he doesn't know why he behaves in these inappropriate ways, that he couldn't remember a given behaviour was against the rules, or that the other child was at fault for suggesting the activity.

Until a recent assessment, it was believed that Adam behaved as he did because of low academic ability. However, a battery of tests has shown his overall ability (IQ) to be average, with his maths skills in the high-normal range and his reading and spelling skills, while delayed, still within the lower range of normal limits. Teaching staff are now at a loss for a new explanation of his behaviour.

AN APPLIED BEHAVIOUR ANALYSIS APPLICATION

Using ABA, the teacher would perform the following steps in addressing Adam's difficulties:

Step 1: Observe the conditions The teacher will need to observe Adam in a range of settings for specified time periods and record in behavioural terms the conditions (antecedents) that occasion his inappropriate behaviour, and the consequences that follow it. In language-based activities, she might notice, for instance, that Adam remains on task for only 2 minutes, following which he chats to a neighbour or leaves his desk for spurious reasons such as wanting to sharpen an already sharp pencil. In so doing, he frequently speaks to or touches other students who in turn become distracted by him.

Step 2: Define a target behaviour Next, the teacher would select the behaviour that is of most concern to her (termed the *target* behaviour) and define it operationally in precise terms. Let's say the teacher is most concerned with Adam's off-task behaviour because it interferes with other students' learning. In that case, she may determine that the target behaviour is disruptive acts such as chatting to other students during desk activities or moving about the room for unnecessary purposes.

Step 3: Define goals (the terminal behaviour) Next, the teacher would define what improvement she aims for in the target behaviour. Instead of distracting after 2 minutes in language-based activities, the teacher wants Adam to remain on-task for 5 minutes, following which his distractions are not to disrupt the other students' learning. The teacher will define what on-task means. For instance, does it include sharpening pencils, and how dull does a pencil have to be before it legitimately needs sharpening? (Note that the teacher would probably avoid such debates by reminding Adam to sharpen his pencil at the beginning of each work period.) Her earlier observations of Adam's off-task behaviour will help to clarify what she will accept as being on-task and what she will not.

Step 4: Change antecedents The antecendents would be altered. For example, Adam may distract his peers to gain the social contact that he cannot achieve in other ways. If so, then his motor, language or social abilities may need addressing to enable him to participate in social play and gain peer approval without having to display inappropriate behaviour at play time or in class. While this intervention is occurring, or if it makes insufficient difference to Adam's behaviour, then the teacher would institute a behavioural intervention program that focused more directly on the target behaviour.

Step 5: Choose a recording method Systematic recording is needed to evaluate the effectiveness of the intervention program. Adam's teacher is reluctant to use self-recording as it may distract Adam since he is easily attracted off-task. For continuous behaviour such as the target behaviour, event recording is unsuitable, and so the teacher will observe Adam for three 5-minute periods during a desk exercise, and record for each minute of that 5-minute span whether Adam was on-task throughout the minute interval or not. (The teacher may find this observation regime is incompatible with teaching other students, and so will need to ask an assistant to observe and record for her, or will have to be less ambitious—and perhaps less accurate as a result—about what she expects herself to observe.)

Step 6: Plan a reinforcement regime Next, a reinforcement program would be planned because enhancing a positive behaviour is more ethical than attempting to reduce undesired behaviour. If Adam is predominantly on task for two of the 1-minute time slots, he will be reinforced. After one week, the demand will increase to three 1-minute intervals before he receives reinforcement, increasing by a minute per week until he must be on-task for 5 minutes to earn reinforcement.

Adam could be asked about his likes so that these form the basis for a choice of reinforcer. The teacher may consider an activity reinforcer such as the chance to do a maths puzzle, but may reject this in case it is too weak a reinforcer to have the desired effect, or in case it adds maths to Adam's already long list of disliked academic activities.

So, the teacher would institute a program that allowed Adam to gain points each time his behaviour met the criterion. Once sufficient points were earned, he could receive a social reinforcer such as collecting the class's lunch orders or being team leader in a sporting activity, or an activity reinforcer such as having time on the school computer, which Adam enjoys. These reinforcers would be chosen in consultation with Adam and, to avoid satiation, would be in place for one week only.

Step 7: Evaluation Recording would be ongoing to evaluate the effectiveness of the program.

Step 8: Reduce undesirable behaviour If Adam's on-task behaviour did not improve significantly with the reinforcement regime, even when a range of reinforcers was tried and the criteria for success refined, then a reductive procedure may also be required. The least intrusive of these has already been instituted, namely differential reinforcement of incompatible behaviours; extinction is unsuitable because the teacher cannot prevent Adam's peers from responding to him when he distracts them, response cost procedures (such as loss of points) are too elaborate for this teacher to feel she can manage, and so she selects nonseclusionary time out because there is no separate time-out room in the school where exclusionary time out could be supervised.

Step 9: Repeat the steps for other behaviours Finally, the teacher would turn her attention to the remaining behaviours and design successive interventions for each of these. The second target behaviour could be Adam's social skills, since his peers will provide the intrinsic reinforcement necessary for maintaining the gains made in his on-task behaviour. Adam's social and play skills may be amenable to a behavioural contract which, following his success in the first part of the intervention, he may be more motivated to undertake and adhere to.

DISCUSSION QUESTIONS

1. Why is it important to define behaviour in observable terms?
2. Why is it important to record behaviour rates in an applied behaviour analysis program?
3. For what reasons is attention to antecedents crucial in designing a behaviour analysis intervention?
4. What is the difference between positive and negative reinforcers?
5. What factors affect the choice of a reinforcer for a particular student?
6. List some guidelines for the administration of effective reinforcers.
7. What is the difference between extinction and punishment?
8. What are the two types of punishment, and how do they differ?
9. Discuss why extinction and punishment should not be among the first procedures used for modifying behaviour under the theory of applied behaviour analysis.
10. Give six potentially harmful side effects of punishment.
11. List some guidelines for the administration of punishers.
12. Discuss some ethical issues raised by behaviourist approaches, and consider how they could be resolved.
13. In what ways can students' rights be protected under behaviour analysis approaches?
14. Re-apply the case study you generated in chapter 2, this time using ABA principles and practices. What are the differences in recommended practices? What effect would these differences have on the individual student? On the whole class? On the teacher?

SUGGESTIONS FOR FURTHER READING

For detailed technical information about behaviour analysis techniques, the advanced reader is recommended to read these titles:

Martin, G. and Pear, J. 1992, *Behavior modification: What it is and how to do it,*
    4th edn, Prentice Hall, Englewood Cliffs, New Jersey
Wolery, M., Bailey, D.B. and Sugai, G.M. 1988, *Effective teaching: Principles and
    procedures of applied behavior analysis with exceptional students,* Allyn &
    Bacon, Boston

Similar detail is provided in a less technical fashion by the following texts. In
addition, the last two titles give approaches for specific difficulties such as
aggression, deficits in social skills, impulsivity and hyperactivity:

Alberto, P.A. and Troutman, A.C. 1995, *Applied behavior analysis for teachers,* 4th
    edn, Merrill, Columbus, Ohio
Kerr, M.M. and Nelson, C.M. 1989, *Strategies for managing behavior problems in
    the classroom,* 2nd edn, Merrill, Columbus, Ohio
Zirpoli, T.J. and Melloy, K.J. 1993, *Behavior management: applications for teachers
    and parents,* Macmillan, New York

4

COGNITIVE-BEHAVIOURISM

The cognitive-behavioral approaches (are) a purposeful attempt to preserve the demonstrated positive effects of behavioral therapy within a less doctrinaire context and to incorporate the cognitive activities of the client into the efforts to produce therapeutic change. (Kendall, 1991, pp. 4–5)

KEY POINTS

- *Cognitive approaches aim to teach students effective ways of dealing with problems independently of the teacher. They promote self-control.*

- *Success at any task depends on the environment, the student's beliefs about herself as a learner, her problem-solving skills, her ability to do the task, and her ability to organise herself to complete it.*

- *Cognitive approaches have been used for complex problems such as aggression, attention-deficit disorder and depression.*

- *Cognitive restructuring can help both teachers and students remain in control of their behaviour and emotions, reducing stress and increasing their personal effectiveness.*

INTRODUCTION

Whereas applied behaviour analysis (ABA) concentrates on content—that is, what a student does—cognitive-behaviourism focuses on the processes involved in an academic or behavioural task. Cognitive-behaviourism is not a unified theory but instead a set of models and strategies loosely tied together by a concern for the thinking processes of the learner (Hall & Hughes, 1989). Throughout this century, cognitive psychology has been present, although subordinate to ABA, with its revival in therapeutic settings occurring in the last 40 years or so and applied still more recently in remedial education (Benson & Presbury, 1989). The educational focus of the cognitive methods has been dual: they have addressed both low achievement and behavioural difficulties of students. This chapter will focus on approaches designed to increase appropriate behaviour, although those that focus directly on achievement—such as attention and memory training—will also indirectly improve behaviour.

PHILOSOPHICAL ASSUMPTIONS

NATURE OF CHILDHOOD

Bernard (1986) argues that people are neither good nor bad: they are just alive, and do some good and some bad things. This implies that the cognitive therapists see individuals as possessing the capacity for both good and bad, and that they make choices about their behaviour.

CONDITIONS NECESSARY FOR LEARNING TO OCCUR

Cognitivists contend that children need to experience the world in order to learn. Cognitive teaching recognises the learner's responsibility for the learning process rather than focusing exclusively on the efforts of an outside trainer.

PURPOSE OF DISCIPLINE

Discipline has both a managerial and a level one educational function (see chapter 1) of promoting student self-discipline.

REASONS FOR INAPPROPRIATE BEHAVIOUR

Cognitive-behaviourists believe that children's actions are shaped both by the environment and by their understanding of it. While they acknowledge the effect of consequences on behaviour, they also believe the following elements also contribute to an individual's behaviour (Kendall, 1991; Meyers, Cohen & Schleser, 1989):

- the individual's *expectations* about anticipated consequences
- the individual's *attributions* about the causes of those consequences
- the person's ongoing *information processing* and *problem-solving* skills
- the individual's *emotional state* (such as self-esteem)
- the child's *developmental level*
- the *social context*.

All these factors are said to influence the person's behaviour and, in turn, the individual's behaviour affects these variables (Meyers et al., 1989).

ADULT–CHILD STATUS

Under cognitive-behaviourism the adult–child relationship is still likely to have authoritarian overtones, although the goals for the student's behaviour and the steps to achieve them are jointly defined by the student and the teacher, rather than being externally imposed by the teacher as in ABA. Therefore, cognitive-behaviourism is placed between the authoritarian and democratic positions on the continuum of theories (see figure 1.1 in chapter 1).

ROLE OF THE TEACHER

The teacher's aim, according to cognitive-behavioural principles, is to encourage the student to decide *for herself* that it is in her interests to satisfy expectations of her actions. The teacher seeks to change how the student makes sense of experiences, by focusing on cognitive content, process and product so that in future the individual changes how she chooses to behave.

COMPONENTS OF TASK COMPLETION

EXERCISE: COMPONENTS OF SUCCESS

Take a couple of minutes to identify the number of triangles in figure 4.1.

Napier and Gershenfeld (1993) assert that when individuals have had previous negative experiences with this type of exercise, they attempt the task half-heartedly, which contributes to a lack of success. Some people do not persist with the task because they do not expect to be able to get it right; some see it as a trick and decide there is no point in trying; some are trained to be competitive and so will persist with the task for an unduly long time to make sure they get their answer right; while others wait to see how other people in the group will answer, and agree with people whom they assess are likely to be correct. (The correct answer can be found at the end of this chapter.)

This exercise demonstrates that there is more to achievement than simple ability at a task. Figure 4.2 illustrates the many other factors that

Figure 4.1   Exercise in the perception of task demands
(Napier and Gershenfeld 1993, p. 4)

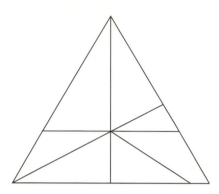

contribute to successful task performance. This model derives in part from Bandura's social-cognitive learning theory (1986), which takes into account the reciprocal feedback between the environment, behaviours, and cognitive and emotional factors. It is supplemented by cognitive restructuring theory and the models developed to account for social skilfulness (see chapter 12).

The resultant model illustrates that when faced with a task, the student first needs the cognitive skills to interpret it and its demands (phase I). Next, her beliefs about herself and her chances of success affect her motivation to carry out the activity (phase II). In phase III, she engages in problem solving to generate a range of behavioural options and to select one that she judges is most likely to work. At phase IV, she acts on this assessment. This last phase requires that the person possess the specific skill needed, and that she be able to organise herself to complete the task in logical steps. All this goes on within the context of the wider environment, which both affects and is affected by the student's behaviours.

THE WIDER ENVIRONMENT

Instead of focusing only on individual stuudents' deficiencies, the cognitivists acknowledge that the social context is a powerful influence on students' behaviour (Burdon & Fraser, 1993) and in turn their actions will shape the environment (Meyers et al., 1989). The environment includes successful teaching practices and school organisation. These will affect the way students view the academic and social tasks they are being asked to complete and will determine what resources are available to support the students' use of their personal skills. Bandura (1986) contends that a very negative context will have an over-riding influence on student

Figure 4.2 Stages of successful task completion

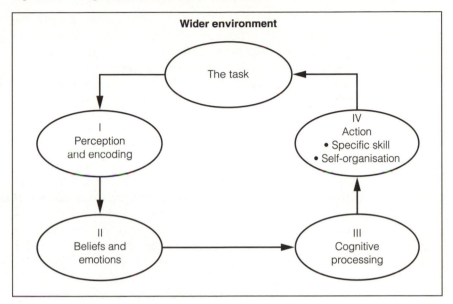

achievement, while in a more neutral or positive context the student's cognitive processes will be more crucial to success.

PERCEPTION AND ENCODING

At phase I, the student will encode or interpret the task she is being asked to complete. As well as this, she will call on information from the past about how she has approached other similar tasks and about the general principles that guide these types of activities. To process this information, the student needs to know something about the type of task being undertaken. For a behavioural task, she needs to know the general principles that govern behaviour, such as consideration of others and acceding to reasonable requests. This information is essential in order for the problem-solving process to begin.

BELIEFS AND EMOTIONS

A range of beliefs about herself and her abilities gives rise to the student's willingness to complete the task (phase II of the model in figure 4.2). Her beliefs will feed and be fed by her self-esteem, and will affect her motivation. These attitudes make the greatest contribution to success, because even if a student has the ability to do the task but no motivation for it, then she will have limited success. This may be especially so for young children who rely more than older children on their emotional interpretations of events (Meyers et al., 1989).

Self-efficacy

This is an individual's judgment about her ability to organise and execute a chosen action (Bandura, 1986). The student must, therefore, be accurate in her appraisal of her abilities, since if she is unduly pessimistic, she will not be willing to undertake and persist at activities. This will cause her to fail and, in turn, she will believe still more strongly that she is incapable. On the other hand, if she has an inflated assessment of her skills, then she may attempt tasks that are too difficult and so could fail unnecessarily (Bandura, 1986).

Self-efficacy is vulnerable to repeated failures and to criticism (Bandura, 1986). Unfortunately, it is not responsive to positive persuasion, which means that a student will need to *experience* success, rather than simply be *told* that she is successful. Therefore, feedback needs to be specific and genuine. That is, the teacher should not tell the student that she has been successful when she has not, and should give feedback that is specific enough for the student to be able to act on the information and correct her errors. Also, the work must be of a level of difficulty sufficient to raise her opinion of her abilities (Bandura, 1986).

The teacher can also acknowledge independent thought more than correct answers, which would benefit a student who has perfectionist standards about getting her work right. While fostering independent thinking, however, the teacher should avoid competition, streaming and teaching the same material to all students since this invites comparisons of their abilities (Bandura, 1986).

Finally, success depends more on hard work than on ability (Bandura, 1986), and so students can be taught to attribute their success to the amount of effort, not to their innate capacities. (See the following discussion of attributional training.)

Learning set

A learning set is an individual's ability to use previous experience to learn. Not drawing on previous experience leads to reduced success and a lack of generalisation of learning. Because of a history of failure, some students—especially those with learning difficulties—may far rather avoid failure than achieve success and so will not apply themselves to a task. Their apparent lack of concentration or other process skills results from their negative learning set rather than any inability to concentrate. Therefore, emotional, not academic, remediation is required.

To develop a positive learning set, students will need to be active in the learning process. This may involve collaborative learning, rather than individual endeavour in which students passively absorb instructions. Also the teacher will need to explain the links between past learning and the present activity, and help the students to identify skills they already have for solving the present problem.

Locus of control

Individuals believe that what happens in their lives is either due to their own behaviour or to outside forces. The first is termed an internal locus of control; the second is an external locus of control and in its extreme form has been called *learned helplessness* (Seligman, 1975). A student with an external locus of control will not be motivated to comply with behavioural expectations or to monitor her own actions independently, because she believes that doing so would make no difference to what happens to her.

The first approach for promoting an internal locus of control is for teachers to give students experience of both success *and* failure, so that they can form a link between their actions and the outcome (Seligman, 1975). If students are always successful, no matter what they do, they feel just as helpless as if they are always a failure, no matter what they do. In either case students will show low tolerance of frustration, poor persistence at tasks, and avoidance of challenge.

A second approach is for the teacher to set work that gradually increases in difficulty, and once the student begins to fail, the teacher can instruct her in how to turn failure into success by changing her approach to solving the problem (Westwood, 1993).

Third, the student can be taught to describe why her approach succeeded or failed, that is, to attribute the outcome to the strategy she used (Cole & Chan, 1990). This is called *attributional training*. It is crucial that the student's attribution is specific and behavioural, however. That is, failure must be attributed to her *actions*, not *herself*. For instance, rather than saying, 'That didn't work, because I'm hopeless at it', the student could comment, 'That didn't work because I didn't plan each step'.

A fourth approach is to negotiate individual contracts that specify what tasks are to be completed, but giving the student discretion for deciding in what order to do them (Westwood, 1993). This gives her experience of being in control of her own learning, although her choice is restricted to *how* to learn, not *whether* to learn.

Self-esteem

A student's beliefs about her capacities to learn (her self-efficacy) and her sense of autonomy are integral to her self-esteem. While self-efficacy is a judgment about one's capabilities, self-esteem is a judgment about the *value* of those capabilities (Bandura, 1986). The cognitivists advise teachers to praise students for positive behaviour in order to highlight their successes and enhance their value to the students.

Motivation

The student's self-efficacy, her learning set, her beliefs about her ability to control success and failure, and her overall self-esteem will affect her motivation to perform a particular task or behaviour. A teacher can increase a student's motivation by employing some cognitive methods, which include the following.

1.   Make sure the task is relevant to the student (Fontana, 1985). The student must see that work is helping her in obvious ways to make a success of her life. The teacher could investigate what sense his class is making of the curriculum being presented, and change that content, rather than obliging the students to change.
2.   This guideline can be adapted to class rules, whereby the teacher explains why the rules are in place so that students see them as relevant and fair, rather than being arbitrary (Conway & Gow, 1990). This would increase the students' motivation to comply voluntarily.
3.   Also, if students play a part in formulating class rules for behaviour, they will be more motivated to comply with them.
4.   When reinforcing appropriate behaviour, where possible the rewards should be intrinsic to the task. Conway and Gow (1990) emphasise using a minimum of extrinsic rewards.
5.   Self-regulation is thought to be intrinsically more rewarding than externally imposed controls (Corno, 1989), because individuals seek to be in control of themselves. If a student's motivation to use self-regulating approaches is suspect, then the program can build in rewards for self-regulation as well as providing rewards for improve-ment in the target behaviour itself.

Conclusion: attitudinal interventions

Problems that had seemed to be due to an inability to organise a task may be resolved when the student develops a more positive orientation to learning in general. This avoids the need for training in self-organisation skills. For example, a student may appear to be distractable, but this could be an avoidance strategy rather than an organisational deficiency, based on the maxim that: 'If at first you don't succeed, deny you were even trying'.

COGNITIVE PROBLEM SOLVING

The third phase of the model in figure 4.2 comprises problem solving. This requires a plan to bring about a desired result. The student examines what needs to be done, scans a range of behavioural options, and selects one that she thinks will be most successful. At this stage the student needs to be capable of paying attention, pacing herself, persisting, and noting feedback, among other skills. Problem solving has the following aspects (Ashman & Conway, 1989; Kaplan & Drainville, 1991; Zirpoli & Melloy, 1993):

1. **Recognition of a problem** The student identifies that an issue exists, and that it can be dealt with appropriately. This requires *interpersonal sensitivity.*

2. **Definition of the problem** This involves accurate interpretation of the task or social demands and isolation of its relevant elements. The student will need *causal thinking*, which is the ability to explain why an event has happened or will happen, and what she can do to make a difference to the problem. Many students have an external focus which means they leave themselves out of the definition of the problem and do not identify what they can do to solve it: they expect the other person to change (Kaplan & Drainville, 1991).

3. **Identification of goals** So that the other person's goals are taken into account as well as her own, the student will need skills in *perspective taking*, which is the ability to understand another person's experience, motives and actions.

4. **Awareness of the relevance of previous experience** and drawing on it.

5. **Generation of alternative solutions** As many solutions as possible are generated.

6. **Decision making** One of the alternative solutions is selected and a plan devised for its implementation. This step requires *consequential thinking*, which is the ability to consider the potential outcomes or consequences of a proposed behaviour, and *means–end thinking*. This refers to the ability to plan the steps needed to achieve a goal.

7. **Verification** that the plan is working and the problem is solved.

Bransford et al. (1986, in Ashman & Conway, 1989) abbreviated these steps into the mnemonic, IDEAL—standing for Identify, Define, Explore, Act, Look.

Problem-solving training centres on teaching students how to deal with the structure of problems, and provides practice in the skills involved. Once appropriate behaviour has been displayed, it may need behavioural reinforcement rather than relying on a purely cognitive approach alone.

ACTION: APPLYING TASK-SPECIFIC SKILLS

Phase IV of the model for task success (see figure 4.2) comprises the ability to enact a chosen behaviour. The first enactment skill involves applying task-specific knowledge. For instance, to complete a maths problem, the student needs to be able to count; to behave non-aggressively, the student needs prosocial skills for solving social disputes.

ACTION: SELF-ORGANISATION SKILLS

Once students have this specific information, they then need to be able to organise themselves to act on it. Students need several skills to be effective and independent managers of their own behaviour (Whitman, Scherzinger & Sommer, 1991):

- They need to be able to monitor their own actions.
- They need the verbal skills necessary for self-instruction.
- They must be able to set appropriate standards or criteria by which to judge their performance.
- They must be able to recognise accomplishments to add to their pool of information that can be drawn on during future tasks.
- They need to self-administer appropriate consequences for their actions.

Kanfer and Gaelick (1986, cited by Whitman et al., 1991) suggest that self-regulation is a complex cognitive skill requiring focused attention, continuous decision making, and an ability to delay both responding and gratification. The main methods for helping students to organise themselves are self-monitoring, self-instruction, self-evaluation and self-reinforcement (or self-punishment).

Self-monitoring (self-recording)

If individuals want to control their behaviour, they have to be aware of what they are doing (Bandura, 1986). Students can monitor their performance outcomes (in terms of quantity, quality or rate of a behaviour) or their attention processes (Bandura, 1986; Maag, Reid & DiGangi, 1993; Reid & Harris, 1993). It may be that students will be most successful when they are able to choose which aspect of their behaviour to monitor, and each aspect may be more or less relevant at given ages and for different tasks (Maag et al., 1993; Reid & Harris, 1993). Less structured approaches may involve simply asking the student whether she is complying with class rules at the time a violation begins.

Self-recording devices need to be portable, easy to use, inexpensive and obtrusive enough to remind the student to record her behaviour while being undetectable by someone else (Shapiro, 1984). Methods include simple tally sheets (perhaps with pictures for younger students) or counting devices. Students can employ time sampling methods or continuous recording, or they can record a behaviour narrative that discloses antecedents and consequences.

The act of self-monitoring may merely inform students, or it can motivate them to change (Schunck, 1989) or even produce a change in the behaviour (Shapiro, 1984), especially when self-monitoring is paired with recording (Maag, Rutherford & DiGangi, 1992) and when the student is observing successes rather than failures (Bandura, 1986). Even when observation is inaccurate, the resulting intervention still has some effect (Whitman et al., 1991). However, to ensure accurate self-recording, most writers recommend matching the student's record with the teacher's for at least some time during the intervention.

Self-instruction

Inner speech can guide our behaviour. Because this inner talk can be adaptive or maladaptive, it will accordingly lead to functional or dys-functional behaviour (Rogers, 1994; Wragg, 1989). Positive self-talk allows students to identify and guide themselves through the steps required to complete the task successfully or to behave appropriately. The aim is for the student to be able to guide her own behaviour using the following steps, which may be written or drawn on cue cards that the student can refer to as a reminder.

1. Pause.
2. Ask: 'What is the problem?'
3. Ask: 'Is what I'm doing helpful to me?'
4. Plan: 'What else could I do?'

The steps are taught to the student in five stages which were first outlined by Meichenbaum and Goodman in 1971 (Alberto & Troutman, 1995; Cole & Chan, 1990; Wragg, 1989). In the first step, *cognitive modelling*, the teacher performs the task while asking and answering questions about the nature of the task and how to go about it, then describing how he is doing each step, and reporting his judgments about his progress. At the second step, *overt external guidance*, the student imitates the teacher's self-instructional routine while student and teacher perform the task together. Next the student performs the task alone while saying the instructions aloud (*overt self-guidance*), then whispering the instructions (*faded self-guidance*), and finally using silent self-instructions (*covert self-guidance*).

A careful analysis of the steps involved in the task is needed, leading to a set of instructions that is as specific as possible. The teacher can build on the strategies the student is already using (Cole & Chan, 1990; Conway & Gow, 1990) and will need to allow the student to work independently from as early as possible. Finally, the teacher needs to provide strategies to deal with failures, and ensure that once mastery is achieved, the student is given time to practise and consolidate her skills.

Self-evaluation (self-assessment)

In this phase of self-regulation, the student compares her performance against a preset standard to determine whether it meets this criterion. Setting appropriate self-imposed performance standards may be the most crucial phase of the self-management process (Whitman et al., 1991).

Students are more likely than teachers to set lenient standards, and yet improvement is more probable if standards are high (Alberto & Troutman, 1995). This implies that a student may need some guidance from the teacher in setting appropriate criteria for success and in judging whether she has attained them.

Self-reinforcement or punishment

Instead of the teacher deciding on the reinforcers and being in charge of delivering them, with self-reinforcement the student determines these. This can begin with teacher administered reinforcers which are faded out as the student learns to self-administer (Shapiro & Klein, 1980, cited by Whitman et al., 1991). The aim of self-reinforcement is to enhance the effectiveness of self-monitoring, although for some individuals, it may not be any more effective than self-monitoring alone (Whitman et al., 1991).

The other aspect of self-delivery of consequences is self-punishment— commonly involving response-cost procedures and loss of tokens in a token economy system. It may be more difficult for students to do the arithmetic involved in subtracting tokens in a self-punishment procedure than to add tokens in a self-reinforcement process (Alberto & Troutman, 1995), and punishment procedures may activate a fear and increased awareness of failure and consequently reduce the students' motivation. Therefore, self-reinforcement is preferred to self-punishment.

Guidelines for self-management training

Behavioural contracts may provide some structure for the self-management program. In addition, the following conditions are desirable when teaching students to manage their own behaviour (Zirpoli & Melloy, 1993).

Student participation

In order to increase the student's motivation to participate, she must be involved in developing the goals, defining the criteria for success, and planning the contingencies involved in the training. If a self-reinforcement element is included in the program, the student needs to be involved in selecting the reinforcer.

Recording method

The recording method needs to be simple enough for the student to use easily. She will need training in how to record her behaviour so that she becomes fluent in self-monitoring. During the intervention phase, she will need prompting to record her own behaviour. Prompts include teacher reminders or beeps sounding at specified intervals. Young children may find it difficult to remember how behaviours are defined, may need more prompts to record them, and will need a very simple recording technique (Shapiro, 1984).

Reinforcement for self-regulation

The student needs reinforcement for self-regulation, as well as for appropriate behaviour. The teacher can compare his ratings with the student's, and give a reinforcer when the two records match. This matching process can be faded once the student becomes more independent in her self-management.

Academic survival skills

The student may need to be taught and given the chance to rehearse practical skills that Rogers (1994) calls academic survival skills. In addition to the cognitive skills—for example, of paying attention—that have already been discussed, behavioural survival skills include staying in one's seat, following classroom procedures, coping with frustration, and so on.

SPECIFIC APPLICATIONS OF COGNITIVE-BEHAVIOURAL APPROACHES

Kendall (1991) describes behaviours in three categories:

* *distorted* thinking (characteristic of depression and anorexia) versus *deficient* thinking (as found in hyperactivity and autism)
* *under-control* (for instance, in hyperactivity) versus *over-control* (demonstrated in anorexia)
* *internal* versus *external* disorders (for example, depression and aggression respectively)

AGGRESSION

Aggressive children and adolescents display some deficits and distortions in their thinking, including an over-sensitivity to hostile cues from others and an under-estimation of their own aggressiveness, which they therefore do not attempt to control (Feindler, 1991; Lochman, White & Wayland, 1991; Wragg, 1989). Aggressive behaviour works for these students, and they lack non-violent solutions to social dilemmas, and so their motivation to change can be limited. Intervention focuses on the deficiencies and distortions in aggressive students' thinking. It involves group training sessions in which they are taught how to identify and deal with their anger; to monitor and manage their own arousal; to think about events before acting; to take another person's perspective; to enact coping strategies such as relaxation; and to generate, evaluate and then use non-violent solutions to troublesome social interactions. The group members manage each other's behaviour, set goals for the behaviour of individuals outside the group, and provide immediate peer feedback to a member about the appropriateness of her actions.

Lochman et al. (1991) report positive results from such programs, although gains are not always evident at six month follow-up. They conclude that the programs need to be more intensive and broad, to include parents, and to focus on prevention with at-risk students rather than waiting for problems to develop.

ATTENTION-DEFICIT DISORDER WITH HYPERACTIVITY (ADD-H)

Children with attention-deficit disorder show deficiencies in coming to attention, sustaining attention (concentration span) and selective attention (Zentall, 1989) with added deficiencies in problem solving, moderating behaviour to suit the context, and self-regulation (Hinshaw & Erhardt, 1991). Their impulsivity is characterised by fast and inaccurate responding (Zentall, 1989). Secondary or associated problems include low school achievement, low self-esteem, poor peer relationships, labile mood and aggressiveness. Negative outcomes in later life are associated with ADD-H symptoms themselves and with the presence of these secondary problems.

Training in a range of skills is considered necessary (Douglas, 1980, in Hinshaw & Erhardt, 1991; Zentall, 1989):

- motivation (to increase attention and effort)
- specific task approaches
- social skills/problem solving
- academic strategies
- self-awareness, to promote accurate reflection about one's own actions (to inhibit impulsiveness)
- self-instruction
- attribution training, to foster an internal locus of control
- accurate observation of peers' behaviour (to overcome an over-sensitivity to hostile cues)
- anger management and other ways to modulate arousal.

Hinshaw and Erhardt (1991) state that programs need to contain all these components since it is still too early to tell which ones are the most effective. They contend that parents need to be involved, and that programs for children and adolescents with ADD-H need to be long term (9–12 months). At the same time, however, Zentall (1989) reports that hyperactive children feel unable to meet the expected standards for their behaviour and that, while improving their skills is important, it is also crucial to ensure that others' expectations of the children are appropriate.

Hinshaw and Erhardt (1991) add that behavioural interventions, such as response-cost procedures and direct reinforcement of alternative behaviours, are especially important with these students. Their final conclusion is that it is likely that cognitive approaches alone will only ever improve on, but not supplant, behavioural and pharmacologic strategies with the cluster of behaviours we call ADD-H.

CHILDHOOD DEPRESSION

While depressed students will need help from psychiatric or psychological professionals, the teacher may need to be able to identify and refer these students since they are at risk of suicide. Also, once the depressed student is receiving treatment, the teacher still has to deal with her while she is at school.

Depressed individuals see themselves, the world and the future in negative terms, with these negative thoughts recurring constantly. This negative thinking is accompanied by negative behaviour such as social withdrawal and physical disturbances such as fatigue, aches and agitation or slow movement. This combination of symptoms makes dealing with a depressed student a challenge, since any one of these symptoms alone is itself difficult to treat (Stark, Rouse & Livingston, 1991). In addition, cognitive interventions require the active involvement of the student, which is less likely when she is depressed.

To overcome some of the therapeutic difficulties, counselling or discussion sessions must be fun. Approaches include training in social skills, problem solving (to help the student consider alternatives in upsetting situations), activity scheduling (to increase her activity level), production of positive self-statements, reattribution and self-control. The student is taught to examine her thoughts more objectively, asking what evidence she has for her negative predictions, what other interpretations are possible, and querying what if the outcome were not as significant and as negative as she is predicting. Next the student is taught to focus her self-observations on positives rather than on negatives, and to deliver self-reinforcement when she uses any of the coping skills being taught (Stark, Best & Sellstrom, 1989; Stark et al., 1991).

While a counselling group is beyond the realm of the class teacher, where appropriate some activities that centre on these themes may be introduced for individuals or the whole class.

GENERALISATION

Cognitive-behaviourism offers some specific strategies to promote generalisation, which has been a vexed issue for applied behaviour analysis. The cognitive approaches motivate students to learn so that negative attitudes do not impair the transfer of learning. Learners can be encouraged to consider generalisation before the task is begun by asking, 'How is this task similar to others?'. Students can then be asked to analyse and examine what they already know about solving the problem at hand (Whitman et al., 1991). If they have the skills already, they need to self-monitor, self-instruct and evaluate whether their approach is working. They also need to identify when they need help. When help is needed, the instructor teaches both the strategy and how it can be used. Finally, students are allowed to work independently, to self-mediate the process. They have now generalised the strategy.

TEACHER SELF-MANAGEMENT

Cognitive approaches can be applied to teachers as well as to students. Teacher behaviour can prevent students from developing a negative perception of learning and of their own ability to learn (Fontana, 1985). For this reason, the teacher will need to regulate his own behaviour so that his manner and actions communicate to students that he is interested in them and their work and that he has faith in their abilities. He will need to present as someone the students would like to get to know. He will need a confident manner, clear and consistent expectations and a willingness to help and guide students. He will need to provide sufficient structure for students to be able to achieve—including being able to anticipate and prevent problems—and to be alert to difficulties when they arise. These teacher behaviours all help students to make sense of the teacher and his role and consequently to understand their own role in the classroom.

To achieve this, knowledge of young people and their perspective is essential, but self-knowledge is also crucial. The teacher's ability to regulate his own actions (and, in turn, to manage the class) is influenced by his own thinking, which includes his beliefs about himself, about his effectiveness in his role as a teacher and about the students.

COGNITIVE RESTRUCTURING

In the late 1950s, Albert Ellis introduced rational-emotive therapy (RET). This is based on the concept that it is not events themselves that bother us, but what we believe particular events mean for us (Ellis, 1962). What we tell ourselves about the events determines what feeling we experience, and the strength of that feeling. Ellis (1973) postulated an ABCD sequence of reactions to events:

- **A**ctivating event
- **B**elief
- Emotional **C**onsequence
- **D**ispute

Ellis contends that the individual's belief (B) about event A can be 'rational' or 'irrational'. If the belief is irrational, the emotional consequence at C is likely to be excessive or 'catastrophising'. These emotional over-reactions are common—for example, our occasional despair at 'having nothing to wear' to a party—but if they are persistently excessive, the individual can become unduly distressed and problems will be inevitable. One characteristic of extreme thinking that engenders high emotion is what Ellis calls 'Absolutist' thinking. This can involve *personalisation*, whereby the teacher over-estimates the degree to which, say, a student's behaviour is directed at him personally. It may include *filtering*, which causes us to notice more negatives than positives, and *over-generalising*, whereby one instance tells us that all other occasions will be the same. When we feel bad, we may *blame* other people, and may castigate ourselves for not being perfect. *Perfectionist* thinking is often characterised by the word 'should'. The individual feels driven to live by these standards, regardless of whether they are functional. Some perfectionist drivers (or 'shoulds') are listed in table 4.1.

We may apply these 'shoulds' or unrealistic standards to ourselves or to students, for instance: 'Students *should* be respectful . . . Students *should* want to learn this: it's important . . . Students *shouldn't* behave this way . . . Students *should* be more appreciative . . .' and so on. They can be extended to parents: 'Parents *should* want to be involved in the school . . . They *should* discipline their children better . . . Some parents *shouldn't* have children . . .' etc.

The corollaries of these and similar 'shoulds' are that when the student or parent does not comply, then: 'They *should* be punished. . .My job is intolerable', or even, 'Why should I try, since my students (or their parents) clearly aren't trying' (by not complying with the teacher's view of how they 'should' behave).

Table 4.1 A teacher's absolutist thinking

---

1. I must be a perfect teacher.
2. My students must always be interested and involved in the lesson.
3. I should have the solution to every problem.
4. I should look after others, never myself.
5. I should never get tired, sick or inefficient.
6. If there's ever anything to be done, I must not relax until it is completed.
7. I must be liked and respected by all my colleagues. Therefore, I must always act to attract this regard.
8. I should worry a lot about bad things that have happened or which could go wrong for me or my students.
9. I have to have someone to rely on: I cannot survive alone.
10. I have problems now (as a person, or as a teacher) because of what has happened to me in the past so I cannot change how I am now. Other people and events control my life.

DISCARDING THE 'SHOULDS'

These beliefs, Ellis contends, make it difficult to conduct a settled and contented life, free of unnecessary stress. He acknowledges that the world would be a nicer place if everyone obeyed our high standards for them, yet this is not going to happen, and getting worked up by wishing it would is not going to make it so, and will only add to our own stress.

Therefore, we need to challenge our inaccurate beliefs. This is called *cognitive restructuring* (Kaplan & Drainville, 1991) and involves the following steps. Once the individual is aware of the event that triggered a maladaptive emotional or behavioural response, first he identifies the beliefs that contributed to his distress; next he acknowledges that these beliefs are irrational, inaccurate or unhelpful; and, third, he sets about contradicting them as vehemently as he has held on to them. It takes effort and persistence to overcome repetitive inaccurate self-talk.

Part of this disputing process is to replace the demand 'should' with the desire 'want'. The *shoulds* compel us to live by standards that are not our own; their more accurate counterparts, the *wants*, are true values. We *want* to do a good job, and when we do not, we feel bad about that, sometimes very bad, but failure does not make us a bad person who has no redeeming qualities. Examples of a teacher's accurate thoughts are listed in table 4.2.

APPLYING COGNITIVE RESTRUCTURING TO STUDENTS

Students too can be taught to change self-defeating talk to helpful self-statements (Rogers, 1994). For instance, 'This is too hard: I can't do it' can be changed to 'This is tricky, but if I use my plan, it will be easier'. Rogers details how to motivate students to change their thinking by using encouragement during rehearsal time and in class, and by giving specific feedback about their progress.

SUMMARY

Cognitive-behaviourism focuses on student self-management, and also offers some advice to teachers in managing their own thinking and consequent approach to teaching. The theory addresses a student's attitude to the learning task or to behavioural compliance, and her ability to organise herself to achieve appropriate standards.

The aim is for the student to become independent in managing her own behaviour, rather than have this managed for her. The rationale for promoting self-management is to increase the student's motivation to comply with expectations, to improve generalisation of new skills, to enhance the effectiveness of the interventions, and to free the teacher from behaviour management.

Table 4.2 A teacher's rational beliefs

1   I would *like* to do a good job and I know I will feel disappointed if I do not. I can cope with that, however, and can take steps to improve my skills for the future.
2   My students are responsible for their own feelings. I can guide them but I cannot force them to learn or behave as I would like. It is their choice and they pay the price of that.
3   I do not have to know everything: I only have to be open to learning what I need to know.
4   Other people will feel disappointed if they want me to do something for them, and I do not. I may be rejected and disapproved of, but I can cope with that and can accept myself and my decision.
5   I would like to do things well most of the time and will feel disappointed when I do not. However, I have the courage to be imperfect.
6   I am allowed to rest when I wish.
7   I would like to be respected by my colleagues and will feel lonely and isolated if I am not. I can cope with this, however, and can take steps to improve these relationships without submerging my own rights.
8   Worrying about things that could go wrong will not avoid them happening. I can live without guarantees and can focus on the good that is present now.
9   I like to have other people in my life although I can survive if I do not receive the support I would like.
10 I may have learnt some ways of dealing with life's stressors that hinder rather than help me. I can continue to use these coping strategies or I can decide to learn new ways which may be more effective and rewarding for me.

CASE STUDY

Adam is seven. He has difficulty with reading, spelling and writing, although he enjoys and is capable at maths. During non-maths lessons, you have noticed that he spends a considerable amount of time off-task, when he frequently disrupts the other students. This is worse in the afternoon than in the morning.

He is in a composite class of six and seven-year-olds. He spends most of his play time with the younger children. Frequently a pair including Adam is apprehended during play times doing such things as harassing passers-by from an out-of-bounds area of the playground which is close to the street, rifling through rubbish bins for food or cans to swap for other items with students, or engaging in fights in and around the toilets.

He seems bemused by the trouble he gets into, usually saying when challenged that he doesn't know why he behaves in these inappropriate ways, that he couldn't remember a given behaviour was against the rules, or that the other child was at fault for suggesting the activity.

Until a recent assessment, it was believed that Adam behaved as he did because of low academic ability. However, a battery of tests has shown his overall ability (IQ) to be average, with his maths skills in the high-normal range and his reading and spelling skills, while delayed, still within the lower range of normal limits. Teaching staff are now at a loss for a new explanation of his behaviour.

A COGNITIVE-BEHAVIOURAL APPLICATION

Under the cognitive-behavioural approach, a teacher might respond to Adam's behaviour with the following steps:

Step 1: Assess the task The teacher would first examine how relevant the curriculum seems to Adam (and other students), including acknowledging that a curriculum is irrelevant if it is too easy or too hard for the student. Possible differences in teaching style between subjects needs to be examined because while Adam's better performance at maths may be due to his greater interest in and ability at maths (as indicated by his assessment results), it may also be due to a closer match between the teaching methods used in that subject and Adam's learning style. This step is similar to the behaviourists' attention to antecedents.

Step 2: The teacher's contribution to the problem Next, the teacher would ask himself whether any element of his reaction to Adam's behaviour is itself adding to the teacher's own stress, rather than the behaviour being the only trigger. The teacher will need to ensure his self-talk about Adam's behaviour is rational, and does not inflame the conflict between them.

Step 3: Emotional factors affecting success: self-esteem Then the teacher would address an anticipated low self-esteem resulting from Adam's repeated failure at school. Praising his achievements would be a key to enhancing Adam's self-esteem.

Step 4: Emotional factors affecting success: locus of control The fourth step would be to challenge the external locus of control that is implied by Adam's denial of responsibility for his infractions of the school rules. This may be done through conversations with Adam, and will be systematised in the later steps of self-management.

Step 5: Emotional factors affecting success: motivation to observe rules Next, the teacher would focus on enhancing Adam's motivation to observe rules. To make rules relevant for students, class meetings would be held to determine the expectations for all students and to decide on the consequences when these rules are infringed.

Step 6: Cognitive restructuring Adam will need training in self-instruction and will need to increase his awareness of his self-talk, challenging his attributions about his failures and about other students. To assist in teaching Adam more positive attributions, he will be told the results of his assessment, so that he hears that he has the ability to succeed.

Step 7: Self-management training To help Adam use positive self-talk to motivate and instruct himself through the steps involved in tasks, the teacher will write verbal prompts on cards for Adam (with cartoons to give extra cues). At first the teacher will prompt Adam to use these cards to guide his thinking, and then will gradually guide him to use them independently.

Step 8: Work contract A contract will be negotiated between Adam and his teacher, stating the expectations for his on-task behaviour, and specifying the activity reinforcer that he will earn if he satisfies this criterion. Wragg (1989) advises that the teacher require a 25–50% reduction in the target behaviour, so this would be the initial criterion, adjusted later if necessary.

Step 9: Self-recording Self-monitoring will be instituted using a tally chart, on which Adam will write how often he completes a task within the allotted time. The teacher will also record Adam's behaviour, until the two records are similar enough that recording will be done by Adam alone. The main focus is on Adam monitoring his actions so that he is less impulsive.

Step 10: Self-reinforcement Adam will give himself points for completing a task to the criterion level established in the contract, and then will trade in his points for the specified activity reinforcer. Accurate recording and reinforcement will earn Adam an occasional activity reinforcer of computer time or a social reinforcer of being class leader for an activity.

Step 11: The wider environment Because of Adam's social isolation, the teacher will offer social skills training sessions for all students, focusing on solving social dilemmas and collaborating in play. The teacher may also observe Adam's play and, where necessary and appropriate, teach Adam the skills needed for the games in which the other students engage at play time. For instance, if Adam has difficulty catching a ball and this activity takes up a good deal of student play time, then it will be difficult for him to become involved unless his ball skills improve.

DISCUSSION QUESTIONS

1. What aspects, in addition to external events, do cognitive-behaviourists believe influence an individual's behaviour?
2. What components contribute to success at a task?
3. Name some key attitudinal components of successful performances.
4. How could a teacher motivate a reluctant student to participate in a self-management program?
5. For what reasons is self-reinforcement preferable to self-punishment?
6. What are some essential elements of successful self-management training?
7. What are Kendall's three classifications of behaviour problems (1991) addressed by the cognitive-behavioural methods?
8. Select a behaviour of interest—aggression, attention deficit or depression—and describe how a teacher would address it using a cognitive-behavioural approach.

9. Under the cognitive-behavioural approach, what role do the teacher's attitude and presentation play in managing student behaviour?
10. What differences and similarities do you see between cognitive-behaviourism and applied behaviour analysis?
11. Re-apply the case study you generated in chapter 2, this time using cognitive-behavioural principles and practices. What new features are introduced into the recommended practices? What effect would these differences have on the individual student? On the whole class? On the teacher?

SUGGESTIONS FOR FURTHER READING

An overview of cognitive-behaviour methods is given in single chapters in each of the following texts:

Alberto, P.A. and Troutman, A.C. 1995, *Applied behavior analysis for teachers*, 4th edn, Merrill, Columbus, Ohio

Kaplan, J.S. and Drainville, B. 1991, *Beyond behavior modification: A cognitive-behavioral approach to behavior management in the school*, 2nd edn, Pro-Ed, Austin, Texas

Zirpoli, T.J. and Melloy, K.J. 1993, *Behavior management: applications for teachers and parents*, Macmillan, New York

Practical programs for cognitive restructuring are outlined by:

Rogers, W. A. 1994, *Behaviour recovery*, ACER, Melbourne

Wragg, J. 1989, *Talk sense to yourself: A program for children and adolescents*, ACER, Melbourne

Therapeutic interventions for aggressiveness, anger, depression, ADD-H and other conditions are described by:

Kendall, P.C. (ed.) 1991, *Child and adolescent therapy: Cognitive-behavioral procedures*, Guilford, New York

---

Puzzle answer

The puzzle contains fifteen triangles: the large one, and six single triangles (which excludes the shape in the bottom right-hand corner since it has four sides), plus eight triangles formed from two or more singles.

CHAPTER 5

NEO-ADLERIAN THEORY: ADLER, DREIKURS, DINKMEYER AND BALSON

. . . each child needs encouragement like a plant needs water. Without it, his growth is stunted and his potential sapped. (Dinkmeyer & Dreikurs, 1963, p. 3)

KEY POINTS

- *The neo-Adlerians aim to increase students' sense of belonging by democratic relationships within the classroom that are based on mutual respect, cooperation and encouragement.*

- *When students feel their appropriate behaviour is acknowledged, they are less likely to act disruptively.*

- *Disruptive behaviour is aimed at being accepted into the group.*

- *Therefore, inappropriate behaviour represents a faulty decision: the student has selected an inappropriate way to meet an appropriate goal.*

- *The teacher identifies which of four goals the student is seeking to achieve, by noting how she feels and responds to the behaviour, and how the student responds to correction.*

- *Once the goal has been identified, the teacher aims to guide the student to achieve the same goal through more appropriate behaviour.*

- *Natural or logical consequences and contracts can be used to deter continued displays of inappropriate behaviour.*

INTRODUCTION

Recent writers such as Rudolf Dreikurs, Don and Don Dinkmeyer (senior and junior, respectively) with Gary McKay and, in Australia, Maurice Balson, who credit Alfred Adler (1870–1937) for their philosophy and theory, have also departed in some significant ways from his writings. Therefore, this chapter will at times compare Adler's foundation writings with the beliefs of his disciples.

PHILOSOPHICAL ASSUMPTIONS

NATURE OF CHILDHOOD

The neo-Adlerians believe that children do more than merely respond to stimuli: they actively assign meaning to events. However, they are at risk of learning inadequate ways of responding to the many demands placed on them, because of their still immature adjustment processes, and the countless pressures they endure (Adler, 1954).

CONDITIONS NECESSARY FOR LEARNING TO OCCUR

Children learn by overcoming feelings of inferiority (Adler, 1954). These feelings are seen to be natural, given children's total dependence on adults for survival. Inferiority engenders ambition and is the driving force behind learning. However, it differs from discouragement, which in contrast leads to despair.

PURPOSE OF DISCIPLINE

Discipline is intended to create the order necessary for learning to occur (the managerial function), to guide individuals to exercise self-discipline (a level 1 educational function) and to promote cooperation within the group (a level 2 educational purpose).

REASONS FOR INAPPROPRIATE BEHAVIOUR

Low self-esteem

The individual's evaluation of himself governs his actions. Adler (1954) lists many adult attitudes which contribute to children's feelings of inadequacy, including the excessive demands of the education system, children not being allowed to take risks, being ridiculed, and not being taken seriously because they are children (which he said was especially true for girls). Later writers asserted that discouragement arises from competition at home and in school (Dreikurs and Cassel, 1990). This fosters the desire to be perfect, which stifles creativity, self-confidence and spontaneity.

Need to belong

Whereas Adler believed self-esteem was the primary force in children, his followers say children's motivation is to belong. The neo-Adlerians write that when our legitimate behaviours are not acknowledged, we become discouraged and so seek to belong in any way we can, even if our behaviour is antisocial.

Faulty choices

Thus, a child's antisocial behaviour is caused by his faulty choices about how to meet his needs, based on some mistaken assumptions about himself, difficulties in the environment, or other people.

Behaviour is purposeful and goal-directed

The neo-Adlerians believe that all individual behaviour is goal-directed and purposive, aimed at satisfying the child's goals. Because children actively interpret their surroundings, consequences, the past, heredity or even emotions do not determine their actions. Instead, feelings are generated to achieve the child's goals, which refer to the future.

Family constellation

In contradiction to these self-directed reasons for inappropriate behaviour, Adler contended that the order of birth in a family makes a difference to the characteristic 'lifestyle' chosen by a child. The later writers have continued to accept this view. Youngest children are said to grow up feeling inferior to everyone else, and will avoid challenges unless they are able to excel; oldest children are conservative and look for power; a second child frequently becomes what the eldest is not; and an only child is characterised as dependent and unable to overcome life's difficulties because his parents deprive him of practice at problem solving by removing all difficulties for him.

ADULT–CHILD STATUS

The neo-Adlerian preventive approaches are based on democratic relationships in schools, which favour individual responsibility. Adler (1954) contended that if we allow individuals to take responsibility for their own well-being, rather than being at the mercy of events outside their control, then we have hope for even those students whose home background or heredity may put them at risk of under-achievement or behaviour difficulties at school. Although its preventive approaches are democratic, this theory is placed between the authoritarian and authoritative–democratic positions on the teacher–student power continuum in figure 1.1, because its interventions rest on the teacher making judgments about the students' motivations, and choosing how to intervene to discourage an antisocial behaviour, without necessarily consulting the student.

ROLE OF THE TEACHER

The teacher must promote students' intellectual, social, emotional and physical development to their optimal levels (Balson, 1992). At the same time, she must enable students to take responsibility for their own actions.

PREVENTION OF CLASSROOM BEHAVIOUR PROBLEMS

The neo-Adlerians espouse three methods for preventing classroom behaviour problems: first, democratic student–teacher relationships; second, a reduction in competition among students and between the teacher and students; and third, the use of encouragement rather than praise, to offset any discouragement the student may feel and which may give rise to mistaken behaviour.

DEMOCRATIC STUDENT–TEACHER RELATIONSHIPS

Democracy comprises a climate of mutual respect, encouragement of students, student participation in decision making, and promotion of student self-discipline (Dinkmeyer, McKay & Dinkmeyer, 1980). Students and teachers enjoy the freedoms but also exercise the responsibilities of living in a democracy (Dreikurs & Cassel, 1990). In contrast, autocratic teaching 'creates an atmosphere in which only a few good children become better, many bad children become worse and the majority are regulated by fear', say Dreikurs and Cassel (1990, p. 16). The distinctions between autocracy and democracy are summarised in table 5.1.

Democratic communication skills

The neo-Adlerians detail democratic techniques for interacting with students individually and in class discussion meetings. Like Gordon's communication roadblocks to be discussed in chapter 6, Dinkmeyer et al. (1980) describe some ineffective listening styles, which they list as: the commander-in-chief, the moralist, the judge, the critic, the amateur psychologist and the consoler. They detail alternatives to these counter-productive styles, including non-verbal communication that the teacher

Table 5.1 Contrast between autocratic and democratic teaching styles (adapted from Dreikurs & Cassel, 1990)

Style	*Autocratic*	*Democratic*
Leadership	Boss	Leader
	Command	Invitation
	Power	Influence
	Demanding cooperation	Winning cooperation
	Domination	Guidance
	Punishing	Helping
	Sole responsibility of boss	Shared responsibility in team
Teaching	Pressure	Stimulation
	Imposing ideas	Selling ideas
	I tell you what you should do	I tell you what I will do
	I tell you	Discussion
	I decide, you obey	I suggest, and help you to decide
Interpersonal	Sharp voice	Friendly, courteous
	Criticism	Encouragement
	Fault-finding	Acknowledgment of achievement

is comfortable with engaging interpersonally with students, and the verbal skills of reflective listening, assertiveness and collaborative problem-solving. These writers acknowledge Thomas Gordon (1970, 1974) as the source of many of these concepts and so the skills will be detailed in chapter 6.

Class discussions

Like the humanists to be discussed in the next chapter, Dreikurs and Cassel (1990, p. 78) advocate the use of class discussion groups on the basis that: '. . . any problem child is a problem for the whole class, and the solution to the problem grows most naturally out of the helpful involvement of all class members'.

Through class collaboration, the discouraged student can begin to feel part of the group, thus reducing his discouragement. Other class members do not feel powerless to overcome the difficulties with the disruptive student, who in turn is not shunned because of his behaviour. The method also demonstrates ways of resolving issues other than through fighting.

The discussion session is structured to occur weekly, rather than only when problems arise. This allows students to postpone attempting to solve the problem alone, since they can anticipate when it will be dealt with by the group. Also issues can be dealt with when they arise, rather than being allowed to escalate to unmanageable levels.

REDUCE COMPETITION

Democratic principles suggest that schools abandon competition, since it does not motivate students for long, and even then motivates only those who can succeed. Competition cuts across cooperation (and in so doing it fosters self-centredness) and it leads to a lack of respect for the intrinsic worth of individuals. Dreikurs and Cassel (1990) contend that focusing on winning and losing detracts from mastery of the task at hand. Some methods of eliminating competition between the teacher and student, and among the student group include:

- use of encouragement by the teacher and students
- promoting peer acceptance, whereby students are asked to pay attention to each other as well as to the teacher, unlike in the autocratic classroom
- giving permission for students to vent their feelings
- allowing students to observe another student solving a similar problem to their own, as happens in class meetings
- promoting peer feedback about each other's behaviour
- focusing on what the students have in common with each other
- fostering student altruism so that they aim to help each other rather than to compete
- giving permission for the classroom to be interactive rather than silent.

ENCOURAGEMENT

The neo-Adlerians prefer encouragement to praise because praise reflects an imbalance of power between teachers and students. In support of this argument, they discuss the costs of praise.

THE COSTS OF PRAISE

Praise signals an inequality of power between the teacher and student, and may even be used to put a student in his place because, by offering judgment, the teacher implies that she has some special competence (Ginott, 1972). Praise aims to manipulate the student into repeating a behaviour, with the teacher deciding what standards to enforce and when to give or withhold praise.

Effect on the student's self-esteem

Praise tells students that the teacher is judging them, and that her opinions of them are more important than their own. This stifles their self-reliance and threatens their sense of being accepted. Even a positive label (such as, 'You're a good boy') can set up unrealistic standards for a student's performance and, in turn, cause him to become discouraged about his ability to meet them.

Interference with learning

The first impact on learning is that when they rely on authority figures for approval, students try to 'read' the teachers for signs that they approve. This 'adult watching' can take valuable energy away from the task they are doing. Second, praise causes students to focus on external rewards rather than on the rewards that come from the activity itself, so it reduces self-motivation and the joy of learning. Third, praise can be intrusive, interrupting students' absorption in their activity. Fourth, praise can teach children to repeat a certain type of work which receives praise, rather than being adventurous and creative or risking mistakes.

Effects on behaviour

Discouraged students, afraid of failing to meet high expectations, may misbehave. Instead of judging their behaviour for them, teaching students to monitor their own successful behaviour improves their behaviour both directly by enhancing their self-esteem and indirectly by giving them skills to regulate their own actions (appropriate and inappropriate).

Ineffectiveness of praise

Praise can be automatic for the teacher and delivered therefore in a meaningless way that lacks credibility (Hitz & Driscoll, 1988). Credibility is also lost when the teacher praises a painting for being a beautiful house, say, only to have the child report that it's a rocket. More importantly, though, praise lacks credibility when the student's evaluation does not match the teacher's. If the praise seems invalid, the student will doubt the teacher's integrity.

Praise is unfair

Considerable expertise is needed to know when and how much praise is fair. Some children become adept at 'pulling' praise from adults 'by smiling or beaming proudly, showing off work, or even communicating an expectation of praise', report Hitz and Driscoll (1988, p. 8). Other students who do not do this receive less praise than they deserve. So praise increases competition between students, who come to feel resentful or jealous if another student receives praise and they do not.

Finally, just like other power based methods, praise is manipulative, which students grow to resent. Also, their frequent experience of the unfairness of praise causes them to reject the adults who administer it.

ENCOURAGEMENT

Instead of praising students, teachers can acknowledge their successes and, in so doing, show students how to recognise their achievements

Table 5.2 Summary of the disadvantages of praise

Effects on the student's self-esteem
- Praise implies the adult's superior position as possessor of all knowledge.
- Praise teaches a child that other people's opinions of him are more important than his own, stifling self-reliance.
- The student does not feel accepted because he is being judged.
- The student may expect himself to be 'good' all the time, lowering his self-esteem when this is impossible.

Interference with learning
- Praised students may engage in 'adult watching', which distracts them from their own developmental tasks.
- Praise causes students to focus on external rather intrinsic rewards. It decreases self-motivation.
- Praise can interrupt the student's concentration.
- A praised student may strive to please and may fear making mistakes, and so may avoid being creative and adventurous.

Provoking misbehaviour
- Discouragement about being unable to meet unrealistic expectations may lead to misbehaviour.
- Praise does not teach students to monitor their own behaviour and so does not give them the skills to regulate their inappropriate actions.

Ineffectiveness of praise
- Praise can be automatic for the teacher, and delivered therefore in a meaningless way.
- The teacher and her praise lose credibility if the student's evaluation of his work does not match the teacher's.

Praise can be unfair
- The teacher needs a high level of technical expertise to use praise well.
- While some students can 'pull' praise from teachers, other students cannot and receive less praise than they deserve.
- Praise increases competition between students.
- Their experience that praise is unfair causes students to reject teachers who administer it.
- Students come to resent being manipulated by praise.

for themselves. This is termed *encouragement*, which differs from praise in the following ways:

1. Encouragement teaches a student to *evaluate his own efforts*: 'What do you think of *that*? . . . Was that fun? . . . Are you pleased with yourself? . . . You seem pleased that you do that so well.' So, encouragement helps a student gain independence from the teacher and raises his self-esteem since he can aim for standards that are relevant to him, rather than imposed by others.

2. Unlike praise, encouragement *does not judge* the student or his work. When the teacher encourages, she may tell the student her reaction to his actions. 'I like the colours you used', replaces the statement that a painting is 'beautiful'. This also avoids having to ask what a painting is, forcing children to draw 'things' rather than to experiment creatively.

Table 5.3   Examples of praise versus encouragement

Praise	Encouragement
You're a good helper.	Thanks for your help. I appreciate your help. Thanks: that's made my job easier.
I'm proud of you for doing so well in your maths exam.	Congratulations. I'm proud for you. Looks like you're enjoying maths. What do you think of *that?* I admire your maths skills.
You're a good girl.	I like you. Thanks for your help.
That's a beautiful painting.	I like the colours you've used. Do you like your painting? Are you pleased with yourself? Looks like that was fun.
Your school play was excellent.	I enjoyed your play very much.

3. Encouragement focuses on the *process* rather than the *outcome*. It highlights the value of learning (Edwards, 1993). A student can be encouraged for what he is doing, rather than for the end product: 'I enjoy seeing you so intent on that' or 'Looks like you're having fun over there', or when the student has a good maths test result: 'I see you're enjoying doing maths'.
4. Encouragement *avoids comparisons and competition* such as, 'That's better', or, 'You're better at that than Richard'. Encouraging statements would describe the action that the teacher appreciated: 'Thanks for being quiet while I concentrated' or 'I appreciate that you put the equipment away'.
5. Encouragement is a *private* event that does not show the student up in public or try to manipulate others into copying a student whose actions have been acknowledged.

Table 5.3 gives examples of praise as distinct from encouragement.

Conclusion

Self-esteem is literally that: *self*-evaluation. To have a positive evaluation of himself, a student needs to be taught how to evaluate his own successes, rather than have these judged by others. He may doubt other people's opinions of him, but will believe his own.

ATTITUDES THAT FACILITATE ENCOURAGEMENT

The first prerequisite attitude that enables the teacher to use encouragement is a guarantee of democratic rights and privileges to all members of the class. Other requirements include: accepting the student as he is; having realistic expectations of students and of oneself; emphasising the process rather than the outcome; and being self-confident (Dinkmeyer & Dreikurs, 1963; Dreikurs & Cassel, 1990).

Accept the student

The teacher who wants to encourage students will need to accept them as they are (not as they could be), so that they can accept themselves. She will need to utilise their interests and focus on their strengths and talents rather than on their weaknesses. This will mean that when commenting on their work, she will avoid pointing out students' errors alone, as this would discourage students from putting in effort in the future (Balson, 1992).

Have realistic expectations

The teacher must set standards that are achievable. Knowledge of child development is crucial. She should communicate to students her faith that they can achieve, and that it is better to try and make mistakes than to do nothing and learn nothing. She should accept a good attempt and show confidence in the student's ability to improve on it another time. Students need to know that their worth does not depend on success.

Emphasise process

The teacher needs to recognise the effort rather than the product. She can foster social cooperation rather than competition and, when dealing with transgressions, she can separate the deed from the doer.

Be confident

The teacher will need to recognise that a student's behaviour does not reflect on her worth as a teacher. The student is responsible for his own choices. The teacher's self-esteem must be high for her to be willing to abandon the superior position given her by autocratic approaches, and to share her power through collaborative learning arrangements and classroom meetings and so enable the students to have a positive influence on each other.

EXERCISE: TURNING PRAISE INTO ENCOURAGEMENT

Since praising can be a very hard habit to break at first, it can be useful to plan in advance and practise altering what you say. To help you do this, take a sheet of paper, and divide it vertically down the middle. On the left-hand side, write down some of the praising statements you commonly use with your students. Next, on the right-hand side, translate each statement into an encouraging one. Planning a change of language in this way allows you to use encouraging statements readily when the occasion arises. With practice, such statements will become automatic instead of feeling awkward.

INTERVENTION WITH DISRUPTIVE BEHAVIOUR

Encouragement prevents students from misbehaving. It is also applied as an intervention when a student is displaying inappropriate behaviour. Let's now turn to other interventive approaches suggested by the neo-Adlerian writers.

GOALS OF BEHAVIOUR

Intervention with disruptive behaviour centres on identifying one of four goals that motivates the student's behaviour and ensuring that this goal is satisfied by more appropriate actions. The student's beliefs about how to meet his goals give rise either to prosocial or antisocial behaviour.

Prosocial beliefs and behaviour turn into antisocial acts if the student becomes discouraged in his attempts to win adult approval and attention. Antisocial behaviour has either an attacking or a defensive mode; these modes equate with active (attacking mode) or passive (defensive mode) pursuit of the student's goal (Balson, 1992). The goals and associated behaviours are listed in table 5.4.

Striving for attention

Adler said that children need affection and power (autonomy) to overcome their feelings of inferiority. The later writers restated this goal as a need for attention, and so was born the concept of *attention-seeking* behaviour. They explain such behaviour as a way of seeking status but observe that the student requires ever-increasing amounts of attention and so is constantly dissatisfied and constantly displaying inappropriate behaviour to get more attention.

As shown in table 5.4, the positive expression of the need for attention is getting involved and making a contribution (Dinkmeyer & McKay, 1982). Its active or attacking negative expression involves provoking the teacher in ways that cannot be ignored—for example, by showing off, being the clown, making mischief, being a nuisance, and other distracting acts such as pencil twiddling or arriving late. Its passive or defending mode engages the teacher unnecessarily by being untidy, cute, shy, fearful, tired, frivolous, in need of help, and having speech difficulties (Balson, 1992).

Power

Power is expressed in its prosocial form in autonomy and self-responsi-

Table 5.4 Goals of behaviour and their expression

Goal	Positive belief	Prosocial behaviour	Discouraged belief	Antisocial behaviour
Attention Involvement	I belong by contributing	Helps Volunteers	I belong only when I am being noticed	Getting attention through disruptiveness; showing off, being a nuisance
Power Autonomy	I am responsible for my behaviour	Shows self-discipline	I belong only when I am in control (bossing others or not being bossed)	Uncooperative, comes into conflict with others, forgetful
Justice Fairness	I belong by cooperating	Returns kindness for hurt; ignores belittling comments	I belong only if I can get revenge	Destructive, cruel acts or sullen and morose
Withdrawal from conflict or challenge	I can belong without getting into conflict	Ignores provocation; withdraws from power contest to decide his own behaviour	I belong only by being inadequate	Under-achievement; absorbed in fantasy, solitary activity

bility (Dinkmeyer & McKay, 1982). Adler asserted that students who continually fail to satisfy their needs because the environment is hostile, because they have disabilities, or because they are presented with insufficient challenges, may either display inadequacy or seek to express power over the environment and dominate others. Dreikurs and Cassel (1990) assert that power seeking becomes antisocial when attention seeking is dealt with inappropriately, and that while the two forms of behaviour are similar, power-seeking behaviour is more intense than attention seeking.

The student seeking to dominate others has come to believe that the only thing he can control is the pleasure or displeasure of the adults in his life. The active or attacking mode of power seeking is behaviour that sends the signal: 'You can't stop me' (Balson, 1992). This includes carrying out forbidden acts, rebellion, defiance, truancy, tantrums and bullying. The passive or defending form of antisocial behaviour aimed at gaining power is based on the motto, 'You can't make me' and includes stubbornness, uncooperative, non-compliant behaviour, forgetfulness, frequent illness, weakness and apathy (Balson, 1992).

Justice or revenge

As can be seen in table 5.4, the prosocial expression of this goal is returning kindness for hurt and ignoring belittling remarks. Seeking revenge (with the justification that it is only fair) is provoked when a student becomes so deeply discouraged because of being disliked and not belonging that he believes he must hurt other people in return (Dreikurs & Cassel, 1990). He blames others for his problems (Balson, 1992) and so believes justice is served by getting back at them.

In the behaviour's antisocial, attacking mode, the student seems unlovable, seeks out those who are vulnerable, is vicious, destructive, and has a delinquent lifestyle involving stealing and vandalism (Balson, 1992). Because of his behaviour, it is difficult for a teacher to convince the student that others like him, as they do not like his behaviour. Dreikurs and Cassel (1990, p. 49) extend this point further: 'Unfortunately those who need encouragement most, get it the least because they behave in such a way that our reaction to them pushes them further into discouragement and rebellion'.

In its defensive form, the student may be sullen and moody and may refuse to participate.

Punishment is ineffective with the revenge-seeking student since it will only provoke further rebellion, and will confirm the student's belief that he does not belong in school (Ansbacher & Ansbacher, 1956).

Withdrawal

An individual must feel inadequate to some extent, as this feeling provides the motivation for learning. The positive expression of withdrawal is the appropriate withdrawal from conflict (Dinkmeyer & McKay, 1989). The antisocial expression is displaying inadequacy. Three reasons cause students to withdraw: they are over-ambitious, over-competitive, or too sensitive to pressure (Edwards, 1993). This type of student sees the environment as hostile or uncontrollable and so he learns to doubt his chances of securing his goals.

For such a student, the short-term goal of avoiding difficulties comes to over-ride the long-term goal of seeking success. He will then demonstrate weakness which adults interpret as a need for help or as a signal to give up teaching him, since he is not trying to succeed. This goal does not have an active mode. Its passive behaviours include: being idle, acting stupid, refusing to mix with others, playing in solitary activities, playing in babyish ways, engaging in fantasy, and acting hopeless and helpless (Balson, 1992).

DIAGNOSIS OF THE BEHAVIOUR'S GOALS

Dreikurs and Cassel (1990) assert that as there are only four goals for a student's misbehaviour, then diagnosis and subsequent treatment is actually fairly simple. Intervention centres on diagnosing the goal, then re-directing it. Diagnosis is based on observing the teacher's emotional reactions and behavioural responses and noting the student's reaction to the teacher's attempts at correction.

The teacher's emotions

The first way the teacher can determine which goals are motivating the student is to note her own emotional reactions:

1. If the teacher feels annoyed, then the student is attention seeking.
2. If the teacher feels threatened or defeated, then the student is aiming for power.
3. If the teacher feels hurt, then the student is motivated by revenge.
4. If the teacher feels helpless, then the student's goal is to withdraw.

The teacher's response

A second way the teacher can diagnose the student's goal is to notice how she responds to the behaviour:

1. If the teacher coaxes and reminds the student, then the student's behaviour is attention seeking.
2. If the teacher tends either to give in or to fight power with power, then the student is aiming to exercise power.
3. If the teacher tries to retaliate, then the student is motivated by revenge.

Table 5.5   Three sets of clues for diagnosing the goals of misbehaviour

If the teacher feels	If the teacher responds by	If the student's response to correction is to	Then the student's goal is
Annoyed	Reminding, coaxing	Stop but then repeat the behaviour	Attention
Angry	Fighting or giving in	Confront or ignore authority	Power
Hurt	Wanting to retaliate or get even	Become devious, violent or hostile	Revenge
Despairing or hopeless	Agreeing with the student that nothing can be done	Refuse to participate or cooperate, be uninterested	Withdrawal

4. If the teacher believes that the student is incompetent and gives up, then the student's goal is withdrawal.

The student's behaviour

A third way the teacher can diagnose the student's goals is by observing the student's responses to correction by the teacher (Balson, 1992; Edwards, 1993):

1. If the student stops the behaviour but then repeats it, then his goal is attention seeking.
2. If he confronts or ignores authority, then his goal is power.
3. If the student becomes devious, violent or hostile, then he is seeking revenge.
4. If he refuses to cooperate or participate or remains uninterested, then his goal is withdrawal.

These three sets of clues are summarised in table 5.5.

CONFRONTATION

The neo-Adlerians contend that while individuals are aware of their behaviour, they are not always conversant with their goals. These writers believe that becoming aware of the reasons for their behaviour (gaining insight) may allow individuals to change. Therefore, once the teacher has identified the student's goal, she then confirms her diagnosis by discussing the possible goals with the student. She confronts the student by asking whether he knows why he behaves as he does and, if not, whether he would like to hear her ideas. Then she asks in a matter-of-fact way each of the following questions (Dreikurs & Cassel, 1990, p. 42):

1. Could it be that you want special attention?
2. Could it be that you want your own way and hope to be boss?

3.   Could it be that you want to hurt others as much as you feel hurt by them?
4.   Could it be that you want to be left alone?

Each of these questions is always asked, in case the student is motivated by more than one goal. Questioning is said to produce a 'recognition reflex' that indicates when the teacher's guess is correct. Young students may admit the goal once it has been explained to them; older students are more likely to try to hide their expression but instead will give off non-verbal behaviour such as a shift in posture that discloses their goal (Edwards, 1993).

Dreikurs and Cassel (1990) assert that this discussion alone might bring about a change in the student's behaviour. If it proves to be insufficient, the teacher may have to institute corrective measures such as encouragement (discussed earlier), goal re-direction, negotiating a learning contract, or instituting consequences.

Goal re-direction

Once the teacher is aware of the student's goal, then she should act to make sure the misbehaviour does not achieve its desired end, and that the student's need is met through more appropriate behaviour.

The teacher is advised to ignore *attention-seeking* behaviour when-ever possible, and instead to give the student attention in unexpected ways when he is not making a bid for it. The teacher is advised to refuse to remind, punish, reward or coax. Encouraging the student when he is behaving appropriately teaches him that he has a place in the group without needing to resort to the antisocial behaviour.

When the student is seeking *power*, the teacher is advised to withdraw from the conflict in the knowledge that fighting or giving in will only increase the student's desire for power. Instead the teacher should collaborate with the student and engage him in leading others, giving him responsibility in cooperative tasks. The aim is to teach him to use power constructively, and to channel his ambitions into constructive areas.

When the student is aiming for *revenge*, the teacher must avoid feeling hurt and must not punish or retaliate, but instead build a trusting relationship to convince the student that he can be accepted without using the antisocial behaviour. If the student is so discouraged that he no longer cares whether he is accepted at school, the teacher may need to refer him for specialist help. Otherwise, the teacher can institute class meetings for negotiating rules and confirming the student's place in the group.

When the discouraged student is *withdrawing* through displays of inadequacy, the teacher needs a sincere conviction that he is capable and can succeed. She must refuse to give up. She must recognise the student's deep discouragement and stop all criticism, acknowledge all positive effort, and not get hooked into pity or into agreeing that the student is hopeless.

Learning contracts

Contracts can specify the criteria by which the student's work earns a particular grade or his behaviour meets the required standard. The student and teacher negotiate these together, although the teacher ensures that the standards are reasonable. The contract can be renegotiated at any time without the student losing face.

Natural and logical consequences

Should the preventive and earlier interventive methods fail to bring about enough improvement in the student's behaviour, then the neo-Adlerians recommend using natural or logical consequences. These are aimed at overcoming the disadvantages of punishments which were listed in chapter 3.

A natural consequence is the natural outcome of an individual's actions, such as when a student trips over untied shoelaces. Logical consequences are arranged by the teacher but, unlike punishment, have a logical, cause-and-effect link with the student's actions. For example, if a student will not cooperate in class (cause) then the effect is that he is asked to go elsewhere until he has changed his mind. The teacher is objective in her aim of guiding the student in learning to take respon-sibility for his actions, with no disguised aim of forcing him to change his decision. The consequence is not a punishment that is imposed by the teacher, but is merely the natural outcome of the student's choice: if he cannot sociably participate in the group, then he cannot participate at all.

Experiencing the results of his choices teaches the individual that while he can behave as he chooses, he must still be responsible for his decisions. (The exception is physical danger.) Reality replaces the author-ity of the teacher (Dreikurs & Cassel, 1990).

Table 5.6 summarises the differences between punishment and logical consequences (Dinkmeyer et al., 1980).

GUIDELINES FOR ADMINISTERING NATURAL OR LOGICAL CONSEQUENCES

1. Dreikurs and Cassel (1990) acknowledge that logical consequences work only if the student cares, so preventive measures must be in place if consequences are to be effective.
2. The student must understand and agree to a logical consequence in advance, and should help to determine what it will be.

Table 5.6   Distinctions between punishment and logical consequences (Dinkmeyer, McKay & Dinkmeyer, 1980)

Punishment	*Logical consequences*
Emphasis on the adult's power	Emphasis on the reality of the social order
Arbitrary and unrelated to the act	Logically related to the misbehaviour
Implies moral judgments	No moral judgment
Emphasises past misbehaviour	Concerned with the present and future
Threatens disrespect	Communicates respect and goodwill
	Treats the student with dignity
Demands compliance	Presents a choice

3. The teacher must provide choices—either that the student return to appropriate behaviour or earn the consequence.
4. The teacher must assure the student that he can change his decision at any time, and return to the group and activity when he is ready.
5. If a student continues to misbehave, then the time away from the activity is lengthened.
6. Dreikurs and Cassel (1990) advise using logical consequences for attention-seeking behaviour, natural consequences for power and revenge seeking, and neither for displays of inadequacy.
7. Finally, logical consequences must be delivered in a matter-of-fact manner, be related to the circumstances at the time, and applied only for harmful or disruptive behaviour that interferes with the teacher or other students.

SUMMARY

The neo-Adlerian writers base their approach on the belief that children strive to belong, and that if they become discouraged about belonging through prosocial behaviour, they will resort to antisocial behaviour to meet this fundamental need. The role of the teacher is to enact democratic classroom relationships that accept all students, reduce competition between them and between the teacher and students, and encourage students. A key principle is to teach students to accept responsibility for their own behaviour through encouragement, contracts and the imposition of natural or logical consequences. The teacher assesses students' motivation for their behaviour, and redirects their actions so that they become prosocial while still satisfying the students' goals.

CASE STUDY

Adam is seven. He has difficulty with reading, spelling and writing, although he enjoys and is capable at maths. During non-maths lessons, you have noticed that he spends a considerable amount of time off-task, when he frequently disrupts the other students. This is worse in the afternoon than in the morning.

He is in a composite class of six and seven-year-olds. He spends most of his play time with the younger children. Frequently a pair including Adam is apprehended during play times doing such things as harassing passers-by from an out-of-bounds area of the playground which is close to the street, rifling through rubbish bins for food or cans to swap for other items with students, or engaging in fights in and around the toilets.

He seems bemused by the trouble he gets into, usually saying when challenged that he doesn't know why he behaves in these inappropriate ways, that he couldn't remember a given behaviour was against the rules, or that the other child was at fault for suggesting the activity.

Until a recent assessment, it was believed that Adam behaved as he did because of low academic ability. However, a battery of tests has shown his overall ability (IQ) to be average, with his maths skills in the high-normal range and his reading and spelling skills, while delayed, still within the lower range of normal limits. Teaching staff are now at a loss for a new explanation of his behaviour.

A NEO-ADLERIAN APPLICATION

The neo-Adlerian teacher may use the following approach with Adam.

Step 1: Prevention The teacher would engage in a democratic relationship with Adam and other students, involving mutual respect, student participation in decision making and a reduction of competition between students and between the students and the teacher.

Step 2: Problem solving The teacher would discuss Adam's behaviour both within a class meeting, and with Adam individually, beginning with listening to him and finding out how he sees the issues. The teacher may then be able to collaborate with Adam in solving the problem, respecting Adam's perspective while ensuring her own needs are safeguarded. The teacher would also ensure that class meetings addressed how Adam (and other excluded students as well) could become a more integral part of the group.

Step 3: Encouragement The neo-Adlerian teacher would cease praising Adam when his behaviour or work was appropriate, and instead would teach him to monitor his own successes through using encouragement.

Step 4: Work contract In consultation with Adam, the teacher would establish a contract for his learning so that he did both more work and work of a better quality.

Step 5: Diagnosis of goals If the preventive approaches did not bring about sufficient improvement in Adam's behaviour, the teacher would examine her own feelings and actions to determine which goal is motivating Adam's behaviour. She may notice that she frequently feels annoyed, and constantly coaxes Adam to improve his work output and his behaviour. This information tells the teacher that Adam is likely to be attention seeking.

Step 6: Confrontation The teacher would then confront Adam with the series of questions about the goals of misbehaviour, beginning with, 'Could it be that you want special attention?', but would ask all four questions of Adam, in case his behaviour has more than one goal. Adam would be expected to acknowledge non-verbally when the teacher's guess was correct.

Step 7: Goal re-direction Assuming Adam's goal does turn out to be attention seeking, the teacher would ignore his inappropriate behaviour when she could, and instead make a special effort to give Adam her attention when his behaviour was neutral or appropriate. She would stop reminding, coaxing, rewarding and punishing.

Step 8: Consequences If these measures were unsuccessful on occasion, Adam would need to experience the natural and logical consequences of his choice of behaviour. For instance, if he cannot confine himself to in-bounds areas of the playground, then he cannot play. If he insists on rifling through rubbish bins, then he is given playground litter duty for a specified period. His off-task behaviour would mean that he is not permitted to work in the classroom since he cannot work without interfering with others. These consequences are decided upon by the teacher, although Adam knows about them in advance.

DISCUSSION QUESTIONS

1. In your opinion, what social changes have given rise to the demand for more democracy in schools?
2. What are some of the arguments against praising students?
3. In what ways does encouragement differ from praise?
4. According to the neo-Adlerians, how does competition negatively affect students and their behaviour?
5. Can you identify reasons for students' misbehaviour besides the ones identified by Dreikurs?
6. What three sets of clues does the teacher use to diagnose the student's goals?
7. In what key ways do punishments and logical consequences differ?
8. Re-apply the case study you generated in chapter 2, this time using neo-Adlerian principles and practices. What new features are introduced into the recommended practices? What effect would these differences have on the individual student? On the whole class? On the teacher?

SUGGESTIONS FOR FURTHER READING

The following text offers an introduction to the concepts of the neo-Adlerian approach:

Dreikurs, R. and Cassel, P. 1990, *Discipline without tears*, 2nd edn, Dutton, New York

For a more detailed description of the theory:

Dinkmeyer, D., McKay, G. and Dinkmeyer, D. 1980, *Systematic training for effective teaching*, American Guidance Service, Minnesota

The Australian reader may wish to refer to:

Balson, M. 1992, *Understanding classroom behaviour*, 3rd edn, ACER, Melbourne

And, for younger children:

Harrison, J. 1991, *Understanding children: towards responsive relationships*, ACER, Melbourne

Parents may be referred to:

Balson, M. 1994, *Becoming better parents*, 4th edn, ACER, Melbourne
Dinkmeyer, D. and McKay, G. 1989, *Systematic training for effective parenting*, 3rd edn, American Guidance Service, Minnesota

6

HUMANISM: ROGERS, GORDON AND GINOTT

(Educational) innovations based on belief in the magic of quantity (more money, more teachers, more services) have not lived up to their promise. What children need and what only teachers can provide is quality of instruction and equality of dignity. (Ginott, 1972, p. 260)

In a democratic school, the emphasis is on eliminating disruptive behaviour, not on punishing malcontents. Teachers are neither prison guards, therapists or [sic] corridor counsellors. They are partners in a mutually-shared enterprise—that of educating and encouraging students to succeed. The teacher does not hold others accountable, but teaches accountability. (Knight, 1991, p. 131)

KEY POINTS

- *Students' achievement and considerate behaviour will be promoted when teachers nurture their students' emotional needs and curiosity about learning.*

- *Teachers do this by establishing democratic relationships with students and by facilitating rather than directing their learning.*

- *Intervention with difficult behaviour begins by classifying whether it is a problem, and then attributing ownership to the person being inconvenienced by the behaviour.*

- *To solve the problem, the particular communication skill recommended—listening, assertiveness, or collaborative problem solving—is determined by who owns the problem.*

INTRODUCTION

The philosophy of Carl Rogers underpins the remaining theories to be discussed in this text, which in chapter 1 were classified as being authoritative and democratic. While his main focus is on the prevention of behaviour difficulties, Rogers' ideas offer only a few practical responses to disruptive behaviour in the classroom. This may be due to democracy itself being reliant on knowledge rather than offering prescriptions for action (Knight, 1991). Nevertheless, when we pair Rogers' philosophy with Thomas Gordon's interpersonal skills, we arrive at a democratic approach to the prevention of and intervention with classroom behavioural difficulties. A third humanist, Haim Ginott, wrote on similarly democratic themes and his ideas supplement those of the two main humanist writers.

The democratic approaches attempt to redress the criticism that school discipline methods based on coercion are out of keeping with the school's educational aims of preparing students for responsible citizenship (Knight, 1991; McCaslin & Good, 1992). Whereas obedience does not safeguard society from the inhumanity of individuals (Gordon, 1991), teaching consideration, tolerance and democratic resolution of disagreements both safeguards society and promotes individual achievement. The humanists believe that the democratic values involved in responding to student behaviour need to be demonstrated and lived in the daily life of the school rather than being taught in an abstract curriculum (Knight, 1991).

PHILOSOPHICAL ASSUMPTIONS

NATURE OF CHILDHOOD

Children are unique beings with the right to respect and to the freedom to evaluate and make decisions about their own experience (Rogers, 1978). Carl Rogers (1951, 1983) believes that when human beings can function freely, we are motivated, make constructive choices, and are trustworthy. Because one of our deepest needs is to belong, our socialisation will be assured, even when we are given substantial freedom.

CONDITIONS NECESSARY FOR LEARNING TO OCCUR

Even when stimulated from the outside, all learning is self-initiated, because 'the sense of discovery, of reaching out, of grasping and comprehending, comes from within' (Rogers, 1983, p. 20). Students' motivation to learn will be facilitated by a non-threatening, accepting, person-oriented climate (Rogers, 1951). Students need meaningful learning that will make a difference to their lives, which implies that curricula must have emotional as well as cognitive content (Rogers, 1978, 1951, 1983).

PURPOSE OF DISCIPLINE

Democratic discipline serves only a minor managerial function. Its main goal is educational, at three levels: teaching self-discipline, promoting cooperative participation in the group, and fostering responsible citizenship, whereby students are given sufficient knowledge and experience to propose solutions to critical social issues (Knight, 1991). The social goal of discipline in schools is to make children humane (Ginott, 1972).

To achieve these educational goals, the individual requires the social support and freedom to grow personally without limiting others (Knight, 1991). She needs the freedom to express herself in all spheres, including emotionally, cognitively and creatively. Because this goal—termed self-actualisation—is so relevant, when given guidance, the individual will provide her own order, and therefore it is unnecessary to impose order from outside.

REASONS FOR INAPPROPRIATE BEHAVIOUR

Every behaviour is a realistic reaction to the student's apprehension of her experiences and the demands of the situation. Gordon (1974) states that the problems of student apathy and other types of discontent which teachers often regard as 'problem behaviour', are only symptoms of a problem, not the problem itself. The way our schools are organised does not meet student needs and gives rise to behaviour that offends or violates the rights of others.

ADULT–CHILD STATUS

The teacher guides rather than controls children. His status comes from being skilled at what he does (authority based on *expertise*) rather than from having *power* over children (Gordon, 1991). However, while respecting children, the adult also respects himself and so will not allow children to over-ride his needs (Rogers, 1978). This is the basis of authoritative dealings with young people.

ROLE OF THE TEACHER

The teacher's main concern is with understanding rather than judging students (Rogers, 1951). To do this, the teacher must be 'real' (Rogers,

1978), which means he should not adopt the role of teacher, but instead relate to students personally and warmly. The teacher's goals will be (Rogers, 1983):

- to establish a climate of trust within which learning can take place
- to nourish and enhance children's natural desire to learn (curiosity)
- to help students to prize themselves, to be confident and to have a healthy self-esteem
- to encourage students' awareness that they are in control of their own happiness instead of this being dependent on outside sources
- to involve students, teachers, and administrators in decision making
- for the teacher to help himself to grow as a person, so that he can find satisfaction from interacting with students.

Skills that students will acquire in a democratic setting include: learning to initiate their own actions and to take responsibility for their decisions; being able to evaluate outcomes; knowing how to acquire useful knowledge; being able to adapt flexibly to new situations; having the capacity to solve relevant problems; and being able to work cooperatively with others (Rogers, 1951).

Since the primary task of the teacher is to teach students how to learn, he will offer materials that allow students to decide what they want to learn and will accept and trust his students and their skills. This aim is contrasted with the goal of absorbing facts only, which usually has little value at the time and even less value in the future, since it does not teach students how to learn or to solve problems.

In summary, Rogers (1983, p. 133) says of the role of teachers: 'They perform almost none of the functions of teachers. It is no longer accurate to call them teachers. They are catalyzers, facilitators, giving freedom and life and the opportunity to learn, to students.'

Rogers (1951, 1983) acknowledges that some students will prefer to be guided by a teacher while others will flourish under self-direction. If they are to be free to learn, all students will need to be free to choose how to learn. Therefore, Rogers suggests that students be divided into groups of self-directed and outer-directed learners. The self-directed students could then be clustered according to their interests.

PREVENTIVE STRATEGIES

A key focus of humanism is the prevention of behaviour difficulties. Central to this are establishing democratic relationships with students, creating a physical environment that is conducive to learning, ensuring the curriculum is relevant to and assessed by the students, fostering cooperative relationships between students, focusing on the process rather than the end-product of learning, negotiating reciprocal learning and behavioural contracts between students and their teacher, and maintaining teacher self-discipline. Finally, students, teachers and parents are encouraged to participate in school administration.

DEMOCRATIC RELATIONSHIPS

In line with his assertions about authority, Gordon's (1974, 1991) key strategy for preventing school behaviour problems is for teachers to deal with students from a foundation of authority based on expertise rather than on power—that is, democratically. The humanists detail democratic communication skills, which are outlined below. Democratic relationships are based on acceptance of students. They avoid labelling students as being deficient, even when they have special educational needs (Knight, 1991).

PHYSICAL ORGANISATION

Gordon (1974) offers specific suggestions for modifying the classroom to facilitate cooperative student behaviour. These include *enriching* the environment—for example, by having a variety of activities and multi-media teaching—or, conversely, *impoverishing* or *restricting* it, to aid the concentration of distractable students. For example, particular activities can be restricted to certain areas in the classroom so that students working there can concentrate. To *simplify* the demands placed on students, complex tasks can be broken into small steps that enable success. Keeping the area safe, and preparing students in advance for upcoming changes, such as a relief teacher, all prevent the expression of behaviour arising out of stress.

RELEVANT CURRICULUM

Rogers (1983) contends that if students are to learn to deal with real problems, then our schools should not insulate them from these, but instead make real problems the subject matter of our classes. This will begin with asking the students what issues confront them, or posing questions that they will need to deal with later in life. This fosters an attitude of inquiry. The teacher will then organise resources (such as reading material, guest speakers and his own knowledge and experience) for students to consult when thinking about the issues raised. Learning would be self-driven rather than taught, and it would not be graded since grades measure only inconsequential types of learning.

STUDENT SELF-EVALUATION

Rogers (1951, pp. 414–15) states that evaluation of learning must be carried out by the students:

> If the purposes of the individual and the group are the organizing core of the course; if the purposes of the individual are met if he finds significant learnings, resulting in self-enhancement, in the course; if the instructor's function is to facilitate such learning, then there is but one person who is in a position to evaluate the degree to which the goal has been achieved, and that is the student himself.

Rogers goes on to say that students experience self-evaluation as another opportunity for growth. It is certainly a difficult task, he contends.

When, however, grades and examinations are imposed by the education system, this issue can become just one more problem for the students and teacher to solve jointly. For example, the students might choose to submit questions for inclusion in a test, or formal results can be supplemented by students' self-evaluations. This safeguards society's need for an accountable education system, while promoting the growth of the individuals who are subjected to its evaluations.

PROMOTING A COHESIVE GROUP PURPOSE

Rogers (1951) recommends that much of what stuudents do at school be decided by the students as a group. The teacher helps to elicit and clarify the purposes of individuals, and will guide their decisions by indicating some of the resources they might use.

PEER TUTORING

In addition to promoting a cohesive group purpose, a second teaching approach for fostering cooperation between students is to use peer tutoring. Although it forms a significant part of the humanist approach, its specifics will not be described here since it is detailed in chapter 10.

FOCUS ON THE TEACHING PROCESS

Ginott (1972) believes that if we motivate and awaken students to their potential, they will learn the skills they need to know. He recommends that we permit mistakes, without ridiculing, excusing or dwelling on them but instead acknowledging that correcting errors teaches skills. In other words, the process of learning is more important than the perfect end-product.

CONTRACTS

Rogers (1983, p. 149) advocates the use of contracts to give, as he puts it, 'both security and responsibility within an atmosphere of freedom'. Contracts allow students to set their own goals and plans for their achievements, so that learning meets their needs but still within the constraints of realistic demands such as course requirements. Contracts allow students to evaluate their work on the basis of standards of quantity and quality that they establish with their teacher. Students accustomed to authoritarian methods may at first need guidance in how to be self-accepting, rather than self-critical, when they are assessing their own work.

TEACHER SELF-DISCIPLINE

The teacher must demonstrate the same standards of courtesy and self-discipline that he wishes his students to observe (Ginott, 1972). He does not allow his students to determine his mood or his reactions and does not use punishment or verbal violence to discipline students, even when provoked. Instead, he allows students to save face, responds to individuals personally rather than relying on his role and status, invites cooperation, and monitors the group to ensure all members are able to participate in the class. In short, the teacher may act spontaneously but not impulsively (Ginott, 1972), practising communication skills so that they become spontaneous and uncontrived.

STUDENT PARTICIPATION

Students have both a right and an obligation to participate in the administration of their school, since only by participation can they acquire a 'deliberative and democratic character' (Knight, 1991, p. 127). However, participation alone is not enough: the issues addressed must be real and debate must produce socially useful results, says Knight.

TEACHER PARTICIPATION

Teachers equally have a right to participate in decisions about school policy and procedures (Ginott, 1972; Rogers, 1983). They have a right to limit intrusions of their work into their personal life and to demand respect and dignified treatment from school administrators (Ginott, 1972).

PARENT COLLABORATION

When a teacher talks to parents about their children, he inevitably intrudes on family dreams . . . What the teacher says about the child touches on deep feelings and hidden fantasies. A concerned teacher is aware of the impact of his words. He consciously avoids comments that may casually kill dreams. (Ginott, 1972, pp. 277–8)

In line with this observation, Ginott (1972) advises that the mood of a meeting will be remembered when the actual conversation will be forgotten, so it is important to set up a quiet uninterrupted meeting place for parent–teacher interviews. The teacher will avoid preaching from his experience or giving advice about what a parent should do, and instead will listen to the parent, respecting his or her ability to find a solution.

INTERVENTION

Gordon's (1970, 1974) key interventive approach has two steps. In the first step, the teacher decides whether he finds the student's behaviour acceptable, based on whether it violates the rights of the student herself, the teacher or other class members, or both the student and the teacher. Gordon advocates a fair distinction between acceptable and unacceptable behaviours: if a teacher finds almost all student behaviours unacceptable, then he needs to examine his expectations and standards. Perhaps he is stressed or is in the wrong job.

The second step is identifying who *owns* the problem. The person whose rights are violated and who is being inconvenienced by the behaviour is said to own the problem—not the person performing the behaviour. The person being inconvenienced takes responsibility for asserting her needs and seeking a solution.

Gordon (1974) outlines four occasions when the teacher needs to deal with interpersonal issues in the classroom:

1. When a student's unmet needs are interfering with her ability to settle to the task at hand, this is the student's problem.
2. When the teacher's needs are not being met, the teacher owns the problem. When other students' needs are being violated, this too may become the teacher's problem, since he must protect all students from harm.
3. When neither student nor teacher is satisfied, both have unmet needs. There is a conflict, so both the teacher and the student own the problem.
4. When a problem seems apparent, but the individual affected can put it aside and focus on teaching or learning then there is no problem.

THE STUDENT HAS A NEED: LISTENING

Listening is more than mere hearing: it is an active process, whose skills require practice. Ginott (1972, p. 77) says that the chronological and psychological distance between students and teachers can be bridged only by listening with genuine empathy, which he describes as 'the capacity to respond accurately to a child's needs, without being infected by them'. Ginott believes that teacher messages to students must be 'sane' to allow students to learn to trust their own feelings and perceptions, without judging them for those. This helps distraught students to deal with their own feelings, and also avoids confusion and unwarranted emotional outbursts. While listening, the teacher's role is to withhold his own opinions and merely act as a sounding board for students.

Step 1: Attention The teacher will make the time to listen when a student has a concern. If the teacher is not available to discuss it just then, he and the student can agree on a suitable time to meet. Alternatively, the student may not approach the teacher, but by 'listening with his eyes' the teacher can notice when the student's non-verbal behaviour indicates that her needs are not being met. For instance, a student who is off-task could be seen to be having difficulties getting down to her work, perhaps because the activity does not seem relevant to her. The teacher could approach the student with this understanding, and examine how her needs could be met more regularly.

Step 2: Invitations to talk Communication theory describes some steps for opening up a conversation. The first step can be a *description* of the other person's body language: 'You look a bit down' or 'You look excited'. This may be followed with an *invitation to talk:* 'Want to tell me about it?'. The teacher could then employ an *attentive silence* that gives the student time to decide whether and how she wants to talk. In this regard, Bolton (1987, p. 48) quotes Robert Benchley:

> Drawing on my fine command of language
> I said nothing.

The teacher might give *minimal encouragers,* saying little (maybe only 'mm-hmm' 'oh' or 'really?') or repeating the last few words the student said. Throughout the conversation, the teacher will ask only *infrequent questions.* These are used to help the student to clarify her feelings, and to follow her own train of thought, not to give the teacher information. As such, the teacher's questions should not require yes/no answers because this closed type of question directs the conversation. Also, questions should be infrequent so that the student does not feel that she is being subjected to an inquisition.

Step 3: Active listening When a student has a problem, it is crucial to accept her feelings, as already mentioned. Before the teacher can do this, however, he needs to listen for them. Identifying the student's feelings can be difficult because she may not be able to label them accurately, or may start by 'testing the water', to see how accepting the teacher will be, before bringing up the real problem.

The teacher can communicate his interest and acceptance by non-verbal behaviours such as: abandoning other tasks when listening, facing the student, and maintaining good eye contact while she is talking with him. These skills take deliberate practice and, although most of us can perform them, we may be tempted to try short cuts, which impoverish the resulting communication.

Step 4: Reflection Having listened to the student's feelings, it can be helpful to reflect these back (sometimes called 'active listening'). For example, when a student says that she hates maths, the teacher's response could be 'You find your maths problems difficult' (if that seems to be the intent behind her words). Ginott (1969) advises that teachers respond to a student's statement about events not only at the content level, but also as a comment on her feelings and relationships. Thus, the teacher can reflect the content, the feeling, or the meaning that is being communicated to him. He can do this by paraphrasing what the student is telling him. Bolton (1987, p. 51) describes paraphrasing as:

- a *concise* response
- stating the *essence*
- of the *content*
- in the listener's *own words*.

Ginott (1969) emphasises that paraphrasing must be brief, so that students do not tune out.

ROADBLOCKS TO COMMUNICATION

Gordon (1970) identifies twelve common roadblocks to communication. Although the listener thinks he is encouraging the speaker to talk to him, instead these roadblocks discourage conversation. The roadblocks fall into three categories: judging, sending solutions and avoiding the student's feelings.

Judging

Responses that convey that the teacher is judging the student include *criticising, blaming* or *name calling*. The student will see these as unfair and will become resentful (Ginott, 1972; Gordon, 1974). She will either reject the message and the messenger, retorting with something negative in reply, or will believe the negative judgment about her. Another type of judgment is *praising* which, as we saw in chapter 5, has many negative effects. The final form of judgment is *diagnosing* or *interpreting*. This is an attempt to tell the student that her stated problem is not the 'real' issue, which ignores her perceptions and judges her negatively for her feelings.

Sending solutions

If a teacher tries to *direct* the student to stop her present behaviour and instead do as the teacher commands, this tells the student that her needs are not important: what the teacher wants is paramount. A solution may also be sent as a *threat*, which can make students fearful, resentful and liable to test the teacher to see if he will carry out the threat. *Preaching* treats students as if they do not know already what the teacher is saying. It is patronising. *Interrogating* is a form of probing that suggests the teacher is about to find a solution for the student instead of allowing her to find her own. Finally, *advising* treats the student as if she cannot solve her own problems.

Of the many responses to students' problems, advising is the most common, because teachers want to help students to feel better. Advising has many disadvantages, however:

1. When the teacher offers his own solution, without having heard why the student feels as she does, he tells her that he will not listen to her.
2. Giving a solution tells the student she is incompetent, that she cannot solve the problem herself.
3. It lowers the likelihood that the student will follow the teacher's suggestion, since she took no part in deciding what was to be done.
4. Therefore, the teacher will have to monitor and enforce the solution.
5. Advising reduces opportunities for a student to develop autonomy which is the ultimate goal of teaching. In the meantime, the teacher will be working too hard to control the student's behaviour.
6. Advising ignores the fact that if a solution were that obvious, the student would have thought of it already. Bolton (1987, p. 22) quotes Hammarskjold:

> Not knowing the question
> It was easy for him
> To give the answer

7. Providing solutions makes teachers responsible for students' problems, which is an unnecessary stress on teachers since students also have skills to contribute to problem resolution.

Avoiding the student's feelings

This is the third group of communication roadblocks. The first form of avoidance is *distracting*, when the teacher tries to take the student's mind off her worries. However, problems that are put off will surface again, and if teachers ignore young people's problems over and over again, they will take important matters and feelings elsewhere, or be left stranded without supports. A second form of avoidance, *logical argument*, tells students: 'Don't feel: think'. And, finally, another avoidance method that looks harmless on the surface but which ignores the depth of students' feelings, is *reassuring*. Like the other avoidance responses, reassuring tells students that they are not allowed to feel as they do because the teacher is uncomfortable when they are upset. Edwards (1993), in describing Haim Ginott's philosophy of discipline, states that when students are told they have nothing to fear, the original problem is compounded by adding the fear of being afraid, anxiety about having to hide their fear but not being able to, and anxiety about having to cope without support.

The thirteenth roadblock

Bolton (1987) adds a final roadblock to Gordon's 'dirty dozen', namely *accusing* other people of using the roadblocks when they communicate with us. We may also blame ourselves for using the roadblocks, which leads to *guilt*. Many people feel discouraged and disappointed in themselves when they realise that their communication habits harm their relationships. However, these habits have simply been learnt from how others spoke to us when we were young, and therefore they can be unlearnt.

PREREQUISITES FOR EFFECTIVE LISTENING

To be able to listen rather than resort in panic and habit to Gordon's communication stoppers, the teacher will first need to accept students and have confidence in their abilities to solve their own problems. The teacher will need to feel genuinely accepting of the student's feelings, even when they are different from his own or when he does not understand why she feels that way. The teacher will need to *want* to help by listening, rather than trying a 'quick fix' solution of his own, and to wait while the student decides whether to discuss her concerns, rather than invading her privacy by probing (Ginott, 1972).

THE TEACHER HAS A NEED: ASSERTIVENESS

Respecting students' rights does *not* mean that therefore teachers have no rights. The basis of democracy is that no one has to exert power over another person (neither person has to win and neither has to lose). The teacher has limits on student behaviour to protect his own rights and the rights of others in the class. He will therefore need to act when these rights are being infringed, being assertive about what he needs. This is done with the formula:

When you (*do such and such*)

I feel (*x*)

because (*my rights are being interfered with in this way*)

ASSERTIVENESS VERSUS AGGRESSION

When the teacher's needs are being over-ridden, he has two options: labelling the student, or labelling his own reactions.

Labelling the student

The teacher could tell a student about herself ('You're a nasty piece of work, you are') or about her behaviour ('That was very selfish'). This, however, lowers the student's self-esteem by blaming and criticising her, damages the student–teacher relationship, and usually is an inaccurate message because it is not really what the teacher wanted to convey. These 'you' messages are what people are referring to when they call someone aggressive. Ginott (1972) describes aggressive messages as insane, and states that labelling students with 'you' messages is disabling because it embarrasses them and may cause them to live down to the negative prediction of them.

Labelling the teacher's response

The alternative to labelling the student or her behaviour is for the teacher to tell the student about himself and his own needs. This type of message begins with that word 'I': 'I am disappointed that you forgot our agreement to share that equipment' or 'I need some quiet now while I concentrate on explaining this clearly'. The 'I' message is non-blaming. It accepts that the student's behaviour does not 'make' the teacher feel as he does: he is responsible for his own feelings.

If the teacher sends an 'I' message with the intent of accusing the student or making her feel guilty, then it is aggressive, not assertive. The teacher must take responsibility for his own feelings, rather than blame them on the students. Some additional guidelines for 'I' messages include:

State feelings accurately

Gordon (1970) advises the teacher to be accurate about the strength of his feeling, that is, not to understate his case. On the other hand, he should not overstate how he feels, because students will learn to ignore exaggeration and in future will not recognise when the teacher is in fact deeply upset.

Express the first feeling, not anger

Ginott (1972) expresses the view that when teaching, anger is inevitable, and he advises the teacher to express what he sees, what he feels and what he expects. At the same time, it can be useful if the teacher does not express anger alone, because that is not the first or most important thing he feels. The first feeling is usually hurt, fright or worry for students' safety. If the teacher lets students know that he was scared or hurt, students will receive the correct message (that the teacher was scared) rather than some inaccurate message ('He's so angry with me. I'm no good').

Be brief

Ginott (1972) advises teachers to be brief when expressing anger or other confronting feelings because both the target student and the observing class close off to talkative teachers. Tirades detract from the excitement of learning.

Do not suggest solutions

The 'I' message tells the student how the teacher feels. It does not, however, tell her what to do about that, since she can find solutions for herself (Ginott, undated; Gordon, 1974).

Listen to the receiver's reaction

The student may feel hurt, surprised, embarrassed, defensive, argumentative or even tearful after the assertive message has been delivered (Gordon, 1974). In that case, the teacher reverts to listening, because now the student has the problem.

ADVANTAGES OF ASSERTION

Considerate behaviour

The first step for a student in learning to consider other people is to hear what they need. By being assertive, students can learn about their teacher's needs and so can respect them more consistently.

Effects on the student's self-esteem

Assertiveness helps students' self-esteem in many ways. First, when students are told what the teacher needs it helps them to predict and understand their world, so that they can feel competent and confident within it. Second, when the teacher decides on his own limits, it prevents students from determining these for him, making them responsible for the teacher's actions and worrying when the job overwhelms them. Being in control of oneself, and not of others, produces a healthy self-esteem. Third, assertiveness demonstrates to students that we all have a right to respect ourselves and our needs. Fourth, students are also told that they are important, since the teacher notices and responds to what they are doing. They *make a difference* to the teacher.

More effective management

If the teacher asserts his needs, he can teach more effectively because he can be consistent. He can work within his tolerance levels, rather than deciding 'to be more patient' than is reasonable, which leads to vacillating between being 'walked all over' and having an inappropriately short temper. Instead, assertiveness avoids building up to anger and lashing out, which may teach students that feelings are frightening, awful or out of control.

Summary of benefits

In summary, assertiveness avoids the disadvantages of non-assertion, which include a lack of respect from others, loss of self-respect, inability to control emotional outbursts that arise when we have pushed ourselves too far, and feeling walked over. On the other hand, it avoids the costs of aggression which are: avoidance by others, loneliness, retaliation, fear, ill health and being overwhelmed by being responsible for so much. Being assertive is honest: it builds relationships.

SHARED PROBLEMS: COLLABORATION

Gordon's third category of classroom difficulties is when the student and teacher both have unmet needs. The behaviour tangibly interferes with the needs of both the student and teacher. Conflict is a natural part of human relationships but nevertheless many of us fear it, especially says Gordon (1974), if we define good teachers as people who never experience conflict in their classrooms or if we feel that we have only two solutions from which to choose—*either* students win *or* teachers win. Both of these approaches, however, rely on power and are doomed to failure. Instead, we can regard conflict as inevitable and healthy, and use its energy to generate workable solutions that protect all participants (Knight, 1991).

Ginott (1972) advises that teachers can side-step confrontations by allowing students to save face, since humiliation of students is to be avoided at all costs. Also, by listening when students express strong feelings and by avoiding demands and commands, the teacher does not unnecessarily provoke a confrontation. When in a particular situation it becomes clear, however, that neither the teacher's nor the student's needs are being satisfied, then they can collaborate to find a solution using collaborative problem solving. This involves six steps:

1. The teacher and student agree to talk it over so that they can *define*

the problem. The teacher finds out what the student's needs are in order to establish where the conflict lies. Gordon (1974) asserts that this is the most crucial step, and requires willing involvement by the student, enough time to become clear about the issues, and a focus on problem definition without any concentration on solutions.

2. *Generate possible solutions.* The teacher and student generate ideas of what they *could* do, so that they both get their needs met. At this stage, they do not evaluate how practical the suggestions are, just brainstorm all possibilities, even silly ones, and write them down.

3. *Evaluate the solutions.* Next, they both examine which of the options they *will* do. They must not choose a compromise, in which neither the student nor the teacher is satisfied, but instead persist until a solution is found which meets both their needs.

4. *Decide which solution* is best, based on the criterion of whether it meets both people's needs. Everyone must be able to agree to try the solution, even if not yet convinced that it will work.

5. *Determine implementation*—when and how to carry out the chosen solution.

6. *Evaluate the solution.* Once it is in place, the teacher checks whether the solution is working. The teacher will need to be on the lookout for commitments made with initial enthusiasm but which later turn out to be unrealistic or unworkable. He will need to be prepared to discard or amend solutions that are not working.

Throughout this process, the teacher uses active listening to clarify what the student needs, and assertiveness skills to state his own needs and what solutions he can accept.

BENEFITS OF NEGOTIATION

Improved motivation

Finding a solution that has been agreed upon means that the student is motivated to carry out the decision because she participated in making it, and therefore the teacher does not have to enforce the solution. Also, helping to decide what should be done develops a student's thinking skills.

Less work

The teacher does not have to work so hard, does not have to have all the answers, and does not have to second-guess what the student needs or wants.

Better solutions

There is more chance of finding a high quality solution, since two heads are always better than one. Also, negotiation gets to the real problem, at what is really the issue. Once this is clear, the solution may then become obvious.

Better relationships

Collaboration eliminates the need to use power, which always leads to a struggle of wills. Instead, teachers and students work with—do not struggle against—each other, which reduces hostility and enhances the student–teacher relationship. Finally, negotiation tells students that their teachers think their needs are important and worthy of consideration.

The method can be equally well applied to conflicts among students, and to establishing class rules within a class meeting. Collaboration benefits relationships most when each source of irritation is dealt with at the time it surfaces, rather than leaving grievances to mount up and hurt feelings to turn to anger.

LIMITATIONS OF NEGOTIATION

This approach will not work when a student is in danger, or when there is true time pressure to get something done. The teacher will need to do whatever has to be done to remove the source of the danger or to get the activity completed. However, it may avoid harm to the relationship if the teacher later explains the reasons for his abrupt action.

NO PROBLEM EXISTS

Gordon's fourth category of interpersonal dilemmas is when the student or teacher has a need but one which can be set aside while each gets on with his or her work. In short, there is no problem to be solved. The main type of non-problem is when there is a conflict of values. Collaborative problem solving will not work for values conflicts for two reasons: first, the student's belief is likely to be strong and, second, a conflict of values seldom harms the other person. The clue to a conflict of values is when the assertive message cannot fit the 'When you . . . I feel . . . because . . .' formula, because in fact it has no tangible effect on the speaker. However, the teacher can still ask for his values to be considered—Gordon uses the example of swearing in front of the teacher—without having any negative effect on the student–teacher relationship. The student may consider the teacher's feelings and change her behaviour even though the teacher can claim no ill-effects if she does not.

ABANDONING AUTHORITARIAN METHODS

The humanists speculate on why the education system is so resistant to changing its traditional stance on teaching.

IGNORANCE OF EFFECTS

Rogers (1983) says that the education system has no information on the effects of its present approach because it does not seek feedback from its consumers (students and their parents). He acknowledges that examinations provide information but only as defined by the system itself. He states that a great deal could be learnt from surveying students' opinions throughout their schooling to ask how school met or did not meet their needs, what experiences were most informative, and how well school prepared them for the next stage of life.

BELIEFS ABOUT WORK FORCE NEEDS

Rogers (1983) contends that schools remain power based because we believe that our industrial society *requires* a conforming work force, but Rogers himself believes that it needs independent thinkers to solve industrial problems, such as pollution.

MAINTAINING POWER

Rogers (1983) and Gordon (1991) both assert that schools will not give up their authoritarian position because this would divest them of some of their power. Gordon goes further to say that the conservative forces in society want to maintain power imbalances—such as between the sexes and generations—in the community and in schools.

DISTRUST OF DEMOCRACY

Gordon (1991) believes that we distrust democracy because we think it is inefficient, bureaucratic and clumsy, and because we lack experience with truly democratic groups, while Rogers (1983) says that we do not believe in people's ability to make the right choices.

MISUNDERSTANDINGS ABOUT CHILDHOOD

Gordon (1991) says that some of our reluctance to embrace democracy in schools is due to our fear of spoiling children, when in fact children will be demanding only as long as their needs are not met.

A second misunderstanding of childhood, in the opinion of the humanists, is the belief, based on the Judaeo-Christian tradition, that children are bad by nature. This idea may not be consciously endorsed by many modern day teachers, although many do believe that children will try to get away with whatever they can. This belief also leads to the 'either–or' thinking, that *either* the student walks all over the teacher *or* the teacher must get in first to ensure his needs are not violated.

CONCLUSION

Rogers concludes that it is not easy to grant freedom and responsibility to students, to trust them to direct their own learning, and to accept their humanity, and asks the question (Rogers, 1983, p. 307): 'Do we dare?'.

SUMMARY

Carl Rogers, Thomas Gordon and Haim Ginott have suggested some fundamental changes in the philosophy that governs how schools and classrooms are organised. The teacher moves from being the expert who holds all knowledge, to a facilitator who encourages inquiry in his students. When a more student oriented approach to learning is in place, intervention with difficult behaviour would rarely be needed. When it is, contracts and peer tutoring are suggested as interventions, with the most comprehensively applied intervention being interpersonal communication about the problem. Gordon's communication model involves two steps. Step 1 is an examination of whether the behaviour is acceptable or not, based on the criterion of whether someone is tangibly affected by it. If no one is inconvenienced by it, then no intervention is necessary. Step 2 involves determining who owns the problem, defined as the person who is being inconvenienced by the behaviour—not the person who is performing it. Then, a communication skill is employed, selected according to whose need is being violated. This is shown in table 6.1.

The humanists describe many benefits of listening to students, including the students' enhanced emotional well-being and their improved motivation and interest in learning. Assertiveness provides a way to ensure that teachers' rights are equally safeguarded, and collaborative problem solving is aimed at finding better solutions without violating the rights of either students or teachers.

Table 6.1 Summary of Gordon's communication skills

Who owns the problem	Appropriate communication skill
The student is in need	Listening skills
The teacher is in need	Assertiveness skills, followed by listening skills if the listener reacts emotionally
Both teacher and student have unmet needs	Collaboration to find a solution, unless the issue is a conflict of values

CASE STUDY

Adam is seven. He has difficulty with reading, spelling and writing, although he enjoys and is capable at maths. During non-maths lessons, you have noticed that he spends a considerable amount of time off-task, when he frequently disrupts the other students. This is worse in the afternoon than in the morning.

He is in a composite class of six and seven-year-olds. He spends most of his play time with the younger children. Frequently a pair including Adam is apprehended during play times doing such things as harassing passers-by from an out-of-bounds area of the playground which is close to the street, rifling through rubbish bins for food or cans to swap for other items with students, or engaging in fights in and around the toilets.

He seems bemused by the trouble he gets into, usually saying when challenged that he doesn't know why he behaves in these inappropriate ways, that he couldn't remember a given behaviour was against the rules, or that the other child was at fault for suggesting the activity.

Until a recent assessment, it was believed that Adam behaved as he did because of low academic ability. However, a battery of tests has shown his overall ability (IQ) to be average, with his maths skills in the high-normal range and his reading and spelling skills, while delayed, still within the lower range of normal limits. Teaching staff are now at a loss for a new explanation of his behaviour.

A HUMANIST APPLICATION

The following steps might be taken by the humanistic teacher when addressing Adam's difficulties.

Step 1: Changing the curriculum The teacher would note Adam's behaviour and take it to be a signal that school work is not meeting his needs. He would ask Adam about his interests and incorporate these into the teaching program.

Step 2: Teacher's role The teacher's own role would change from being the expert presenter of information to being a facilitator, whereby the students could research topics of interest to them, with the guiding support of the teacher who would arrange for materials to be available for them.

Step 3: Negotiation of rules Rules would be established in collaboration with the class. These would be few in number. Consequences for violations of rules would be related to the act. These would be renegotiated if they became unsuccessful in practice.

Step 4: Collaborative learning Small work teams would be established for various projects, allowing students to help and learn from each other and to develop cooperative skills. This would also be aimed at helping Adam's play difficulties, by helping him gain entry to the group during class time.

Step 5: Peer tutoring Another student may be given the task of tutoring Adam in his weaker subjects, and Adam may tutor one of his peers in maths.

Step 6: Work contract A contract would be written with Adam, whereby he established some goals for his own achievements, and specified how he would assess when he had reached these. The teacher would need to guide Adam in how to be self-accepting and responsible in his evaluations.

Step 7: Identifying who owns the problem If Adam's behaviour was disruptive or if he violated the contract, the teacher may assess that this is the teacher's own problem. In that case, he would deliver an assertive message stating how Adam's behaviour directly affected him (the teacher). Once the teacher has delivered his assertive message, he may need to revert to listening if Adam becomes upset or defensive about the teacher's statement.

Step 8: Collaborative problem-solving On the other hand, in many instances the teacher is likely to see the behaviour as a signal that Adam's needs are not being met, but then neither are the teacher's. In that case, a time would be made to renegotiate the contract and to solve the problem collaboratively. This process would be pursued until a solution which satisfied both the teacher and Adam were reached.

Step 9: Self-responsibility for homework Ginott (1972) recommends that students who do not do their homework submit a formal note stating what was not done and when it will be completed. The reasons why it was not done are not given, since this would teach children to make up excuses and lies and because it is taken for granted that the student has her reasons for not completing the work, and that homework is her personal responsibility. When the homework is completed, the note is returned to the student. This intervention would be applied to Adam. At the same time, Adam's parents would be guided in how to give indirect help so that Adam can manage the process of getting his homework done, without themselves taking responsibility for helping him with the content or for changing his feelings about homework.

DISCUSSION QUESTIONS

1. For what reasons does Rogers regard teaching as 'over-rated'?
2. What are his goals for facilitated learning?

3. What does Gordon's distinction between the two types of authority (expertise versus power) imply for teaching discipline?
4. What criterion determines who owns the problem being signalled by difficult behaviour?
5. What are the roadblocks to communication, and how do they interfere with listening?
6. What distinguishes assertiveness from aggression?
7. Under humanism, how are shared problems addressed?
8. Why does Gordon suggest that assertiveness is not appropriate for a conflict of values?
9. Give some reasons why we find it difficult to abandon authoritarian teaching methods.
10. Contrast the humanists' democratic practices with those of the neo-Adlerians. Do you see any significant differences in their underlying philosophy and practices?
11. Re-apply the case study you generated in chapter 2, this time using humanist principles and practices. What new features are introduced into the recommended practices? What effect would these differences have on the individual student? On the whole class? On the teacher?

SUGGESTIONS FOR FURTHER READING

Any of the following texts will provide a description of the humanist philosophy, with communication and teaching skills also outlined:

Ginott, H. G. 1972, *Teacher and child*, Macmillan, New York
Gordon, T. 1974, *Teacher effectiveness training*, Peter H. Wyden, New York
——1991, *Teaching children self-discipline at home and at school*, Random House, Sydney
Rogers, C. 1983, *Freedom to learn for the 80s*, Merrill, Columbus, Ohio

7

CONTROL THEORY: WILLIAM GLASSER

It is the responsibility of each individual child to work to succeed in the world, to rise above the handicaps that surround him; equally it is the responsibility of the society to provide a school system in which success is not only possible, but probable. (Glasser, 1969, p. 6)

KEY POINTS

- *Schools will motivate students to do quality work and behave responsibly if they are democratic and if curricula are relevant to—that is, meet the needs of—students.*

- *Teachers will motivate students if they satisfy students' need to belong by developing warm relationships with them and by promoting strong peer relationships.*

- *Curricula need to focus on mastery rather than on learning facts, using self-assessment and voluntary homework to further students' learning.*

- *A counselling approach aims for an agreement that disruptive students will use more considerate ways to meet their needs.*

- *When a student is disruptive in class, the immediate response is a reminder about expectations. If the student cannot immediately correct his behaviour, he is given time to plan how he can.*

- *Coercion (punishment and praise) are not used, as these remove individual responsibility.*

- *The strong preventive emphasis of Glasser's approach means that whole school commitment is necessary, not only to the practical management issues, but also to supporting teachers, parents and the whole school community to encourage responsible behaviour and quality learning.*

INTRODUCTION

Glasser's approach fits within the democratic framework introduced under humanism. He draws on the humanist tradition plus cognitive therapies to yield a theory of individual self-responsibility and social obligation. His philosophy has a strong preventive element, without which his interventions would be inadequate. While the school system receives much criticism from Glasser, preschools observe many of his recommended practices, and so their approach fits comfortably within his philosophy.

PHILOSOPHICAL ASSUMPTIONS

NATURE OF CHILDHOOD

Glasser does not specifically address the nature of childhood, except to say that children are capable of adopting self-responsibility.

CONDITIONS NECESSARY FOR LEARNING TO OCCUR

Glasser (1992, p. 174) says that education is the process of 'discovering that learning adds quality to our lives'. Because there is no basic need to do schoolwork, students will learn only when doing so satisfies their basic needs, and when they have a meaningful relationship with their teachers. If what students are doing satisfies one of their basic needs, they will work hard; if it does not but they care for their teacher, they may still work well. Learning must also be fun, especially for younger students, who have so much to learn and at the same time have a particular need for fun.

PURPOSE OF DISCIPLINE

Students who are not in good order at school cannot be at school (Glasser, 1992). Discipline enables the individual to make rational rather than emotional decisions about meeting his needs, without at the same time interfering with the needs of others. This clear managerial purpose to discipline goes hand-in-hand with a three-part educational purpose. The first educational goal of discipline is to have students exercise self-responsibility. The second educational function of discipline is to enhance students' belonging with the group, which includes freeing them from intrusive control and giving them the power to be self-determining. The third and most broad educational purpose of discipline is to enable students to participate fully in making decisions in their school so that

they experience—rather than only learn about—the democratic responsibilities that they will need to exercise as adult citizens.

REASONS FOR INAPPROPRIATE BEHAVIOUR

Glasser offers two reasons for disruptive student behaviour: first, he
believes that the school system itself brings about failure because teachers
are not sufficiently involved with their students and curricula are irrelevant
to many students and, second, school learning does not meet students'
needs. These features lead to failure, and students' belief in themselves
as failures leads to apathy, delinquency and withdrawal from school and
home, all of which lead to loneliness.

Glasser (1969) contends that if school failure did not exist, students
from even the most impoverished circumstances could overcome their
backgrounds. He believes that teachers use poor home backgrounds as
an excuse for the poor academic performance of many students, whereas
the major problem in Glasser's opinion is the way we teach these
students. Instead of the school offsetting home disadvantage, homes are
expected to offset the failure that children experience at school, but this
cannot be overcome by even the most loving home.

ADULT–CHILD STATUS

Glasser believes that no one can make anyone do anything: each of us
is responsible for his or her choices and goals. This means Glasser has
both a philosophical and a pragmatic commitment to democracy in
schools: he believes coercion is destructive, and that it does not work.
Students comply with coercion because they judge that, all things
considered, it would be better for them not to resist, but they resent
being coerced and will do only the absolute minimum of what they have
been asked (Glasser, 1992).

ROLE OF THE TEACHER

The teacher's instructional role is to show students how doing quality
work at school will add to their quality of life, either now or in the
future (Glasser, 1992). The teacher's managerial role is to establish rapport
with students so that they gain the strength to take responsibility for
themselves (Glasser, 1986). The teacher aims to give students the
necessary mental tools for dealing effectively and rationally with new
situations or difficulties and for not fearing challenges (Glasser, 1969).

PREVENTIVE APPROACHES

Students will behave appropriately, accept responsibility for their actions and will be motivated to learn if education is of a high quality and meets their emotional needs. This creates a school that is a good place to be.

SCHOOL BECOMES A 'GOOD PLACE TO BE'

Tauber (1990, p. 130) describes Glasser's basic preventive philosophy: 'Before any classroom management strategy can be expected to succeed, students must first perceive school as a good place to be'.

What makes school a good place is its emphasis on quality. Quality is evidenced by the students' belief that if they do some work, they will be able to meet their needs enough to encourage them to keep working. Glasser (1977) says that a quality school is characterised by courtesy, reasonable rules, laughter, good communication, and self-responsibility. The teacher is a leader who is engaged warmly with her students. She sets up a class that has reasonable rules, that works cooperatively, and in which teaching and learning are fun and of use to the students either now or in the future. The teacher is supported by the school hierarchy.

MEETING STUDENTS' EMOTIONAL NEEDS

Glasser acknowledges that students' physical or survival needs for food, shelter, and security must be satisfied before any learning can take place. He states (1986, p. 20): 'Teachers are well aware that hungry students think of food, lonely students look for friends and powerless students for attention far more than they look for knowledge'. This quote introduces Glasser's list of the basic emotional needs (1986), which he considers to be equally important: belonging (love), power, freedom and fun. In his earlier writing, Glasser (1969) spoke of an identity need, which could be equated with self-esteem, although this need is not mentioned in his later works.

Belonging (love)

This need is reciprocal: the student needs both to receive and to give affection.

Power

This refers to the student's need to control what happens to him. By control, Glasser does not mean that the individual manipulates others, but that he chooses for himself and is self-determining. He steers his own life, just as he would steer a car. Or as Strohl states (1989), power lies in our perception that we are making a meaningful impact on the world.

Freedom

Freedom refers to the need for independence or freedom from control by others. Power and freedom are opposite sides of the same coin. If an individual has too much power, then he restricts the freedom of others. Therefore, ensuring the freedom of others counter-balances the need for personal power. The need for freedom or independence can also be at odds with the need to belong, since an individual cannot belong if he is too different from his peers.

Fun

This is the 'intangible joy' (Glasser, 1986, p. 28) we experience with the spontaneous satisfaction of our needs.

SATISFYING STUDENTS' NEED TO BELONG

Like the neo-Adlerians, Glasser believes that the need to belong is a central motivation for human beings. He reports that (Glasser, 1992, p. 48): 'Students are saying that it is very hard for them to satisfy their needs in academic classes because most work is done alone and there is little or no class discussion'.

Cooperative working teams

Learning should be conducted within cooperative groups, since learning together within a small team satisfies students' need to belong and to be independent of the teacher. These groups should be of mixed ability, so that more able students can receive satisfaction from helping other students, while the less able can still achieve. In this way more in-depth understanding of the work can be achieved by all members, and working with other members can provide a comparison against which students can assess their own progress.

Peer tutoring

Strong students would be trained to act as peer tutors for any student needing one-to-one tutoring, so that no student would sit in class needing but not receiving help. Glasser (1992) suggests that in exchange for tutoring, the tutor could receive credit in a course called 'academic leadership' or added credit in the subject being taught, in recognition of his effort and commitment.

Class meetings

Glasser (1969) states that teachers must be given time to meet with their classes to discuss and resolve problems. Each class is a working, problem-solving unit. Class meetings are held daily in primary school and two to three times per week in secondary school to deal with issues as they arise. Glasser describes three types of class meetings: social problem solving, open-ended and educational-diagnostic meetings.

Social problem solving meetings deal with class disturbances (behavioural difficulties) that are of concern to any student, teacher or parent. Glasser (1969) advises that these meetings should focus on finding a solution rather than finding fault with individuals. As Glasser's other measures are enacted within the school and the class, these meetings will become rare.

Open-ended meetings allow the students to discuss any issue relevant to their lives, including any dissatisfaction with school.

Educational-diagnostic meetings are related to what the class is studying. These are aimed at establishing whether the teaching procedures are effective in producing in the students a living, working understanding of the concepts being taught, rather than a pure theoretical or fact-based learning.

The meetings are held in a circle, not in the usual seating arrangements as these do not promote discussion. The change of seating arrangements also signals a special form of communication. In the meetings, the teacher is non-judgmental because judgments would imply solutions, when the aim is for the group to arrive at these independently. The teacher gives opinions sparingly, and when she does so, her opinions carry equal weight with the students' views.

SATISFYING STUDENTS' NEED FOR POWER AND FREEDOM

Glasser's theory states that individuals have the need for power balanced by a respect for the freedom of others. In breach of students' need for power—that is, for control over their lives—teachers use a form of management that places them in charge of students. Glasser calls this *boss* management, in contrast with *lead* management. His distinction equates with Thomas Gordon's distinction between authority based on power versus expertise (1991). Boss management involves imposing academic work and standards of behaviour on students, without their input. It is detrimental because it limits work quantity and quality and it produces the discipline problems teachers are trying to prevent (Glasser, 1992). While boss management appears to work for many students, Glasser contends that instead, these students' success is due to their home backgrounds and occurs despite, rather than because of, the school system.

Boss management burdens the teacher with a method of management that is bound to fail no matter how competent she is in other respects.

The boss believes that students can be motivated from outside themselves, but finds that she cannot motivate students to learn and so feels responsible for their shared failure. And because schools have very few rewards available to them for coercing students positively, these external control methods frequently become very negative. The contest between the student and teacher uses much of their energies, which creates inefficiency and self-defeating behaviour. Students regard the teacher as an adversary, and ridicule or ignore her, or see her as an obstacle to getting the job done (Glasser, 1992).

In contrast, an effective lead manager combines what students are looking for with what she asks of them. Students become self-driven. Lead management in schools has four essential elements which define quality teaching (Glasser, 1992). First, the leader facilitates student self-responsibility by providing the appropriate atmosphere, tools and environment for achieving the task. Second, the teacher engages students in a discussion about the quality of their work, how they are to complete it, and within what time limits. Third, the teacher demonstrates the activity so that students are sure about what is required and can suggest more appropriate ways of completing it. Finally, the students evaluate their own work for its quality.

> A boss drives. A leader leads.
> A boss relies on authority. A leader relies on cooperation.
> A boss says 'I'. A leader says 'We'.
> A boss creates fear. A leader creates confidence.
> A boss knows how. A leader shows how.
> A boss creates resentment. A leader breeds enthusiasm.
> A boss fixes blame. A leader fixes mistakes.
> A boss makes work drudgery. A leader makes work interesting.
>
> Glasser (1992, p. xi)

Reasonable rules

A lack of coercion is essential for warm relationships and for enabling students to be accountable for their actions. Reasonable rules have a clear cause-and-effect relationship to the behaviour. For instance, walking in corridors (cause) leads to fewer accidents (effect) (Tauber, 1990). If this cause–effect relationship is not apparent to students, they will not abide by the rule or believe that school is a good place to be. Glasser (1992) contends that lead managed schools need very few rules and that, in contrast, boss managed schools have many rules that themselves provoke defiance. This in turn provokes a need for coercion, which engenders more defiance.

QUALITY EDUCATION

Glasser (1992) believes that to prevent students' misconduct and under-achievement at school, the school itself must be reorganised and curricula reshaped to expect and support quality work. Quality work is a product of fair, warm and caring relationships which do not use coercion and which respect the expertise of all members. It produces outcomes that are useful, that involve all members of the group, and which satisfy the participants who assess it on their own criteria of quality.

Greater depth of study

Glasser (1992) believes we must cover less ground in our academic curricula, and present what we do cover in more depth and more slowly, so that students finish with a good grasp of the content. This is the basis of quality work.

Involvement with teachers

If teachers engage students in a warm relationship that accepts them and their right to have their needs satisfied, then students will be motivated to learn and to accept responsibility for their actions. Teachers will listen to students whose behaviour is inappropriate so that it can be solved in a way that meets both their needs, rather than assuming the students are in the wrong.

Emphasis on thinking

Glasser believes that schools do not capitalise on the school entrant's openness to learning acquired in the preschool years. Instead of solving relevant problems, the student is required to memorise. This focus on learning facts arises from what Glasser (1969) terms the *certainty principle*, which holds that there is one right answer to every question. This leads to rote learning by able students and to increasing numbers of children being identified as having learning difficulties. Low student satisfaction results because no thought is involved in memorising facts (Glasser, 1969). At the same time as facts are learnt, social issues which may not have an answer at all, or certainly not one single solution, are not addressed. This leads to our being able to land on the moon before being able to solve the problem of racial and sexual discrimination, says Glasser.

If we abandon the certainty principle, then we can teach:

- An understanding of the social issues of the day, rather than an examination of more superficial facts.
- Questioning, rather than being told.
- Decision making and following through on choices made. These involve strength, responsibility, commitment and judgment (synthesis

of many facts). They also require self-confidence, which can arise only from success in the past.

- Tolerating uncertainty, so that we can make a decision, for example, without worrying that it is *the* right one: instead it can be *an* answer, one that can be changed if it does not work.
- Fostering creativity and originality while no longer seeking certainty.

Curriculum relevance

Not only is the school curriculum frequently unrelated to students' lives outside school, but also students' opinions, experience, interests and observations that they bring from home are not valued at school (Glasser, 1969). While some students tolerate that school has nothing to do with home (and vice versa), many do not. This second group of students becomes unmotivated and isolated from the first. Glasser states that we must prevent this separation from occurring naturally, and that we must not formalise it by streaming classes according to ability. Streaming leads to student hopelessness and dropping out, lower standards for the slower students, lack of teacher appreciation for the attempts of slower students to improve, and a self-fulfilling prophecy of lack of success for those students whom teachers do not expect to succeed.

Ways of making the curricula relevant include allowing a two-way exchange between home and school, reinstating the emotional content of school teaching which presently is emotionally dull to many children, refusing to teach facts for memorisation, ceasing to grade students' work, and not assigning homework. Students would address questions of why, when, where and how the information could be used by them or someone else, now or in the future (Glasser, 1992). This suggests that teachers should teach skills (as opposed to facts) that students will need in their daily life and in the future, and explain to them exactly how the skills will benefit them. Glasser lists relevant skills as: reading, speaking, writing, arithmetic (but not higher mathematics as it is not necessary for life) and problem-solving (Glasser, 1969, 1992).

Of this list, Glasser (1969) states that the most important and relevant skill for students to attain is reading, as reading can be used to acquire any other information. He advises that reading be taught usually in heterogeneous groups, except where students have considerable behavioural and reading difficulties. In that case, in any school, there are sufficient numbers of students with reading difficulties to establish a separate group for daily reading lessons taught by the remedial teacher, with students graduating back to the regular class as their reading skills improve. Meanwhile, for all other lessons, these students remain in their regular classes. However, in his later writing, Glasser (1992) argues that writing is more important than reading, because people who can write well can read well, but those who can read do not necessarily write well. (He does not mean the act of handwriting as such, but communicating ideas in written form.)

Assessment

Grades are intended to give students a sense of achievement and to motivate them to work harder. However, grades do not have this effect on students who do not care about their teacher's evaluations of them or their work (Glasser, 1992). Only their own judgment about their grasp of useful skills (that is, self-evaluation of a relevant curriculum) will motivate students to achieve quality. Grades are used to force students to learn irrelevant material, can seldom be fair, and so for these and other reasons (detailed in table 7.1), Glasser (1992) advocates teaching students to judge their own individual and collaborative work. They learn how to do this by taking their time to know the subject matter, and so to know whether they have covered it in a quality way, and by comparing their evaluation with their teacher's so that the teacher can guide them in making realistic assessments that are not too harsh. Students would be taught not only how to evaluate their own work, but also that doing so is the most important part of their education (Glasser, 1992).

Glasser (1992) observes that at times we must still measure progress to establish where a student needs help and where he needs to do more work, but that the teacher can ask the students to nominate when they are ready to take the test. (The test would be open-book since memorising facts is foolish.) Students who do well on the test would proceed to new material; those who do not would be given the opportunity to practise further and master the material. In this way, the student is given a chance to improve on the work and be re-assessed. Glasser (1992, p. 65) defends this suggestion with the observation that: 'If we are not going to try to improve what we do, there is little sense in assessing it'.

Glasser contends that his system of assessment could be handled by providing two streams for the one course: each course would cover the same content but one would take one year and the other two years. Another suggestion is that students who wish to prepare for public examinations could elect to do courses towards these while others could select courses whose content is not dictated by examinations and which can cater for students whose skills fall outside the usual academic curricula (Glasser, 1992). Glasser also suggests that by learning the answers to his who, why, when and how questions, students would find it easier to remember the otherwise irrelevant facts these public examinations call for and so most students receiving quality teaching would be more successful at exams.

Table 7.1   Negative effects of grades

Low quality work
- Grades tell students and their teachers that no learning is worthwhile unless it can be measured (that is, unless it is graded). This means that students will study only what is to be tested, and so academic standards are lowered. Grades become more important to students than getting an education.
- Academic standards are again lowered by the anxiety that grading engenders in students, reducing their ability to study.
- Closed-book examinations are based, says Glasser (1969, p. 72) on the fallacy that 'knowledge remembered is better than knowledge looked up' and yet rote learning is suitable for a relatively small range of material, whereas research skills are useful for a vast array of material and for learning how to solve problems.
- Coercion (through tests) to memorise irrelevant information causes students to cheat, not because they lack ethics but because, 'there is no virtue in learning nonsense' (Glasser, 1992, p. 217).
- Coercion (through tests) to memorise facts causes many students to hate the subject matter, which 'is worse than just not knowing it' (Glasser, 1992, p. 231).

Demarcations between students
- When the curriculum is irrelevant, grades will encourage only the academically successful students to learn.
- Grades increase competition between classmates.

Unfairness
- While grades are supposed to be an objective measure of students' progress, it is hard to make any finer distinction than pass–fail. Attempts to do so are inaccurate, unfair and phoney.
- Grades are not a good indicator of success at anything other than school work, and are poor indicators of students' ability at work or higher education.
- Students are aware that although a C grade is considered a pass, the only decent grades to achieve are a B or an A. Since grading is done according to normal distributions, most students will never achieve these good grades, and many will become despondent.
- There is no recognition of late maturing and no second chance to redeem a poor school record—school failure damns one to failure for life.

Poor interpersonal relationships
- Finally, grades reduce human involvement between teachers and students, which is central to student motivation.

Homework

Compulsory homework is a fundamental source of coercion and irrelevance in schools (Glasser, 1969, 1992). A Glasserian teacher would not assign homework because of its disadvantages (summarised in table 7.2), among which is the high price students who complete homework pay for their conscientiousness. However, if students could not achieve quality work within the time allotted in class, they could be counselled about what extra work they could do voluntarily at home, and many students would choose to revise and practise at home just as adults choose to take their work home (Glasser, 1992).

Table 7.2 Disadvantages of compulsory homework (Glasser, 1969, 1992)

Reduces student motivation and achievement
- Homework reduces the quality of students' lives.
- Homework is irrelevant, especially until the most senior years of high school.
- The student has no choice about doing homework.
- Homework allows students to make the same mistakes over and over when studying at home without teacher supervision, and therefore they learn wrong approaches.
- Most homework is more easily and better done at school.

Contributes to student drop-out and burn-out (stress)
- Homework is excessive, tedious and as irrelevant as the general school curriculum.
- Homework causes students to hate school and learning.
- Homework reduces available time for relaxation which would offset stress.
- The bright student who is conscientious about doing homework has no time left afterwards to pursue other recreational activities; the less able student does not do the homework but because this defines him as a failure, he does little else either. Thus, both groups of students are denied other learning and enjoyable activities. And by adulthood, they have not developed ways to enjoy their leisure time.

Contributes to demarcations between students
- Students from middle class homes have the facilities at home for quiet study whereas students from working class homes have not, leading to a widening of the differences between their academic achievement levels.
- Just as it contributes to class differences in achievement, homework highlights academic differences between students, since only academically able students complete their homework.

Contributes to antagonism between teachers and students
- Compulsory homework leads to conflict between students and teachers, which in turn leads to low quality work that exacerbates the friction between students and teachers . . . and so the cycle repeats (Glasser, 1992).

Prevents quality teaching
- Assigning homework prevents teachers from planning exciting instruction (Glasser, 1992).
- Homework must be graded, with all the disadvantages of grading.
- Failure to do homework must be punished, which violates all the principles of a quality school.
- To avoid arguments, teachers accept low quality homework, sending the message that low quality work is acceptable.

Family tension
- Compulsory homework creates tension between parents and children, since parents frequently believe that it is their role to oversee the completion of homework and so they nag their children, whereas since the school sets the work, the school should supervise it.
- Voluntary homework that involves talking to adults could help bring parents and children together, whereas compulsory homework only creates antagonism.

COUNSELLING INTERVENTION

Glasser's control theory gave rise to reality therapy whereby, as the title implies, the individual's behaviour is contrasted with reality in order to check that it does in fact meet the person's own goals. This approach has been applied to non-achieving or disruptive students to arrive at long-term solutions, and may be the context in which disruptions are handled immediately, using the ten-step discipline program (see page 144). The fundamental principle of reality therapy is to reach a commitment to a plan for improved behaviour, with no excuses accepted for violating this agreement. The teacher knows that changing behaviour can be difficult, so while she accepts a student's feelings, empathises with a difficult home life or with traumatic events that happened to him in the past, she will not allow him to use these as an excuse for continued failure and suffering. Permitting excuses communicates a lack of caring and lack of interest in the student's success. Instead, the teacher is interested in when and how the student can adhere to the plan. When the behaviour changes, the student's feelings will change accordingly.

Glasser (1992) makes the point that counselling does not have to take a long time when the counsellor has an ongoing, positive relationship with the student: most of the time in formal counselling between strangers is spent in building up this relationship. Therefore, a therapeutic conversation between student and teacher can be brief. Its aim is to enable a change in the student's behaviour so that it still meets his emotional needs but also does not violate the needs of other people. Hammel (1989) describes the steps that comprise the counselling approach:

1. The teacher secures the student's involvement, both in school and in the student–teacher relationship. In other counselling theories, this would be termed 'building rapport'.
2. Next, the teacher guides the student in identifying his problem. The focus is on present rather than past misdemeanours or past 'causes', as these become excuses. This step is facilitated by the teacher's warm involvement with the student, established in step one, and by the student's knowledge that there will not be any punishment or criticism of him for his choices.
3. The teacher helps the student to identify what he wants from school.
4. The teacher asks him to judge whether his behaviour is working for him—that is, whether it meets his goals. This is a cause–effect judgment, not a moral one, since moralising connects the behaviour to the child's character and judges him.
5. The teacher seeks the student's commitment to finding other ways of meeting his needs.
6. The teacher and student plan a new behaviour, with the student taking responsibility for this, just as he has for his inappropriate behaviour.
7. Having formulated a plan, the student must then agree to pursue it.
8. The teacher evaluates whether the plan is working. She accepts no excuses for failing to abide by the plan as excuses are past-focused. She does not punish transgressions. Instead, she modifies the plan

if it is shown to be unsuitable, or reconfirms the student's commitment to pursuing it.

IMMEDIATE INTERVENTION: HANDLING DISRUPTIVE BEHAVIOUR

Even when preventive approaches have been put in place to avoid most occurrences of disruptive behaviour, on occasion a student may still behave disruptively. If the individual concerned has a history of difficult behaviour, the counselling approach will already have established how he can meet his needs in school; in addition, an immediate intervention will be necessary. This is intended only for disruptive behaviour, not for students who are just off-task (Glasser, 1976).

THE PHILOSOPHY

No punishment

Glasser (1992) points out that we often punish young people for offences that hurt no one but themselves (such as absenteeism) when we do not punish adults for offences that cause harm to others. We think we are teaching young people a lesson, but instead punishment detracts from students' quality of life and so interferes with their motivation to learn and their willingness to take responsibility for their actions. In saying this, Glasser clarifies that he is not arguing for more punishment for adults, but for more mercy for young people. If we do not punish young people, it will be harder for them to be angry at us (Glasser, 1992).

Instead of punishment, Glasser advocates only two types of consequences for disruptive behaviour: to restrict freedom, or to remove privileges, both temporarily, until the student can figure out a way to follow sensible rules. The student has control over when his freedom or privileges are reinstated; in contrast, with punishment the teacher has control.

Just as the lead teacher refuses to administer punishment, she also does not deliver rewards because they too represent an imbalance of power between the teacher and student and remove the student's responsibility for his own behaviour.

Expect to find a solution

Glasser (1992) advises the teacher not to take the student's behaviour personally and to act as though no harm has been done by it (since it hasn't). The only permanent harm would result if the teacher could not find a way to help the student to work out his problems and get back to doing useful work.

Never give up

Students may take a long time to be willing to run the risk of abandoning tried and true methods of gaining control, even when these attract a high price. They may not trust that other, unknown, methods would work better. The teacher must persevere, and must never revert to boss management while the student experiments with change. How long is 'never'? asks Tauber (1990). In answer, Glasser (1977, p. 61) offers this guiding rule: 'Hang in there longer than the student thinks you will'.

THE PRACTICE: THE TEN-STEP DISCIPLINE PROGRAM

Glasser (1977) lists ten steps for immediate management of those students who disrupt the classroom. They reflect the awareness that the student's behaviour represents a decision about how to satisfy his needs, even though the chosen actions may be ineffective or disruptive. The lead teacher communicates that the student's disruption is his problem, not the teacher's, and that the teacher is confident about how to respond.

The ten steps form clusters, with steps 1 to 3 focusing on the teacher's role in preventing or contributing to the behaviour, steps 4 to 6 clarifying expectations, and steps 7 to 10 involving a counselling process. They can all be embedded within the longer-term counselling approach given earlier, and are based on the foundation already established by the preventive approaches. Without these preventive strategies as a context, the ten steps will fail.

The teacher's role

1. Because, like her students, the teacher is choosing her own behaviour, she should ask herself: 'What am I doing that contributes to the problem?'.
2. The teacher can choose to change her behaviour if she wishes. Glasser (1976) advises teachers that if what they are doing is not working, they should stop it.
3. Next, the teacher is advised to make an effort to do something different. She might acknowledge a student when he is undisruptive, for instance. This is a preventive step, inasmuch as it builds a respectful relationship within which the student will care about the teacher's needs and will value school as a good place to be.

Rule clarification

4. If the student behaves disruptively, the teacher needs to deal with the behaviour matter-of-factly, without anger. Glasser (1976) suggests the teacher ask a question that is quick and sharp and to the point: 'What are you doing?'. Alternatively the teacher could acknowledge that the student has a problem, and offer to help him sort it out,

either now or as soon as the teacher is available. These questions are confronting but not threatening: they call the student's attention to his behaviour without criticising him (Glasser, 1992).

5. If the student continues with the disruptive behaviour, the teacher adds the further question: 'Is what you're doing against the rules?' or, 'Is it likely to work for you?'. With this reminder, the student may be willing to resume appropriate behaviour, because he knows that it will have the long-term benefit of satisfying his needs. If the student will not respond to the question, the teacher can make the statement, 'This is what I saw you doing, and it is against the rules'.

6. The reality therapy step begins with the statement: 'We've got to work it out'. The student and teacher problem solve a way to resolve the issue. The aim is to reach an agreement on a plan whereby the student will behave more appropriately.

The counselling process

7. For primary schools: when the child continues to be disruptive and refuses to work it out, the teacher will isolate him from active participation in the class, giving him space and time to think through what he wants and how he is to achieve it. This exclusionary time out (see chapter 3) is not a punishment: it can be as pleasant as the teacher wants to make it, although the child must stay until he is ready to 'work it out'. Exclusionary time out is not suitable for older students.

8. The primary school student who disrupts in the quiet area, or an older student, is sent out of the class. He remains in a time out room until he is ready to solve his problem, but is not hurried to get ready to return to the class. A teacher staffs the time out room throughout the school day. This teacher should not argue with the student or negate his complaints about the work or his teacher, but neither will she accept these as excuses for the student's behaviour.

9. If the student disrupts in the quiet area, then he is sent home, since he cannot be in school until and unless he is willing to learn. (In his later writings, Glasser makes no mention of this step.)

10. If the student is unwilling to attend school and obey the rules, the school does not have the resources to solve this. The school should advise the parents of community agencies they could consult.

The above steps have been softened somewhat in Glasser's latest book, *The Quality School* (1992). His later writings advise teachers not to involve the student's parents except to pass on positive information or to collaborate with solving non-discipline problems, such as a child's difficulty with making friends. This sends two messages to the student: first, that his teachers believe he can solve the problem independently of his parents and, second, that they want to solve the problem, not punish the student, and they do not want his parents to punish him either.

SUMMARY

Glasser's approach requires a fundamental revision of the content and processes in schools. It begins with ensuring that students regard school as a good place where teachers expect and support responsible behaviour and quality work. Glasser calls on teachers to offer a useful curriculum and to explain how it will meet students' needs. He suggests that the curriculum be deepened to allow for quality work, rather than broadened to cover a wide range of content, some of which is nonsense.

Glasser's preventive approaches include developing warm relationships between teachers and students, working collaboratively as teams and in class meetings, and instituting reasonable class rules. At the same time, schools need to be managed more democratically, with teachers providing leadership rather than coercion to facilitate student engagement and orderly behaviour.

When students behave disruptively, Glasser's recommended interventions comprise a longer-term counselling approach, and an immediate response to disruptive behaviour. In both approaches, the teacher's role is to help the student find a way of returning to orderly behaviour without being coerced or shamed. The long-term counselling approach asks the student to determine what he wants from school and examine whether his behaviour is helping him achieve that. However, a more immediate response is required if a student violates this agreement or behaves disruptively. In these instances, the teacher gives a reminder and, if this fails to produce appropriate behaviour, then the student is removed from the learning environment. Once away from the class activity, the student must write a new plan of how he will behave within expectations.

Glasser's democratic principles extend beyond student–teacher relationships, to include the school hierarchy and how it affects all members of the school. Principals need to have faith in the school staff and in the students' ability to make responsible decisions. School councils would involve students, teachers and parents in making genuine decisions about the administration of the school.

CASE STUDY

Adam is seven. He has difficulty with reading, spelling and writing, although he enjoys and is capable at maths. During non-maths lessons, you have noticed that he spends a considerable amount of time off-task, when he frequently disrupts the other students. This is worse in the afternoon than in the morning.

He is in a composite class of six and seven-year-olds. He spends most of his play time with the younger children. Frequently a pair including Adam is apprehended during play times doing such things as harassing passers-by from an out-of-bounds area of the playground which is close to the street, rifling through rubbish bins for food or cans to swap for other items with students, or engaging in fights in and around the toilets.

He seems bemused by the trouble he gets into, usually saying when challenged that he doesn't know why he behaves in these inappropriate ways, that he couldn't remember a given behaviour was against the rules, or that the other child was at fault for suggesting the activity.

Until a recent assessment, it was believed that Adam behaved as he did because of low academic ability. However, a battery of tests has shown his overall ability (IQ) to be average, with his maths skills in the high-normal range and his reading and spelling skills, while delayed, still within the lower range of normal limits. Teaching staff are now at a loss for a new explanation of his behaviour.

A CONTROL THEORY APPLICATION

The Glasserian teacher might apply the following strategies to handling Adam's behaviour.

Step 1: Prevention The teacher would look at which aspects of the school system might be provoking Adam's behaviour. The first of these may be irrelevant curricula. The teacher will be aware that the curriculum is set down to a large extent, but she can ask Adam about his interests, and ensure that these are included in school-based learning, and she can explain how established curricula are useful and relevant to students.

Step 2: Satisfying students' emotional needs The teacher would aim to satisfy Adam's emotional needs so that his work output would increase. His lack of motivation is regarded as being due to the work itself being unmotivating for him. Some ways of increasing his motivation are:

- Students would be grouped into teams to allow them to meet their social needs through collaborative work. The teacher may need to institute social skills programs to ensure the students have the skills to negotiate team work in socially acceptable ways.
- With reading being a high priority for education, the teacher would ensure Adam received remediation in this area especially. Built into a remedial program would be a way for Adam to assess his own progress, rather than using an externally applied grading system.
- The teacher would cease assigning compulsory homework, although she would counsel Adam about extra work he could do if he was willing.

Step 3: Class meetings Daily class meetings would be undertaken. The teacher would ensure a balance between social problem-solving meetings, open ended meetings, and educational-diagnostic meetings. Early meetings would establish class rules and discuss the consequences for infractions. These consequences would include restricted freedom while the child reconsidered his behaviour. In social problem-solving meetings, students may be able to suggest other ways Adam could be involved in their play besides his present antisocial play activities.

Step 4: The teacher's role: rapport The teacher would build rapport with Adam by taking notice of him when his behaviour is neutral or acceptable, so that their relationship becomes warmer.

Step 5: Changing the teacher's behaviour Next, she would consider what she is doing that is keeping Adam's behaviour in place, and would stop doing that. An instance may be her constant berating and interrogation of Adam following an infraction of the rules.

Step 6: Reality counselling With greater closeness between herself and Adam, the teacher would next help Adam to make a plan to meet his needs at school. She would ask him what he wanted from school, and how he thought he could get that. Is his present behaviour helping?

At the time of an infraction, the teacher would ask Adam what he did in the particular circumstance—she would not tell him herself. She would not invite excuses by asking him why he acted as he did, and would not accept excuses (such as, that it wasn't his fault because another child suggested or started the misbehaviour or because Adam didn't remember the rule). Next, the teacher would ask Adam to describe the consequences of his actions. She might recite these together in summary and next, ask him whether he likes these consequences. Finally, she would ask Adam what he wants to do about his behaviour when it attracts these costs.

Step 7: Writing a plan Now that Adam no longer accepts his behaviour and its consequences, a plan would be written requiring him to produce quality work and to abide by the rules set by the whole class. The conditions under which he will do so would be specified.

Step 8: Agreeing on consequences Consequences for infractions of the rights of others would be specified. If, for instance, Adam's off-task behaviour were disrupting other students, or if his play were breaking an agreed rule and he continued with this after a reminder such as 'What are you doing?', the teacher would observe: 'You're interrupting others, Adam, and this is against our agreement. We need to work this out'. If Adam were unable to stop the inappropriate behaviour, he would be asked to withdraw until he was ready to abide by the agreement. If the school had a counsellor, she would talk with Adam in a separate isolation room; otherwise the teacher could arrange with Adam to review their agreement in her next free period, and in the meantime he would stay separate from the class (perhaps still in the room) until willing to write a plan about how he will cease the inappropriate behaviour.

Step 9: Parental collaboration Until now, the teacher has avoided bringing in Adam's parents so that his school behaviour does not create a problem for him at home. However, if the school based intervention does not work, the teacher may ask for parental input, as long as it remains clear that the teacher expects to solve the problem herself and is not looking for the parents to do this for her.

Step 10: Referral If neither the parents nor the teacher can suggest a solution, then the teacher may advise the parents of counselling agencies they could consult.

Step 11: Suspension Suspension from school is the final consequence. Glasser (1992) contends that because a quality school meets students' needs and is a good place to be, students do not feel they are getting away with anything or hurting the school when they are suspended. As soon as they can commit themselves to a plan to work out their behaviour, they can return to school.

DISCUSSION QUESTIONS

1. What does Glasser believe causes students to behave disruptively in schools?
2. Glasser coins a term to refer to democratic management of classrooms. What is this term?
3. What, according to Glasser, are people's emotional needs?
4. What aspects does Glasser contend are necessary for a quality education?
5. What academic skill is the most important, in Glasser's opinion?
6. What does the concept of self-responsibility imply?
7. What aspects of classroom management does Glasser believe will contribute to students' belief that school is a good place to be?
8. What are the components of the counselling approach based on reality therapy?
9. What three parts are involved in Glasser's steps for the immediate handling of disruptive behaviour?
10. Apply Glasser's recommendations to the case study you generated in chapter 2. What key features does Glasser introduce that have not been used by earlier theorists? What effect would these differences have on the individual student? On the whole class? On the teacher?

SUGGESTIONS FOR FURTHER READING

Any of Glasser's texts, listed in the reference section, would give an outline of his philosophy. His titles include: *Schools without failure* (1969), *Control theory in the classroom* (1986) and *The quality school* (1992).

Useful overviews of Glasserian theory and its application are provided by:

Charles, C.M. 1996, *Building classroom discipline*, 5th edn, Longman, New York
Edwards, C.H. 1993, *Classroom discipline and management*, Macmillan, New York

8

SYSTEMS THEORY

You cannot solve the problem with the same kind of thinking that has created the problem. (Albert Einstein in de Shazer, 1993, p. 84)

KEY POINTS

- *Systems theory has a single purpose: intervention with, not prevention of, chronic behaviour problems.*

- *There are four main branches of systems theory; the one highlighted in this chapter—brief strategic therapy—believes that behaviour problems (complaints) arise when behaviour is accidentally mishandled and so an attempted solution has not worked.*

- *Change, then, is brought about by changing how the behaviour is handled. To do this, the teacher needs to identify previous solution attempts.*

- *To motivate people to try a new solution, a new way of thinking about the problem is encouraged (reframing).*

- *This new view of the problem can then give a new rationale for using any solutions from the other theories or from systems theory itself.*

INTRODUCTION

Systems theory is different from the individual theories that concentrate on the person with the disruptive behaviour. The individual theories see the person as a whole, made up of parts. In contrast, systems theory sees the individual as part of a whole system or group. A system is any ongoing group—such as a family, school, class or work group—that has characteristic patterns of organisation. These patterns may comprise

communication patterns, allocation of roles, established rules and consequences for infractions of rules, and so on. The word *system* implies that
the group interacts in systematic ways that obey implicit rules and
expectations. Systems theory focuses on these patterns of interactions,
observing that the system's rules can become so inflexible that the
problem—in our case, difficult behaviour—cannot be solved successfully.

Systems theory represents a way of thinking rather than one specific
method for addressing student behaviour (Kral, 1992). It provides a new
way of organising our ideas and then employs intervention techniques
from the other theories, but with a new rationale for their use.

PHILOSOPHICAL ASSUMPTIONS

Family therapy, the counselling discipline that sprang from systems theory,
has been applied to the full range of human behaviour, so does not
specifically discuss the six philosophical dimensions we have used to
introduce the earlier theories. Nevertheless, it is possible to infer systems
theory's position on these dimensions.

NATURE OF CHILDHOOD

Childhood is a time of restricted responsibility in which the child needs
adults to be in executive control of the system, although at the same
time is accountable for what she does (Combrinck-Graham, 1991). Despite
unequal responsibilities, however, the child and adult still have equal
rights.

CONDITIONS NECESSARY FOR LEARNING TO OCCUR

Learning new behaviours does not require insight—that is, self-awareness
of the reasons for our actions. Instead, learning or change requires three
things: first, some discomfort with the results of the present behaviour;
second, information about alternative ways to act; and third, because
change is difficult, we need strong motivation to adopt a new behaviour.

PURPOSE OF DISCIPLINE

Systems theory would not regard itself as an instrument of discipline and
makes no statements about the purpose of discipline. It can be inferred,
however, that because it is a purely interventive approach, its role is to
repair order in classrooms. It does so by reinstating a healthy hierarchy
in which the teacher has executive duties in the classroom and the
students assume increasing responsibilities as they age. Its purpose is

managerial—that is, to permit teaching and learning to occur, although it also has a therapeutic purpose of ensuring less personal distress to participants.

REASONS FOR INAPPROPRIATE BEHAVIOUR

Most individual theories begin with an attempt to diagnose the cause of a student's difficulties that gives rise to the behaviour. This is a linear view of cause and effect: that cause A (origins) leads to effect B (a consequence) (Fisch et al., 1982). In contrast, systems theory does not look for causes of difficult behaviour, but simply identifies the interactions that are maintaining it, based on the concept of *circular causality*. It observes the repetitive interactions that surround the difficult behaviour: the student behaves, and the teacher responds, to which the student responds, and the teacher responds to the student, and so on. What an observer regards as a cause and what as an effect is purely arbitrary in a circle. This implies that it is not necessary to identify a *single* cause (or the beginning of a problem) because there is no beginning or end in a circle.

The different branches of systems theory have slightly different explanations about the interactions that come to surround difficult behaviour. (The reader interested in pursuing the differences between the various branches of systems theory could refer to Hayes (1991) or Smyrnios and Kirkby (1992).) One branch of systems theory that is most readily applied to school based problems is brief strategic therapy. It believes that problematic behaviour arises when everyday developmental challenges or crises are accidentally mishandled. The methods that were aimed at solving the problem unintentionally maintain or intensify it (Amatea, 1988; Fisch et al., 1982). Despite the failure of their methods, participants persist with their solution, not because they are mad, foolish or illogical, but because they conscientiously follow the wrong advice, namely that if at first you don't succeed, try, try again (Fisch et al., 1982).

ADULT–CHILD STATUS

Systems theory makes no judgments about how groups should be organised, but it does observe that when members are confused or disagree about the system's organisation, then problems can result (Carlson, 1992). One aspect of organisation is that members must have sufficient power to carry out their roles. In the case of student behaviour, the teacher must be higher in the class hierarchy than students, so that he can make executive decisions about the functioning of the group, such as deciding that there will be rules for the students' behaviour, although the teacher and students can collaborate to determine those rules. The teacher and students share equal status but have different roles.

ROLE OF THE TEACHER

Unlike the predominantly school based theories discussed in earlier chapters, systems theory does not enunciate principles of good teaching for prevention of behaviour problems. It is purely an interventive approach: it is an attempt to address the occasions when teachers find themselves doing the same unsuccessful thing over and over again in response to a student's behaviour.

Because of the concept of circular causality, systems theory advises the teacher to interrupt the cycle of action and reaction that has come to surround the problem. Change by any participant will bring about a change in the whole interaction pattern and, since it is easier for the teacher to change himself than to change the student, the teacher's job is to respond in new ways to the student's repetitive behaviour.

PROCESS OF ASSESSMENT AND INTERVENTION

Systems theory focuses both on what to do when assessing and intervening with difficult behaviour, and how to carry out these recommendations. First, let's examine some of the processes for conducting systemic assessment and intervention, and then describe the content of both phases.

COOPERATE WITH OTHERS' PERSPECTIVE

Cooperation is both an attitude and a technique for acknowledging that one person's perspective on the problem is as likely to be true as any other person's. This invites the practitioner to look at the other person's perspective to arrive at a new understanding of the problem. Any new understanding that helps the teacher behave differently towards the complaint has the potential for solving the problem. Not all perspectives will be equally useful, though: those that focus on the past, or on diagnosing an individual as deficient or helpless in some way, are usually negative and will defy finding a solution.

In the language of other therapies cooperation is called empathy. However, rather than being directed only at the individual, the systemic worker's empathy focuses on individuals' predicament as a group and as individuals, both now and in their history (Perry, 1993).

An extension of the concept of cooperation is given by Molnar (1986) who notes that often we experience a student as *resisting* our attempts to teach her. We blame the student for being uncooperative, but cooperation is a two-way street: if a student is not accepting our input, then we may need to change our approach instead of asking the student to change.

BE NEUTRAL

Systems need both stability and the ability to change. If an external force favours one of these, the individual (or system) will counteract the pressure and favour its opposite. For this reason, the principle of neutrality holds that advocators of change *must be neutral* on the issue of whether someone else *should change* or stay as she is. In presenting a balanced case for and against change, the teacher can point out to a troublesome student that change is risky and difficult and may not be successful; her present behaviour works to some extent (it may be fun) although it has its penalties. The choice between her two options is hers alone.

This may seem dishonest. It *feels* as if you would have more success if you tried to talk her into changing her ways. However, four arguments favour neutrality: the first is the democratic principle that no one can coerce another to change. Second, it can be seen that the more the adult tries to convince the student to mend her ways, the more the student resists, setting up a vicious cycle that solves nothing. Third, neutrality is *not* the same as reverse psychology. With reverse psychology, the individual does not believe the suggestion and is trying to arrange for the other person to behave in a certain way; the principle of neutrality requires the individual to believe the suggestions, or not use them. Fourth, *neutrality* on the issue of whether the other person should change or not, is not the same as being *impartial*, although the two concepts are related. Impartiality means not taking sides, while neutrality means that you can express your bias and your values, but without arguing that the problem bearer should change.

AVOID MORE OF THE SAME

Although a range of solutions—such as telling a student off, time out, detention, visits to the principal's office and sending notes home to the parents—may have already been tried, they usually all have the same theme, commonly trying to discourage a student's inappropriate behaviour. This type of change is called first-order change, whereby the teacher make changes within a class of interventions. In contrast, second-order change refers to a change of type.

At times, solutions fail because they represent 'more of the same' solution even when they appear to be different. For this reason, and others to be discussed later in this chapter, the teacher is unlikely to begin by addressing the student since that is how previous attempts at a solution have failed. Instead, he will be looking at changing the type of solution altogether, since a problem has become chronic because of failed attempts to solve it, and repeating failed attempts will not work. This means that the teacher will examine his own part in the problem, rather than the student's.

NOTICE CHANGE

Once an intervention has begun, it is crucial to notice changes, even those that do not appear to be related to the problem or its solution. Since chronic problems represent a lack of change, old patterns can be revisited if those involved do not notice progress. On the other hand, change should not be praised because praise argues for change (is not neutral), and the system will attempt to stabilise by reverting to old patterns. When change has not occurred, the worker can compare bad days with worse days and ask about what creates the difference (McLeod, 1989).

USE HUMOUR

Chronic problems can make participants feel desperate and will generate inflexibility about finding a solution (Molnar & Lindquist, 1989). Instead, finding humour in an intense situation may in itself solve the problem, or at least be a vehicle for doing so.

BE SINCERE

The teacher needs to accept that there are many ways to view a problem, all equally hypothetical, and that any one view is as likely to be true as any other. In choosing between views, however, it is crucial for the teacher to use his own personal and professional judgment. To be able to persist with an intervention, he needs to believe in the new view on which it is based, or he would revert to the old management method and would appear hypocritical.

TAKE TIME

Often, desperation leads to a sense of urgency about finding a solution. However, if a solution were that obvious, the participants would have found it long ago. Therefore, a teacher using a systems approach will need to buy time and not let himself be pressured into acting prematurely (Fisch et al., 1982). Also, because systemic interventions may appear illogical to observers, the teacher will need to lay the groundwork carefully with other involved staff before instituting a systemic intervention (Amatea, 1989).

SYSTEMIC ASSESSMENT

Most systemic assessment is conducted by interviewing the participants in the complaint. However, if the teacher is applying systems theory to the difficulties of his own students, then he cannot interview himself and so instead he may use formal and informal observations, as well as talking with any other participants. While this is highly subjective, it is not necessary to assess 'reality' because participants act as if their explanations *are* reality, and so it is enough to understand how participants perceive events (Fine, 1992). Therefore, an assessment and subsequent intervention needs to understand the participants' perceptions and be framed within their belief system, even if their explanation differs from what someone else may regard as the 'facts'.

The aim of assessment is to find out who is involved in the complaint, what the complaint entails, how that is a problem, and to whom it is a problem (Fisch et al., 1982). The aim is not to find diagnostic explanations, but simply to understand how the problem is manifested.

DEFINE THE PROBLEM

Watzlawick, Weakland and Fisch (1974) describe *difficulties* as unfortunate but natural events that respond to commonsense solutions or that go away without intervention being necessary. Steve de Shazer and colleagues (1986) are speaking of the same phenomenon when they describe teaching (and life) as 'one damn thing after another'. *Problems*, on the other hand, come about when solutions do not work or, put another way, when difficulties are accidentally mishandled. The teacher then becomes engaged in doing 'the same damn thing over and over'. The issue or *complaint*, then, is not just the target behaviour but also the irritating need to respond to it repeatedly. So, a complaint is defined as both the problem behaviour *and* the efforts of the problem bearer and others to solve it. This repetitive cycle of interactions is defined as the complaint and so becomes the target of assessment and intervention.

The complaint, then, is defined as interpersonal rather than being due to any individual's personal deficiency. This means that the teacher would not seek to diagnose a student's emotional or other disturbances because even when diagnosis is possible and accurate, knowing a cause does not necessarily imply how to solve the problem. This belief is especially useful for school practitioners who need quick solutions to severe problems (Dicocco, Chalfin & Olson, 1987). Assessment shifts from searching for a cause to searching for solutions to the complaint and, in doing this, it aims to identify the resources participants already possess which could be applied to finding a solution.

Also, the teacher will not be focusing on individuals' thoughts and feelings (Kral, 1988). Their behaviour is more easily accessible for observation and change, and a change in behaviour will have a 'ripple effect' that will alleviate distressing feelings without having to focus on them directly.

DETERMINE WHOM TO INVOLVE IN ASSESSMENT AND INTERVENTION

The teacher applying systems theory to school behaviour difficulties would work with those people already most directly involved in the problem. A change in those people most connected to the complaint will have a ripple effect on those less involved in it, so those on the fringes need not be included directly in the intervention. Those most involved may be only the problem bearer (for instance, a student with performance anxiety), or it may include two or more people, depending on who has been engaged until now in trying to find a solution to the problem (Amatea, 1989).

To assess the motivation of participants and therefore decide whom to involve in the intervention, de Shazer (in Kral, 1992) distinguishes three roles of those involved. The first role is occupied by the *visitor*, who attends because she must, but who is not interested in change. The student with the difficult behaviour is usually in the visitor's role. The worker needs to develop a positive relationship with the visitor, under-standing events from her point of view, but should not make her do anything during the intervention phase. The second role is that of the *complainant*, who wants to talk about the problem but is not ready yet to do anything about it. The worker will give the complainant tasks that are aimed at improving the worker's understanding of the dynamics of the problem, but the complainant is not asked to act. The third role is that of the *customer*, who responds to a more direct approach because he or she is the one most inconvenienced by the behaviour and so wants to do something about it. It is likely that this person is the problem bearer's teacher or parent.

As can be seen from this characterisation of roles, the teacher is least likely to intervene directly with the student because she usually is not motivated to change. A second reason not to focus on the student is that she has least power in the system, and so will be least able to affect it. Therefore, the teacher himself and his part in the repetitive interactions around the student's behaviour would be the main focus of assessment and intervention.

DEFINE GOALS

Having identified the participants, the worker will ask them about their goals for behaviour change, because it is easier to get somewhere if you know where you want to go (de Shazer et al., 1986). Participants will need to state how they will know when the behaviour has improved, and in what ways the improvement will be different from the presenting pattern. The goals must be small, realistically achievable, and stated in specific, concrete, behavioural and measurable terms (Berg & de Shazer, 1989). Goals need to specify what participants want to see continue, rather than what behaviour they want stopped, because the absence of something is difficult to notice. One question these writers suggest would lead to goal clarification is: 'Suppose one night while you slept, a miracle happened, and the complaint was solved: what would you notice was different when you woke up?'.

ASSESS CONSTRAINTS

Because any solution must fit within the system's constraints, the teacher must be aware of the constraints surrounding the problem (de Shazer et al., 1986), such as parental unwillingness to be involved, or lack of support from the school administration. Assessing constraints means that the teacher will note what aspects of the problem are out of his control, compared to those he can control. Only those he can control will be included in the assessment and intervention. This means that only those willing to be involved will be invited to contribute to the intervention.

IDENTIFY PARTICIPANTS' BELIEFS AND THE RESULTING
INTERACTION PATTERN

Using a brief strategic approach, the teacher will assess the participants' beliefs about the complaint (Amatea, 1989). This serves two purposes. The first is that by becoming aware of the participants' beliefs about the problem, the practitioner comes to an understanding of why the problem has persisted. The beliefs account for why participants have attempted one solution and not others. They have given rise to repetitive interaction patterns of behaviour and response that have become a problem. The second purpose of assessing participants' beliefs is that during intervention the practitioner will be giving them a rationale for trying something different. When this is framed within their own belief systems, they will be motivated to try a new solution.

Mostly these beliefs are implicit in what people say and how they describe the complaint and the student's motivation for persisting with it. This can make it difficult to assess the participants' beliefs. It is doubly difficult if the teacher is attempting to intervene in a problem in which he is involved, and therefore he has to analyse his own beliefs. Likewise, if discussing the complaint with a colleague who shares the teacher's own beliefs, it may be difficult even to notice that they *are* beliefs rather than facts (Amatea, 1989).

Nevertheless, asking for or observing specific examples of the sequence may allow the teacher to identify some common themes or patterns being repeated over and over again (Amatea, 1989):

- Belief that the problem bearer cannot help her behaviour: it is involuntary. If the student believes this about herself, she avoids overcoming the problem. If the teacher believes it about a student, the teacher will avoid making demands on the student, which can lead to inconsistent handling and low expectations for the student, which she lives down to.
- Belief that the problem bearer is deliberately being disruptive. This leads to attempts to force compliance, which in turn creates a cycle of coercion and resistance. Both participants feel angry, frustrated and victimised by each other.
- Attempts to gain voluntary compliance. An example of this is a parent of a school truant who will not insist that the child attend school unless she feels comfortable about going, when instead the child will not feel comfortable until she attends school and confronts the issues that are upsetting her.

Once the teacher can identify the sequence of events that surrounds the complaint, then the way is open to disrupt that sequence during the intervention phase (Fine, 1992), giving a rationale that incorporates rather than opposes the participants' beliefs about the problem.

OBSERVE EXCEPTIONS

Change is inevitable; stability is an illusion (Chang & Phillips, 1993; Kral, 1988). Instead of focusing on the apparent stability of the problem, the teacher should expect something worthwhile to be happening as well, and should anticipate that it will continue to happen (de Shazer & Molnar, 1984). By noticing the times when the behaviour does not occur, the teacher can question the beliefs that have been used to explain it. For instance, Hsia (1984) noted that a student with apparent separation anxiety leading to school phobia frequently separated from the parents in situations that did not involve school, and that therefore separation anxiety was not the reason for the truancy as had been assumed.

OBSERVE SYSTEM STRUCTURES

Systems have three characteristics that are equally vital to their survival. They are *organised* into patterns of communication, roles, rules, rules about rules and their infraction, hierarchies, boundaries between subsystems (which refers to the separateness of individuals and how clearly they differentiate their various roles). Systems also have a need for *stability*, and a competing need for *flexibility* (change). Common dysfunctions of these basic characteristics include:

- Disturbed hierarchies, in which those who should be in charge are not.
- Unclear boundaries: people take responsibility for other members' behaviour or fail to take responsibility for their own. This can happen within or between groups, such as when parents are asked to solve school based behaviour problems or the teacher is pressured to rescue parents from their distress.
- Triangulation: when the level of tension between two members of the system is intolerable, a third person (usually the symptom bearer) is brought in to deflect the tension. As well as occurring between two members of a system, these patterns can also happen between groups—for instance, when the school and family try to prove to each other that their approach to a child's difficult behaviour is the correct one.
- Inflexibility, in which an unsuccessful way of solving the problem is persisted with, because it is seen to be the right way to act even though it is not working.
- Too much change, such as when a child is removed from home into foster care, and in the process loses her parents, siblings and home and also changes schools, and so loses peers and familiarity with the school's organisation. This can give rise to the same difficult behaviour which caused her to be removed from home, and which is seen to reflect her underlying emotional disturbance, when instead systems theorists would see it as reflecting too much change in the systems to which the child belongs and would attempt to stabilise her circumstances.

While the teacher's role is not to force the system to change how it has organised itself, awareness of imbalances in the system's structure can help frame an intervention. For instance, intervention for a student who has been placed into foster care would centre around stabilising her family or school system. This can be contrasted with an individual intervention which would counsel the student about her emotional problems.

ASSESS THE TEMPORAL CONTEXT

As well as examining the social interactions that surround a complaint,
systems theory also addresses how the complaint has developed over
time. The question 'Why now?' is addressed, asking why the complaint
has presented as a problem now rather than some time ago or some
time later. Also the teacher will seek to know who has become involved
in trying to solve the problem throughout its life, what effect those
attempts have had, and who is presently most involved and most
concerned—and conversely who is least involved and least concerned—
about the problem now. This information can help formulate an intervention, not the least of which is avoiding repeating a solution that has
already been tried and has failed.

NOTE PARTICIPANTS' STRENGTHS

The worker will need to identify when the participants have been able
to solve similar problems in this student's life, or for other students with
similar problems. By highlighting these effective and useful actions the
participants can do or have done, the systems thinker can encourage
them to do the same again.

SYSTEMIC INTERVENTIONS

On the basis of these observations, the worker determines what intervention the participants are most likely to accept and perform. Because
the problematic behaviour has unwittingly been maintained by the
attempted solutions, then the aim of an intervention is to enable the
participants to let go of an ineffective solution so that they can try another
one instead (Fisch et al., 1982). The new solution lies in changing the
interactions that have come to surround the difficult behaviour. Although
problems can be quite serious, one small change in the interaction
sequence can snowball to effect a large change, and therefore: 'big
problems don't necessarily require big solutions' (Kral, 1988, p. 3).

Just as a key does not need to be an exact fit to open a lock, an
intervention does not need to be elaborate: it only needs to open the
way to a new solution (de Shazer et al., 1986). And just as a skeleton
key will open many locks, a particular intervention may be suitable for
many different problems. This is the principle of *equifinality* or, in
colloquial terms, the principle that there is more than one way to 'skin
a cat'.

STORMING THE BACK DOOR

Molnar and Lindquist (1989) use this term to refer to an indirect way to build a more constructive relationship between the teacher and a troublesome student. Without focusing at all on the particular behaviour causing concern, the teacher comments favourably on something positive or neutral about the student's behaviour. Because all interactions are linked, changing any one interaction—even when it has nothing to do with the problem—changes the relationship and so changes the problem.

FOCUSING ON NON-PROBLEMATICAL ASPECTS

The teacher can expect to find occasions when the problem does not occur. He will observe what is currently happening that he does not want to change, and the things he is already doing well. The steps involved in locating exceptions are (Molnar & Lindquist, 1989):

1. Identification of situations when the problem does not occur.
2. Identification of which aspects are present when the behaviour does occur versus when it does not.
3. Selection of a non-problem behaviour or situation that is easy to increase in frequency.
4. Formulation of an approach for increasing the incidence of non-problem behaviour.

COMPRESSING TIME

Instead of dealing with many behaviours presented by the one student, the behaviours are compressed into one pattern that might be likened to a 'career' or pathway in life. This allows just one intervention to be applied. The student's behaviour is described how it was, how it presents now, and how it is likely to extend into the future. For instance, rather than dealing with a full gamut of aggressive and disruptive acts, the teacher could describe an aggressive student as having a career as a delinquent. Compression of time must be paired with the principle of neutrality that requires that the teacher deliver the description of the student's career in a neutral manner which does not try to talk her into changing.

PRESCRIBE THE SYMPTOM

As implied by the concept of cooperation, the teacher accepts that the student's perspective is legitimate, and that her behaviour (the 'symptom') makes sense to her given her view of it. The logical next step, then, is to allow the student to perform the behaviour, since she has good reasons for behaving as she does and should not be required to abandon something that works. Refusing to continue to struggle with the student about her behaviour often has two effects: first, the student may feel understood for the first time and, second, she may begin cooperating with the teacher in return (Molnar & Lindquist, 1989).

However, the behaviour can continue only within limits that make it less disruptive to the teacher and other class members. Some changes to the old complaint pattern include (de Shazer et al., 1986):

- changing the location of the pattern
- changing who is involved in the pattern
- changing the order of the steps involved
- adding a new element or step to the pattern
- increasing the duration of the sequence
- introducing random starting and stopping
- increasing the frequency of the pattern.

For instance, a student who leaves her seat repeatedly can be seen to have a need to take a break from her work. Since this need is legitimate, she can be given permission to continue with it, although with some modifications, such as taking a break before activities begin instead of during them.

REFRAME

Individuals understand behaviour using the most logical explanations suggested by their experience and training. They then enact solutions based on these explanations. When a problem has become chronic, however, this is a clue that their understanding about it is unproductive (Molnar & Lindquist, 1989). Present solution attempts are failing because they are based on an explanation that has remained stable over time, producing in turn interventions that have remained the same over time. A solution will require a new way of looking at the problem.

The technique for changing our description or explanation of a problem is termed *reframing*. Building on the concept of cooperation, reframing embodies the belief that problem behaviour can be legitimately interpreted in a variety of ways (Molnar & Lindquist, 1989). Reframing is the process of producing a new description of the behaviour but one which is still plausible to the participants. The reframe or new under-standing of the behaviour must fit the interactions that surround the behaviour, must be acceptable to the participants, and should help to design an intervention. If it does not, then another view that is more suitable needs to be arrived at. The new interpretations are usually positive since if we are critical of others, they are less likely to change.

At the same time, however, the reframe must not downplay the significance of the complaint, because to call it something nice without implying a solution would only allow the disruptive behaviour to continue unabated, which is against the interests of all participants.

The steps involved in reframing are (Molnar & Lindquist, 1989):

1. The teacher describes in specific behavioural terms what the student does, when, and in what circumstances. He identifies who else is involved.
2. Next, he describes how he usually responds to the behaviour and what effect that has.
3. The teacher identifies his present explanation for the student's behaviour. He will note those descriptions that look into the *past* for *causes*, which contain hypotheses about the individual's *personality*, or are *blaming*. These are his clues that his explanation will not be helping to solve the difficulty.
4. The teacher will create a range of positive alternative explanations for the behaviour. This is the reframing step.
5. Next, he selects a positive explanation that will seem plausible and honest to those experiencing the problem.
6. The teacher describes this new explanation in a sentence or two. This may or may not be delivered to the student concerned, because insight is not necessary for change to take place.
7. Finally, the teacher acts in a way suggested by the new explanation. The new explanation is intended to promote new ways of interacting, since the complaint now has new meaning and so cannot be responded to in the old way.

Reframing may be difficult to undertake because a teacher does not wish to appear to be lowering his standards by cooperating with a negative behaviour, or may find it hard to see anything other than the negative aspects of the problem. However, fixed views of the problem have brought about fixed solutions, so a change in approach can only be achieved by a change in thinking.

The teacher can reframe how he understands the student's *personal characteristics*, he can reframe what he understands to be her *motive*, or he can take a fresh look at what effect the behaviour is having.

Positive connotation of personality

Labels blame the problem on one person's supposed deficiencies or on the past, neither of which can be fixed (Molnar & Lindquist, 1989). A label directs attention away from the interactions that surround the behaviour, and usually ignores what the individual does well. In this way, labels can make difficulties unsolvable by de-normalising the problem and suggesting first-order solutions (doing more of the same).

The concept of positive connotation of personality is illustrated when a person who has been labelled as lazy, is instead described as being expert at getting others to do things for her; a 'crazy' person could instead be described as eccentric (Haley, 1980), or as an expert at failing; a 'non-compliant' student could be seen to be a non-conformist, which is much less blaming; a school phobic may be staying home to look after a depressed parent, if this fits the remainder of her behaviour, or she may be seen to be giving herself a well earned rest from her studies—again, if her truancy seems to be a way of coping with stress.

Positive connotation of motive

We mostly attribute negative motives to a student whose behaviour is intrusive or disruptive. Positive connotation of motive requires us instead to identify a positive motive for the behaviour on the understanding that people do the best they can, given their perspective. Although the behaviour remains negative, changing the hypothesis we hold about the student's motives allows us to change how we respond, which in turn can bring about a change in the behaviour itself.

For instance, a student who is clowning around during class could be termed 'defiant' or 'attention seeking' but the teacher could equally well interpret her behaviour positively, by observing that the student is sacrificing herself by being willing to entertain her peers, even when it gets her into trouble.

Positive connotation of effect

Just as behaviour can have a positive motive instead of a negative one, so too it can have a positive effect rather than a purely negative one. If we can identify this positive effect, then we can respond to the behaviour more positively. For instance, a student who does little work creates little marking for the teacher. The teacher can simply thank the student for contributing to his lighter work load. The reframe does not imply the student's intent, but simply describes a positive outcome of her behaviour.

DO SOMETHING DIFFERENT

Unlike reframing that is based on changing our thinking about the problem, doing something different merely requires observing the usual response to the problem, and doing something entirely different from that, regardless of whether any of the participants understand how the teacher's response has been maintaining the student's behaviour. However, to give participants a rationale and so motivate them to perform what is a radical departure from their previous solution attempts, it may be necessary to use reframing as well.

The advice to do something different rests on systems theory's belief that the problem has come about because participants have unwittingly responded in the same way whenever the difficult behaviour has occurred. They persist because they believe in their solution and also because they have no other resources and ideas for solving it (de Shazer & Molnar, 1984). However, Bateson (1979, in de Shazer et al., 1986) said that for change to occur, a source of randomness must be introduced. Therefore, de Shazer and colleagues advise that if something isn't working, don't do it again; do something else. Or, put another way, 'Always change a losing game' (Fisch et al., 1982).

To interrupt the usual sequence surrounding the complaint, the new response must be a noticeable departure from the old pattern. To this end, Amatea (1989) suggests that the new solution be the opposite of previous solution attempts:

- Where the problem has been defined as involuntary, it is now described as voluntary. The teacher will highlight instances when the problem bearer has successfully overcome temptation and has behaved appropriately, which proves that the problem bearer has some control.
- If the teacher thinks the student is being deliberately disruptive, then he will try to stop her behaving that way, while the student will resist this persuasion. Instead, the teacher might impose the student's response, rather than oppose it—that is, use symptom prescription.
- If the participants have been engaged in a fight, then one person will instead submit.

The teacher identifies the most appropriate new solution by observing which previous solution attempt has been most crucial, then identifies the biggest departure from that. Next, he ensures that this new solution can be readily incorporated into his daily routine so that it can happen often enough to have an impact on the complaint.

WARN ABOUT RELAPSES

Relapses will occur naturally during the process of change. However, they often unnerve and discourage participants. To rob relapses of their discouraging effect and to normalise them, the teacher can predict them in advance and advise participants simply to do something different from what they were doing when the problem was first referred (de Shazer & Molnar, 1984).

Even without any forewarning, a relapse can be presented in a more encouraging light. For instance, it can be described as a difficulty but not a problem, as a reminder about the 'bad old days' of the problem, or as a legitimate use of an old method for coping, but one which has altered inexorably during the intervention and so is no longer the same.

BORROW APPROACHES FROM OTHER THEORIES

Systems theory provides a new way of looking at a stale problem. Once the new way is arrived at, the teacher can use any treatment approach that fits within the new perspective. He might, for instance, set up a contract for restricted practice of the symptom under a symptom pre-scription approach. He might use notes home to parents to highlight changes made, although he would steer away from praising the changes as this violates the principle of neutrality. Or he might formalise his instructions and feedback to the student if when he observed exceptions, he identified that the student required more structure.

Whenever an intervention is borrowed from another theory but is applied for a different reason, its flavour is different, and so under the umbrella of a systemic approach, the application is expected to have very different effects.

WORKING WITH STUDENTS

Lusterman (1985) suggests that school pressure for a student to perform more satisfactorily can stress even a well functioning family, and can add intolerable stress to an already dysfunctional family, setting the student up for victimisation by both school and home. Within the context of chronic problems, students are the least powerful members of the dual systems and so should not be the direct focus of intervention unless no other focus is possible. Amatea (1989) recommends that if the student must be the focus, then the teacher must be careful to avoid using the same solution that has led to the present problem. She recommends that the teacher address an issue that is central for the student, taking her perspective. This may mean agreeing that school is unfair, for instance, and that change on the student's part is just a way of getting other teachers off her back.

WORKING WITH PARENTS

Lindquist, Molnar and Brauchmann (1987) characterise three types of school related behavioural difficulties: problems in the family that disturb the school, problems at school that disturb the family, and problems at school that do not disturb the family. Distinguishing the type of problem, they contend, helps the teacher decide whether to focus on the school, the family, or the school and family's interactions. However, although brief strategic workers are aware that the family is the prime influence on the student and that upsets in the family structure can lead to behaviour difficulties at school, the teacher would not focus on the family because family counselling is not within his role as a teacher. Also, a change in the student at school will bring about a change in how the family view her, and so the disturbed situation at home can be improved without being intervened with directly. Nevertheless, when the teacher regards the problem as stemming from home, he would look for signs that a school focus was failing because it was not involving the key participants, and would refer the family to a family therapist if they were willing.

While focusing on school based issues, the teacher may involve parents from the outset in collaborating to find a solution, he may simply liaise with them to apprise them of his approach, or he may inform them of the success of his intervention once it has ended. Whatever role the teacher adopts, systems ideas can encourage parents' cooperation, and ensure that the teacher and parents can support each other's efforts. This is a significant reversal of the pattern of uncooperative and unproductive relationships between families and school that often becomes entrenched when the student has a school based behaviour problem (Lindquist et al., 1987; Lusterman, 1985).

The guidelines for collaboration with parents are identical to those already given for working with other participants (such as cooperation, sincerity, noticing their strengths), although in addition work with parents requires that the teacher confirm the parents' status as family leaders who have the skills to solve their own difficulties.

The teacher would collaborate with other agencies involved with the family, or refer to a family therapist to coordinate interventions if relationships between the school, the family and outside agencies have become complex. If the teacher is unaware of or ignores other agencies involved with the student, then the workers may undermine each other's attempts at a solution. The end result will be that the complaint can remain the same among the confusion, and that each agency applies the same unsuccessful solution. The family's chaos is mirrored by a chaotic helping system (Reder, 1983) which perpetuates and even adds to the family's difficulties.

STEPS FOR SUCCESS

Start small

Molnar and Lindquist (1989) observe that because a small change can have a significant impact, the teacher can start by aiming for a small improvement. These writers also recommend that the new initiate to systems ideas begin with small problems rather than crises.

Cooperate

The teacher will need to use the other person's language, and adopt the other person's perspective.

Go slowly

The teacher might begin by practising one technique that interests him and waiting to observe its effects.

Check the technique

If the intervention is less than successful, the teacher will need to check that he implemented it correctly, and that he was sincere. After an initial attempt, did he revert to old ways of responding? If the intervention was accurate, the teacher will have to persist: it may be necessary to repeat the intervention.

Try another approach

When an intervention is failing, the teacher can ask if there is another part of the system that can be involved.

Involve others

The teacher will need to consult with colleagues in order to maintain his creativity.

PROBLEMS UNSUITABLE FOR SYSTEMIC INTERVENTIONS

Teachers should use the simplest intervention that is likely to work, and employ more complex strategies only when problems do not respond to simple corrective action (Amatea, 1989). While systems theory is aimed at complex problems, there are times when even these are not amenable to systemic interventions. Amatea (1989) excludes those times when a recent trauma causes the student emotional turmoil, where her family is so disorganised that she lacks the stability needed to learn predictable behaviour—in which case specialist family intervention is necessary—or when the student's difficulties are due to specific learning deficits that lead to academic difficulties. However, Frey (1984) observes that young people may behave more helplessly than their condition warrants, and therefore a systemic intervention, while not ameliorating a learning difficulty entirely, can partly address under-achievement.

SUMMARY

The systems perspective is a circular view of the world. It is different from the individual theories. Whereas individual psychological theories see the individual as a whole made up of parts, systems theory sees the individual as being part of a larger whole. Robinson (1980, p. 187) confirms this, noting that the whole is more than the sum of its parts, and saying that: 'Any attempt to understand the "whole" by breaking it down into its component "parts" will always miss the nature of the relationship between the "parts" and the quality of their interaction'.

Although many of the approaches of systems theory could be explained using the framework of other theorists covered in this text, Molnar and Lindquist (1989) advise against the transfer of ideas. They assert that using ideas from individually based theories could perpetuate the teacher's present description of problem behaviours, in turn maintain the present solution, and so maintain the problem. Instead, when these theories have not suggested a solution, the teacher will need to try something different. In the words of de Shazer and colleagues (1986):

If something works, do more of it (Look for exceptions)

If something isn't working, stop it (Do less of the same)

If something isn't working, do something else (Do something different)

CASE STUDY

Adam is seven. He has difficulty with reading, spelling and writing, although he enjoys and is capable at maths. During non-maths lessons, you have noticed that he spends a considerable amount of time off-task, when he frequently disrupts the other students. This is worse in the afternoon than in the morning.

He is in a composite class of six and seven-year-olds. He spends most of his play time with the younger children. Frequently a pair including Adam is apprehended during play times doing such things as harassing passers-by from an out-of-bounds area of the playground which is close to the street, rifling through rubbish bins for food or cans to swap for other items with students, or engaging in fights in and around the toilets.

He seems bemused by the trouble he gets into, usually saying when challenged that he doesn't know why he behaves in these inappropriate ways, that he couldn't remember a given behaviour was against the rules, or that the other child was at fault for suggesting the activity.

Until a recent assessment, it was believed that Adam behaved as he did because of low academic ability. However, a battery of tests has shown his overall ability (IQ) to be average, with his maths skills in the high-normal range and his reading and spelling skills, while delayed, still within the lower range of normal limits. Teaching staff are now at a loss for a new explanation of his behaviour.

A SYSTEMIC APPLICATION

The teacher using systems ideas will first assess and then intervene in the interaction pattern comprised of Adam's repeated behaviour infractions and the teacher's repeated attempts to resolve them.

PHASE ONE: ASSESSMENT

Step 1: Define the problem An individual theory would suggest that Adam has some learning difficulties and is not taking responsibility for his own behaviour. In contrast, the systems thinker would define the problem as including not only Adam's behaviour but the irritating need for someone (mostly his teacher) to respond to it. Therefore, the problem is the repetitive interactions that occur when Adam behaves inappropriately.

Step 2: Identify who is involved (roles) Given that our case is hypothetical, for the purposes of demonstrating a systemic approach we need to make the assumptions that either: (a) the teacher wants to deal with the issue at school rather than engage the parents in the intervention; or (b) the parents have few problems with Adam at home and so would not fit a customer role. Neither, however, does Adam, who could be said to be a visitor, since he is not concerned about his behaviour. Therefore, the teacher puts himself in the role of customer, being the main one concerned about the behaviour, the one who most often responds to it, and the one most able to make a difference to it.

Step 3: Define the goals The teacher examines his goals. He would like Adam to achieve more, and would like his behaviour not to disrupt the other students as often. He would like to have to remind Adam less often to abide by agreed standards of behaviour and to produce an acceptable standard of work. In short, he would like Adam to 'apply himself better'.

Step 4: Assess beliefs Given that the teacher has defined himself as the customer and is in the best position to instigate changes, the teacher will examine his own beliefs about the reasons for Adam's behaviour. Until the recent assessment, he had thought that Adam had significant learning difficulties that caused his off-task behaviour. The teacher also assumed that these apparent learning problems caused Adam to be unable to remember rules. On the other hand, the teacher has also believed at times that Adam was being wilful in defying the teacher's directives.

Looking at the issue from Adam's perspective, it is possible that Adam believes his teacher is picking on him. From this perspective, his behaviour of being a passive victim of his own inadequacies makes sense. The only thing he can do in the face of unfair and coercive treatment is to assert his autonomy whenever he can, which is most readily through disruptive acts.

Step 5: Identify the interaction pattern To design an intervention for Adam's behaviour, the teacher needs to describe the sequence of events that has surrounded his repeated infractions. The teacher has coaxed and reminded Adam to attend to the task at hand, and has chastised him for his apparent forgetfulness of the school rules. It could be seen, then, that the teacher has tried to coerce appropriate behaviour, and Adam has been resisting these attempts.

Although the teacher thought his responses to Adam were different over time, he now realises that they have in fact all been of the same class (*first-order solutions*). All have attempted to coerce compliance. The teacher has reminded and coaxed, he has required Adam to complete school activities at home, but Adam frequently 'forgot' to take them home or to return the 'completed' work to school the next day. To overcome his noncompliance, Adam's parents were asked to sign a homework notebook, but again Adam did not return the notebook to school, reporting that he 'forgot'. Other attempts at coercion have involved time out whereby Adam had to complete his work while separated from the rest of the class, or even in recess when other students were not available to distract Adam or to respond to his inappropriate behaviour.

In summary, the teacher has vacillated between believing Adam is misbehaving deliberately, and at other times believing that Adam cannot control himself. Correspondingly the teacher has alternated between using coercive tactics and expressing helpless frustration. The thrust of these interventions has been to 'get Adam to apply himself better'. Closer examination also reveals that the teacher has alternated between being too patient with Adam, and then berating him when his (the teacher's) patience has run out.

Step 6: Observe exceptions The teacher needs to examine exceptions to the problem, especially those that might challenge his beliefs about the reasons for it. The teacher's belief has been that Adam is incapable, and cannot remember. However, he notes an exception—that Adam remembers his swimming gear (and Adam loves swimming)—and yet cannot remember school rules. This demonstrates that Adam does not have a learning or memory problem, but that he lacks motivation to remember certain things.

PHASE TWO: INTERVENTION

Step 7: Reframe The teacher realises he needs to do something different, since the old solutions of coercion and becoming exasperated are not working. He will look for a new solution that would be a big departure from these two previous solutions. To help with this step, the teacher tries to find a new way of looking at the problem (*reframing*), to provide a rationale for a new approach. He wonders if his patience with Adam and his beliefs about Adam's learning disabilities have in fact given Adam the impression that he (the teacher) thinks Adam cannot do any better and is incompetent. If this were so, then Adam's behaviour is only an implicit agreement with this judgment. Adam is conforming to the teacher's view of him. This is a new and more *positive connotation* of Adam's personality, which in the past has been described as noncompliant. It is important that this reframe seems plausible to the teacher so that he can accept it sincerely. It is unlikely that the teacher would convey the reframe to Adam since insight is not necessary for change: instead, Adam will feel the effects of the reframe in the resulting change in the teacher's interactions with him.

Process note: cooperation The teacher knows that change is difficult, and so he will assume that Adam would be afraid of being more competent, especially when no one believes he can be successful. This more empathic view of Adam will allow the teacher to be more positive with him. The teacher may be able to build a more constructive relationship with Adam (*storming the back door*) which in itself will be beneficial and will also give Adam the confidence to try a new solution. The teacher may make an extra effort to encourage Adam (but not praise him as praise is not neutral).

Process note: neutrality The teacher will stop coaxing and reminding Adam (applying the principle of *neutrality*), so that Adam receives the message that he is capable of making decisions for himself. The teacher will also inject some humour and fun into his relationship with Adam and the class.

Step 8: Do something different The new reframe that Adam is agreeing with his teacher's low expectations may imply that the teacher needs to give Adam explicit directions about his work and how to remain on-task, in the expectation that Adam can be more successful. However, this solution may be so similar to the previous coercive attempts that Adam could not tell the difference. Therefore, the teacher decides to be clear with Adam that he now realises two things: (1) that Adam is a capable lad (as evidenced by his assessment results) and (2) that Adam is in charge of his own behaviour. The teacher will tell Adam that from now on he will refuse to remind and coax him, since he is able to remember when he chooses to.

To add a practical challenge to the myth that Adam cannot control himself, the teacher may assign Kral's task (1988) which is aimed at adding some random starting and stopping to the behaviour pattern: Adam is to toss a coin each night at home, with heads signifying that tomorrow he will have a good day at school, and tails signifying a bad day. If he has a good day when the coin had turned up tails the night before, then he has overcome a negative injunction; if he complies with the coin's instruction then he is clearly in control and can do as directed. In this way, it becomes clear to Adam that his previously 'involuntary' behaviour is under his control. An additional element might be added, namely that the teacher is to guess which way up the coin landed the night before.

Step 9: Symptom prescription It has been understood that change is difficult, and Adam's behaviour works for him, at least partially. Therefore, he will not be obliged to change it. At the time of Adam's disruptions, the teacher will approach him quietly and reaffirm that Adam needs a way to cope with school pressures and since this is the only way he knows, he must use it. At the same time, however, his coping strategy stresses the other students, and so the teacher will invite Adam to withdraw from the room until he feels on top of the demands of his work. He can do whatever he likes in a nearby area, and come back when he feels he can cope again, at which time he will be welcomed. (Note that this may look like ABA's time-out procedure, but it is merely time away from stress and is not a punishment: if it conveys the flavour of a punishment, it will fail.)

Step 10: Evaluate If the new approach does not work, the teacher may generate a different reframe. The number of new solutions or reframes is limited only by the teacher or therapist's imagination (and time), and so in theory any number can be tried until one is successful.

Alternatively, the teacher may involve Adam's parents to give him advice about what they do at home that works. If in this conversation it turns out that the problems are experienced by both school and home, they may be solved jointly or the teacher may refer Adam and his parents to a family therapist.

DISCUSSION QUESTIONS

1. According to brief strategic therapists (the branch of systems theory covered in this chapter), how do behaviour difficulties develop into chronic problems?

2. What is the difference between a difficulty, a problem and a complaint?

3. What are the crucial approaches for conducting a systemic assessment and intervention—that is, what process variables are identified as important?

4. For what reasons is diagnosis and labelling avoided under systems theory?

5. What roles are typically held by those involved with a chronic behaviour problem?

6. What two purposes does assessment of participants' beliefs serve in making an assessment and choosing an intervention?

7. Think about a student's behaviour with which you have been involved. How could it be reframed? What difference would the new view of the problem make to the type of response it received?

8. Generate some completely different approaches to that behaviour problem, even if there is no rationale for using them. What effect would you anticipate from these new responses?

9. Think of an intervention approach suggested by another theory of your choice. What would be a systemic rationale for its use? How would the systemic rationale alter the effect of the intervention compared with the original theory?

10. In what ways does systems theory's approach to dealing with students differ from the other approaches examined in this text?
11. How would systems theory recommend you approach the student in the case study that you generated in chapter 2? What effect would its unique recommendations have on the individual student? On the whole class? On the teacher?

SUGGESTIONS FOR FURTHER READING

For a description of system theory and practice applied to student behaviour problems:

Amatea, E.S. 1989, *Brief strategic intervention for school behavior problems*, Jossey-Bass, San Francisco

Molnar, A. and Lindquist, B. 1989, *Changing problem behaviour in schools*, Jossey-Bass, San Francisco

For some case studies unrelated to school based problems but which give an introduction to the breadth of interventions used in systems theory:

Haley, J. 1973, *Uncommon therapy: the psychiatric techniques of Milton H. Erickson, M.D.*, W.W. Norton, New York

——1980, *Leaving home: the therapy of disturbed young people*, McGraw-Hill, New York

——1984, *Ordeal therapy*, Jossey-Bass, San Francisco

Lang, T. and Lang, M. 1986, *Corrupting the young (and other stories of a family therapist)*, Rene Gordon, Melbourne

9

CRITIQUE OF THE THEORIES

Obviously . . . we see theory as important and indeed necessary for
. . . practice . . . Yet—in either of two ways—theory can also lead to
difficulties and errors. First, theory may be over-elaborated or taken too
seriously—reified—until it hampers direct observation and simple interpretation of behavior . . . the other danger from theory arises when it
is inexplicit . . . we all have general ideas which form the context for,
and thus guide, our specific thinking and behavior. But these general
views may be implicit and taken for granted. Then they are more
influential, since they are less open to review, questioning, and possible
revision. (Fisch, Weakland & Segal, 1982, pp. 6–7)

KEY POINTS

- *The limit-setting and ABA theories are criticised for their authoritarian
  approach. This focus on training students to be compliant is said to
  conflict with the teacher's aim of educating students to make rational
  choices for themselves.*

- *Of the theories, ABA has the strongest body of research evidence about
  its effectiveness. On the other hand, it has many practical limitations
  for the classroom teacher.*

- *Cognitive-behaviourism aims to harness the benefits of ABA while
  avoiding its deficiencies by teaching students to manage their own
  learning and behaviour.*

- *Neo-Adlerian theory recommends democratic preventive practices,
  although its interventions are controlled by the teacher and are based
  on her subjective diagnosis of the student's goals for his behaviour.*

- *Humanism advances the benefits of democratic relationships in
  schools both for promoting students' emotional well-being and for
  preventing behaviour problems that arise when students' needs are*

not met. However, in so doing it lacks methods for repairing classroom order when students behave disruptively.

- *Control theory concurs with and enlarges on humanism's democratic preventive approaches, and adds long-term and immediate interventions to be used when a student behaves disruptively.*

- *Systems theory is applied only to chronic behaviour problems that have not responded to lesser interventions. It aims to facilitate new solutions to old problems. However, being a new way of thinking, its concepts can be difficult for the new practitioner to learn.*

INTRODUCTION

The first point of comparison between the seven theories introduced in this text is their philosophical assumptions, which are summarised in table 9.1. Next, this chapter will offer a critique of each theory with its strengths and weaknesses discussed from the standpoint of its opposing theories. Some of this information comes directly from the authors; other points are inferred from their writings.

LIMIT-SETTING APPROACHES

STRENGTHS

Practical recommendations

The skills focus of the limit-setting approaches equips teachers with practical skills for establishing order in a classroom (Charles, 1996).

Parent involvement

Many would applaud this approach's clear guidelines about involving parents when their son or daughter is disruptive in school. Glasser, however, advises teachers not to contact parents because he does not want parents to punish students for problems they are having at school. Teachers will need to make up their own minds about which advice is likeliest to produce positive outcomes.

Order

The limit-setting approaches will achieve order in a classroom, although too much control can limit learning (Doyle, 1986; McCaslin & Good, 1992).

CRITICISMS

Lack of research evidence

Despite the widespread popular support for assertive discipline, there is little research evidence supporting its effectiveness (Charles, 1996; Jones & Jones, 1995).

No educational philosophy or theory

The approach has no educational theory to guide a teacher's use of its practices (Jones & Jones, 1995), which can lead to inappropriate practice. It also leads to contradictions between the limit-setting and competing theories, with the latter presenting a clearer rationale for their methods. An example is Jones' recommendation (1987a) to penalise a whole class for individual noncompliance which is contrary to research findings on the benefits of collaborative learning.

Teaches obedience

Teaching obedience does not guarantee considerate behaviour or a safe society (Porter, 1996). It also increases children's vulnerability to abuse since they are taught to comply with all adult commands without judging their merits.

Skills are not comprehensive

Assertiveness is just one of three fundamental communication skills. The remaining skills of reflective listening and collaborative problem solving—which are included by the humanists—are ignored by Canter and Canter (1976, 1992).

Authoritarian stance

Many writers decry authoritarian approaches for being too harsh and militant, too overpowering for young children and demeaning to older students (Charles, 1992), although in his later edition, Charles (1996) reports Lee Canter's defence that this program is harsh only when it is implemented improperly. If this is so, then one might conclude that—at best—the program is open to misuse or—at worst—violates students' autonomy.

The essence of criticism of the authoritarian methods—which includes the limit-setting approaches—is that they are *ineffective* because they train obedience, without having any instructional components to pass control back to students. Teaching obedience 'dilutes and obstructs' the educational goals of teaching problem-solving skills and critical thinking (McCaslin & Good, 1992, p. 12). That is, neither behavioural nor educational goals are satisfied, with token rewards leading to token learning (Levine & Fasnacht, 1974, in Thompson & Rudolph, 1992) and students who lose

Table 9.1 Philosophical assumptions of theories of student behaviour management

Philosophical assumptions	Limit-setting approaches	Applied behaviour analysis	Cognitive-behaviourism
Nature of childhood	Children need clear limits	Children's behaviour follows the same laws as adults'	Children have the capacity for both good and bad
Conditions necessary for learning	Learning requires order	Learning is the acquisition of new behaviours	Children learn by experience
Purpose of discipline	Managerial (establish, maintain and repair order)	Managerial (repair order)	Managerial Educational (teach self-discipline)
Reasons for children's inappropriate behaviour	Lack of parental guidance; non-assertive teachers	Consequences that reinforce desirable behaviour and reduce inappropriate behaviour have not been enforced	Consequences plus the child's expectations, beliefs, skills and context all influence behaviour
Adult–child status	Authoritarian	Authoritarian	Teacher is controlling, although consults with the student
Role of the teacher	Establish order	Arrange conditions to alter the rate of behaviour	Encourage student self-responsibility

sight of intrinsic rewards and who work only if external rewards are available. In the words of McCaslin and Good (1992, p. 13): 'We cannot expect that students will profit from the incongruous messages we send when we manage for obedience and teach for exploration and risk taking'.

Gordon (1991) argues that external controls are ineffective, because they work only while the student is dependent on the teacher, but that by adolescence the teacher runs out of the power to coerce compliance. Gordon (1991, p. 94) states this argument: 'It's a paradox: Use power, lose influence'. At the same time that the student has no power and does no work to control his own behaviour, the teacher works increasingly hard to control him by coercion.

Punitive methods have two negative effects on students' self-esteem: they are likely to teach students that they are accepted only if they conform, and they rob children of control over themselves which is a key component of self-esteem.

Table 9.1 continued

Neo-Adlerian theory	Humanism	Control theory	Systems theory
Children actively assign meaning to their experiences	Children are rational and trustworthy	Children are capable of self-discipline	Children have restricted responsibilities
Children learn by overcoming feelings of inferiority	Children learn when curricula are relevant and teachers are personally involved	Children learn when curricula meet their emotional needs and teaching is of high quality	Learning requires discomfort, new ways to act, and good reasons to change
Managerial Educational (self-discipline and group cooperation)	Educational (self-discipline, group cooperation, democratic participation)	Managerial Educational (self-discipline, group cooperation, democratic participation)	Managerial (through reinstating a healthy hierarchy) Therapeutic
Low self-esteem Need to belong is not met at school Discouragement Faulty choices Family constellation	Schools provoke disruptive student behaviour by being emotionally cold and academically unstimulating	Low quality education Students' emotional needs are not met at school	Behaviour has been maintained by unwitting mishandling Behaviour stabilises the system
Democratic preventive methods; authoritarian interventions	Democratic/ authoritative	Democratic/ authoritative	Democratic/ authoritative
Promote student development and self-responsibility	Facilitate learning Relate warmly Nourish curiosity Promote self-actualisation	Promote student responsibility and personal growth through leadership	Change solutions to chronic problems

Authoritarian methods are likely to provoke *resistance, rebellion, retaliation, escape* or *submission* (Gordon, 1970, 1991). These are the very behaviours which teachers are trying to control and which they most dislike in students. They give rise to further punishment; escape and withdrawal lead to alienation from adults; while submission leads to problems with peers because other youngsters do not like compliant, dutiful children.

Power based approaches *destroy trust* between teacher and student and so the young person leaves the relationship (including leaving school) as soon as he can. Controlling methods also heighten rivalry and competitiveness within groups, as the children compete for adult approval and favours. The teacher's power is tenuous and is threatened if she is seen to change her mind about a ruling, to be flexible or open to

Table 9.2   Disadvantages of authoritarianism

Ineffectiveness
- Authoritarian methods teach obedience, in direct opposition to the educational purpose of teaching self-discipline.
- Authoritarian methods become ineffective as students get older.
- Teachers overwork; students can be irresponsible.
- Students may refuse to work unless rewarded.

Effects on the recipient's self-esteem
- Punitive methods teach the child that he is valued only if he conforms.
- He is not independent in controlling his own behaviour, which is a key source of self-esteem.

Effects on the recipient's emotional state
- Power based methods provoke resistance, rebellion, retaliation, escape and submission.
- These reactions are maladaptive and excite further punishment or rejection.

Social effects on the recipient
- Controlling methods teach children to distrust adults.
- The methods heighten rivalry and competitiveness within groups and families.

Effects on the administrator and society
- The coercive relationship is based on fear and will inevitably disintegrate.
- The teacher's power is constantly under threat. This means she cannot be flexible and so loses students' respect.
- Obedience is used to excuse antisocial behaviour.

negotiation. Yet at the same time, these management approaches engender respect.

Finally, Gordon (1991) asks whether societies actually want obedient youngsters, since more crimes against humanity have been committed in the name of obedience than in the name of rebellion. Furthermore, teaching obedience allows miscreants to escape responsibility for their actions by blaming someone else for their misdeeds.

Glasser (1992, p. 277) refutes advice that teachers should get tough with students because 'that's all they understand', saying that, 'If we continue to get tough with them, it is all they will ever understand'.

APPLIED BEHAVIOUR ANALYSIS (ABA)

STRENGTHS

Precision

Proponents of ABA argue that its methods and philosophy are clear and therefore can be applied readily by teachers and parents. Nevertheless, applying ABA techniques is more complex than it looks and their effective and ethical application takes considerable competence (Alberto & Troutman, 1995). The approach's clarity gives teachers confidence but it can also dictate their actions.

BEHAVIOURAL OBSERVATION

ABA has set the standard for rigorous observation of behaviours, avoiding diagnosis and interpretations—which can be biased—and instead requiring the observer to specify exactly what behaviour took place, under what conditions and to what effect. With the exception of neo-Adlerian theory, all theories of student behaviour uphold this standard of impartial observation of behaviour.

Effectiveness

Applied behaviour analysis began as an answer to psychoanalysis, with its lengthy investigations into the client's subconscious and past life events. The early behaviourists believed that clients presenting for help about their present life circumstances needed help *now*, not after years of therapy. Behaviourism, therefore, aims to give more effective help more efficiently, since this is more humane than leaving people to suffer during prolonged therapy.

This goal is vindicated by a considerable body of research that has demonstrated the effectiveness of the ABA approach (Alberto & Troutman, 1995; Kaplan & Drainville, 1991). However, most studies take place in rigorous conditions not normally replicable in the average classroom (Kaplan & Drainville, 1991), so ABA's effectiveness in classrooms is not firmly established.

Its very effectiveness raises objections from the humanists about manipulation of others, however. In answer to this criticism, Bailey (1991) says the trouble is not so much the practices of ABA, but the words used to describe them, such as *manipulating* variables, describing individuals as *subjects*, or employing *control* conditions. Research writings, Bailey says, fail to give a rationale for changing individuals' behaviour, namely, to give them the dignity of success, and to expand their options and personal freedom (Alberto & Troutman, 1995; Bailey, 1991). ABA also avoids other more intrusive interventions (such as drug or electro-convulsive therapies), meaning that the approach not only helps individuals achieve their goals, but also does so efficiently without unnecessary suffering. Therefore, by definition the approach must be humane, these writers contend.

CRITICISMS

Authoritarian stance

Humanists criticise ABA for being authoritarian, and for denying students freedom of choice. Kaplan and Drainville (1991) acknowledge this but state that if we do not restrict students' choice to fail, their options as adults will be restricted for them.

Prevention

Because of its precision, ABA is mainly used to treat rather than prevent difficult behaviour. While antecedents are considered, the observer takes into account only those events that immediately surround an undesirable behaviour, rather than viewing the behaviour in its broader social context.

Superficial change

Because ABA is directed at outer behaviours, some critics claim that the underlying problem is not really treated (Kaplan & Drainville, 1991).

Inefficient

The cognitivists criticise ABA for ignoring the student's thinking, and thus ignoring an ingredient that would be useful for solving his difficult behaviour and teaching him to be self-directed (Bandura, 1986). This makes ABA less efficient, and also means that the method of classroom management is at odds with the educational goal of teaching children to think for themselves.

Disregard of motivation for the behaviour

Most other theorists believe that motivating the student to find more suitable ways to meet his needs is more effective than manipulating the student externally to change his behaviour. It is also more ethical to take into account the valid emotional need that may underlie the person's behaviour.

Practical considerations: jargon

Having to teach parents and teachers a new set of jargon both uses up time that could be spent intervening with the behaviour, and lacks respect for their present skills. This can undermine their confidence or make them less open to suggestions for practice.

Feasibility for classrooms

Focusing as it does primarily on individually tailored interventions, ABA is impractical for teachers whose main focus is on managing groups (Doyle, 1986). ABA can only repair order, and then only by detailed and demanding interventions.

One factor making ABA less suitable for use in groups is the possible contagion effect. An ABA program may begin by targeting a single student or a priority behaviour but then spread to other behaviours of that student or to other students. Peers can think it unfair that the student with the poorest behaviour receives the most attention and reinforcement, and might copy the target child's behaviour and in turn require a behavioural program themselves.

Time demands

The observation and data gathering required for a behavioural program can be prohibitive for the teacher (Wolery et al., 1988). This argument is met, however, with the acknowledgment that handling disruptions ineffectively takes up a considerable amount of teacher time (perhaps as much as 50%, reports Jones (1987a)), so an ABA program may reduce demands rather than increase them (Kaplan & Drainville, 1991).

Trivial focus

Writing behavioural objectives also demands a great deal of time. These can be so precise that they may apply only to specific skills and not broader, more relevant, abilities such as creativity. These criticisms are partially addressed by ensuring the objectives are functional, realistic, beneficial to the student and not limited to factual knowledge only, and by incorporating the students' goals into the objectives (Wolery et al., 1988).

A wider criticism of triviality is that behaviourists focus on specific behaviours, rather than on patterns of behaviour over time (Thompson & Rudolph, 1992). This can reduce the focus to minor behavioural infractions, and can also swamp the teacher with detailed interventions for each and every behaviour.

Negative effect on learning

The controlling approach of ABA may reduce on-task behaviour (Doyle, 1986).

Maintenance of gains

ABA has been criticised for failing to maintain behavioural gains achieved during intervention, even when it specifically teaches generalisation by manipulating schedules of reinforcement, fading external reinforcers, and training the target behaviour in a range of settings and with a range of trainers (Kaplan & Drainville, 1991).

User unfriendliness

Bailey (1991) agrees with the criticism that technical reports of behavioural studies make their information inaccessible to teachers, especially compared with the polished workshop presentations that motivate and enthuse disciples of competing theories.

Teacher noncompliance

Teachers often refuse to enact behavioural interventions (Benes & Kramer, 1989) first, because they disagree with ABA's philosophy that all behaviour is determined by outside forces (Bailey, 1992; Miller, 1991; Wolery et al., 1988). Second, teachers are less likely to comply with behavioural recommendations when they have played no part in deciding how to intervene. Their exclusion can come about because ABA is so complex that interventions need to be designed by specialists (Kutsick, Gutkin & Witt, 1991).

Ethical objections

Many practitioners have ethical objections to ABA's philosophy and procedures. Aversive methods attract particular criticism, which focuses on two separate problems: the methods' openness to misuse (Wolery et al., 1988) and the ethical issues that arise even with their correct application (Alberto & Troutman, 1995). Behaviour analysts offer guidelines (see chapter 3) to address ethical dilemmas, about which Kaplan and Drainville (1991, p. 23) conclude: 'behaviour modification (ABA) is simply a tool; as such it has no morality. In the hands of moral people, it is moral, and when it is abused . . . it becomes immoral.'

COGNITIVE-BEHAVIOURISM

STRENGTHS

Increased motivation

When he is in control of the intervention, the student becomes more motivated to change his behaviour and more persistent at using skills that lead to school success (Fontana, 1985). He can also develop an internal locus of control, attributing his performance to his own efforts rather than to external forces. Both will improve the student's self-esteem.

Better educational and behavioural results

Cognitive strategies directly teach self-management skills, such as social problem solving, which students will need as adults. These skills are more relevant than many others that we teach students, and are more likely to generalise (Kaplan & Drainville, 1991). This means that private behaviour, occurring in the absence of a teacher, can still be controlled, since the controller is the student himself, not an adult (Grossman, 1995).

Benefits for teachers

Teachers do not have to solve all their students' problems or oversee their behaviour constantly, since it is assumed that students have skills

Figure 9.1   Inter-relatedness of achievement, behaviour and self-esteem

and can govern their own behaviour. Teachers have the freedom to vary in their expectations of students, since the students themselves provide their own consistency by controlling themselves. Finally, teachers benefit from the fact that cognitive methods may more closely align with their own belief systems, and they avoid some of the ethical problems inherent in authoritarian procedures (Grossman, 1995).

Efficiency

Students frequently present with a constellation of difficulties in three areas: school achievement, behaviour and self-esteem. The self-regulatory skills of self-monitoring, self-instruction and self-evaluation promote self-discipline and therefore a resolution of problems in all three areas at once. The link between the three areas is represented in figure 9.1.

Wide applicability

Self-management skills can be taught to students with a wide range of abilities and ages. Cognitive techniques are more suitable for older and more able students than behaviourism alone (Kaplan & Drainville, 1991). Nevertheless, they require some language and intellectual sophistication, which may preclude students with severe intellectual or language disabilities.

Ethics

Cognitive-behaviourist approaches overcome some of the ethical dilemmas of imposing controls externally.

CRITICISMS

Authoritarian stance

Humanists would be critical of the level of adult control that is still possible under cognitive–behavioural theory.

Imprecision

Many behaviourists find the strategies of cognitive-behaviourism vaguer than pure behaviourist approaches (e.g. Lee, 1993). They also criticise cognitive theory for having a less sound research basis (James, 1993; Lee, 1993) and less data on efficacy, especially with children (Hall & Hughes, 1989). The fact that cognitivism is not a unified theory, but a confused collection of approaches, means that application can be incoherent and ill-advised (Benson & Presbury, 1989). On the other hand, the complexity gives flexibility and gives rise to interventions that are designed for individuals (Dyck, 1993; Dobson & Pusch, 1993).

Remedial focus

There are few cognitive approaches for preventing behavioural problems, or for enhancing the problem-solving skills of non-disabled children (Meyers, Cohen & Schleser, 1989). However, some approaches have potential for preventing dysfunction, including: social skills training, suicide prevention, substance abuse prevention, protective behaviours and stress reduction for teachers (Conoley, 1989).

Continued reliance on behavioural methods

Cognitive treatments still have to be supplemented by behavioural interventions (James, 1993), with all the criticisms that these attract from humanists.

Self-esteem

Neo-Adlerians (e.g. Dinkmeyer & Dreikurs, 1963) contend that using praise and other rewards suggested by the cognitive-behaviourist approach, will not enhance self-esteem. The student must form his own evaluations of himself, and this is achieved by encouragement (internal judgment) not praise (an external evaluation).

Diagnosis

Cognitive methods rest on determining where the individual's problem-solving processes are going awry; systems theorists say that diagnosing an individual's deficiencies in this way ignores the environmental, developmental (Meyers et al., 1989) and social causes of the student's present level of functioning.

Practical disadvantages of cognitive strategies

A student may not wish to modify his behaviour and so it may be difficult to engage him in the process of self-management (Grossman, 1995). However, when the teacher models cognitive processes, teaches a high level of mastery of each skill before adding another component, gives the students experience of using cognitive strategies in a variety of settings, and explains the relevance of strategies, then the student's motivation to use cognitive approaches can be increased (Kaplan & Drainville, 1991).

The cognitive and linguistic demands of the cognitive methods may be too demanding for children (Hall & Hughes, 1989).

Ideas about the time it takes to teach students to manage their own behaviour are mixed: some authors say it requires less teacher time and improves generalisation of skills compared with ABA (Kaplan & Drainville, 1991), while others say it takes considerable teacher time to teach these skills and evidence of improved generalisation is promising but not conclusive (Grossman, 1995; Hall & Hughes, 1989), especially when treatment gains are to be generalised to the classroom (Meyers et al., 1989). The difference in opinion may reflect the target group: complex conduct difficulties such as aggression, social problems and depression are certainly time-consuming to treat. Perhaps also the time demands reflect the fact that learning self-management is a life-long process for all individuals.

NEO-ADLERIAN THEORY

STRENGTHS

Democratic preventive methods

Neo-Adlerian theory is the first we discussed which advocates democratic relationships between students and teachers, avoiding the disadvantages already listed that arise from authoritarian interactions. However, its interventive practices are not as democratic as its philosophy or the humanist practices.

Encouragement

Encouragement allows students to regulate their own actions and to maintain an intact self-esteem. The practice of encouragement is consistent with this theory's democratic stance, conveying respect and avoiding competition.

Clear prescriptions

Dreikurs and Cassel (1990) said that since there are only four goals of behaviour, it is very easy to diagnose and intervene with behaviour. Accordingly, the teacher is provided with very clear guidelines for action.

Parent training

Studies comparing behavioural with neo-Adlerian parent training courses, for instance, found that the neo-Adlerian model was more effective with both parents and children (Thompson & Rudolph, 1992).

CRITICISMS

Authoritarian interventions

Under humanism and control theory, the teacher and student collaborate to decide how to deal with inappropriate behaviour but, under neo-Adlerian theory, the teacher makes a judgment about the student's goals and is in charge of most of the decisions about intervention.

Unrealistic standards of behaviour

The neo-Adlerians require children not to respond to provocation, to return kindness for hurt and to ignore belittling remarks. If they cannot, then their behaviour is deemed to be antisocial and to have one of four negative goals. These expectations reflect middle class values, are unrealistic and are probably undesirable, since teachers do not want children to become passive victims of bullying or even incidental insults.

Narrow list of emotional needs

Glasser would criticise the neo-Adlerian view that all behaviour has one single motivation: to belong. He acknowledges this goal, but adds four others (including survival). He would argue his list is a more comprehensive description of human emotional needs (Glasser, 1986).

Reliance on diagnosis

Systems theorists (for instance, Fine & Holt, 1983) argue that categorising students into pigeonholes according to their assumed goals is not helpful for solving problematic behaviour; neither is there any evidence for these goals (Thompson & Rudolph, 1992).

Subjective diagnosis of goals

It is illogical (and a violation of cognitive theory) to assume that the student *makes* the teacher feel a certain way, and that this feeling is an accurate predictor of the child's intent. When one teacher finds the behaviour acceptable and another does not—or the same teacher feels differently about the behaviour on different occasions—has the student's goal changed? It is illogical for the goal to differ according to an observer's subjective assessment that the behaviour is inappropriate, especially when that observer may not have seen the sequence of events that gave rise to the behaviour. Systems theorists would argue that diagnosing children's goals is based on a confusion between the *intent* of the student's actions, and their *outcome*.

Disrespect for individuals' self-awareness

The teacher is charged with the skill of understanding the student's goals better than the child does himself. This involves one of Gordon's communication blockers—namely, mind-reading—which is likely to alienate the student, rather than give him insight into his own actions, and subsequently the motivation to change them. Glasser would seek to help the student become aware of his own goals and to decide *for himself* whether his behaviour is likely to satisfy those.

Negative characterisation of individuals

Unlike the democratic theories, neo-Adlerian theory uses negative and judgmental terms to describe the goals of children's behaviour (Thompson & Rudolph, 1992), despite Adler's contention that the child's behaviour arises from discouragement. The negative descriptions of children give rise to authoritarian interventions. Perhaps instead each goal could have been given a more positive connotation, for example:

1. Attention seeking could have been called a quest for *confirmation.*
2. Power seeking could be referred to as a need for *self-determination.*
3. The goal of revenge could instead be seen to reflect a belief that one is *unaccepted* and *unloved.*
4. Withdrawal could be framed as a feeling of *hopelessness.*

Blocking goals

Balson (1992, p. 27) asserts: 'As all human behaviour has a purpose, the key to understanding and modifying a child's behaviour is to identify the purpose and then act in such a way that the behaviour does not achieve its intended goal'. This signals teacher opposition to the student's goals, despite Adler himself, and also Dreikurs, contending that the individual's goals are a natural and valid response to his social interactions.

Inequity between adults and children

It is legitimate to ask that, if the goals apply to children's behaviour, and the theory is democratic, then why do the same goals not apply to adults?

Logical consequences

While natural consequences fit squarely within the democratic paradigm, logical consequences do not, says Gordon (1991). He argues that a natural consequence, which is an outcome arranged by nature (such as a student whose undone shoelaces cause him to trip over and hurt himself), does not harm the student–teacher relationship. On the other hand, logical consequences (that are arranged by the teacher) do harm that relationship. Gordon argues that a 'logical consequence' is a clear attempt to control the child punitively and is identical to punishment in the ABA sense.

Criticism of parents

Neo-Adlerian writers assert that much of children's difficulties are due to parental mishandling, as exemplified by Balson's statement that (1992, p. 44):

> Parents are the initial source of a child's discouragement. They refuse to accept children as they are . . . Tasks which are completed imperfectly are corrected by parents; offers of cooperation are declined; and children are denied an opportunity to discover their own strengths and abilities.

This blaming, and the belief that problems will be resolved if parents are offered the 'right' training, convey an undemocratic disrespect for the skills parents already possess and may undermine parents' confidence.

Lack of social focus

Neo-Adlerian theory is very individually focused and does not take the social context into account. Acknowledgment of birth order is one exception, but the assertion that birth order predestines one to certain behaviour does not suggest a solution to demanding behaviour since the family birth order cannot be changed. The concept may also come to excuse a student's actions (say, by blaming the 'middle child syndrome'). Balson (1992) addresses this in part by stating that the birth order may not in itself be significant, but that the adult's beliefs about it and consequent handling of children may cause the problems these writers associate with birth order.

HUMANISM

STRENGTHS

Preventive focus

The humanists believe it is more humane to prevent a problem from occurring than it is to deal with it once it has arisen. The central theme of their philosophy is *prevention*.

Self-responsibility

The student is enabled to act in ways that meet his needs, and is taught to consider the rights of others. He also moves from relying on the evaluation of others to forming his own self-judgments (Thompson & Rudolph, 1992).

Enhanced learning

Carl Rogers (1978, 1983) believes that democratic classrooms enhance students' learning and social and emotional development.

Addressing the real cause

Gordon (1974) argues that student apathy and anger are *symptoms* of undemocratic relationships with young people: they are not the *problem* itself. The problem, he says, is the way schools are organised. Humanism addresses this issue by considering the school's contribution to disruptive student behaviour.

Positive view of children

Unlike the other theories discussed previously, all the democratic perspectives attribute a positive motive to students' behaviour, even when that behaviour presents difficulties for others.

Living democracy

Student, teacher, and parent participation in the administration of the school promotes their equal involvement, which not only teaches about democracy but also lives it.

CRITICISMS

Unscientific theory and methods

Skinner (1989), the leading behaviour analyst during the latter half of this century, is cutting in his criticism of what he calls the antiscience stance of humanism. He contends that only information gained through scientific methods is valuable, and he rejects humanism for its lack of rigour and uselessness for understanding human behaviour.

Lack of efficacy data

Following from this criticism that humanism lacks scientific rigour is the accusation that it lacks efficacy data. However, McCaslin and Good (1992) argue that Baumrind's work differentiating authoritarian, authoritative and laissez-faire discipline styles does supply convincing data on the superiority of authoritative—that is, democratic—methods.

No recommendations for remedial teaching

The cognitivists might suggest that it is not necessary to focus on the student's feelings such as low self-esteem since these would improve if the student were simply more successful at schoolwork. They would criticise humanism for its lack of remedial approaches in addressing students' under-achievement.

Lack of interventions

Some theorists contend that, aside from contracts and collaborative problem solving, the humanists offer no direct interventions for disruptive behaviour. Neo-Adlerians would argue for the need for logical consequences, while Glasser adds a counselling approach and the ten-step program for responding immediately to disruptive behaviour.

Superficial focus on relationships

Systems theorists would argue that while the humanists have a social focus, they look only at the content of interactions, rather than at their meaning.

Impure democracy

Some accuse humanism of not being democratic, since decisions are not made by majority vote and teachers still have control (McCaslin & Good, 1992). However, while the humanists would agree that the teacher is authoritative (because of her expertise), she nevertheless has the same rights as students to get her needs met. The democratic label for the humanist, control and systems theories is not a statement about equal roles, but about equal rights.

Practical considerations: communication skills

Gordon's system of active listening, assertion and conflict resolution demands considerable interpersonal sophistication, especially on the part of the teacher. Gordon may also have given insufficient guidance on framing assertive messages, giving only the 'When you . . . I feel . . . because . . .' formula for assertive messages. This may be unduly limiting. Jakubowski and Lange (1978) list other forms, which are included in chapter 10.

Time demands

Humanist methods may also be time consuming. It is likely, however, that the teacher presently consumes much time in less effective methods of dealing with behavioural issues.

Students will not respond immediately

Duke and Meckel (1984) also note that students may 'test' the negotiation process, but Gordon says that students will come to accept the approach and believe in the teacher's integrity when she does not resort to coercion during this testing phase.

Verbal sophistication

Both students and teachers will require sophisticated verbal skills which may preclude students with intellectual or language disabilities from participation in negotiation processes.

CONTROL THEORY

STRENGTHS

Self-responsibility

Glasser has stated that because of its notion of self-responsibility, control theory offers hope for those whose background would otherwise condemn them to school failure and unfulfilling relationships. Its focus on their present decisions, with optimism that they can change these to meet their own needs (without violating the rights of others), and gentle but firm guidance for doing so, provides a democratic framework for change. This focus also ensures socialisation, since the student is required to act in ways that do not interfere with another person.

Takes context into account

Control theory takes into account more than just the psychology of the individual student. Instead, it asks educators to take into account the effect of the school system on students.

Living democracy

Control theory endorses the other humanist writers' contention that democracy must not be taught solely as a topic in politics, but must be lived within the classroom. Without this, says Glasser (1969), children learn about democracy, but also learn that it does not apply to them.

Removes heat from student–teacher conflicts

Glasser (1992) contends that many teachers respond to student disruptions with a righteous attitude that students shouldn't behave that way. Instead, Glasser regards students as rebelling against the system, not the teachers, and so teachers can remove some of the heat from their exchanges with the students by not taking their rebellion personally.

Positive view of individuals

Glasser's theory is less blaming of disruptive students (compared with neo-Adlerian theory, for instance) and so is more likely to engender improvement in their behaviour.

Effectiveness of whole-of-school approach

Thompson and Rudolph (1992) report that Glasser's method reduced the recidivism rate at one school from 90% to 20% in a short period of time. They argue that it is clear that control theory works well when the whole school and parent population is involved, endorsing the philosophy and providing practical support such as a time out room. An individual teacher can use Glasser's approach to problem-solving in isolation from the rest of her school (Charles, 1996), although it is likely to be less effective than when the entire approach is comprehensively applied.

Applicability to students with learning difficulties

Glasser (1986) contends that because control theory interventions are verbal, they cannot be used by students who cannot talk, and therefore will be inappropriate for students with severe or profound intellectual disabilities. He reports that his approach has been used for young students and people with moderate disabilities, however, with no major modifications.

Additional approaches

Control theory adds the counselling approach and ten-step discipline program to the interventions recommended by the humanists, providing a broader range of intervention options.

CRITICISMS

Role of the teacher

Whereas the cognitive restructuring approach gives teachers a framework for examining their own thinking and feelings about students and their behaviour, Glasser does not attend to this aspect of teachers' contribution to students' behaviour difficulties.

Openness to misuse

The humanists would offer a caution that Glasser's ten-step discipline program can be easily misused and transformed into a punishment. It has at times been adopted from steps 6 to 10 only, without the preceding steps (Lewis, 1991), which negates its democratic values base. Tauber (1990) suggests that the steps are like the ingredients in a recipe, that just as you cannot expect a cake to turn out well with some ingredients missing, so you cannot expect student behaviour to improve unless all the steps are followed.

The teacher needs to be a skilful communicator

A related issue is that it may be difficult for teachers to communicate with students about their inappropriate behaviour without resorting to controlling methods or imposing their own solutions. It is also difficult to avoid responding in a way that allows students to make excuses for their behaviour (Edwards, 1993).

Criticism of schools and teachers

Systems theorists might query Glasser's criticism of the school system since this may engender defensiveness in teachers, making them less willing to take up his ideas because blame and criticism tend to stifle action.

Practical issue: time demands

Glasser's approach (such as counselling and holding class meetings) is time consuming (Duke & Meckel, 1984; Edwards, 1993). However, if these measures prevent problems, then teaching time is not wasted later by having to intervene with difficult behaviour.

Verbal skills of students

As with the other theories that rely on verbal problem solving, students with language difficulties may not be able to participate fully in the counselling and goal setting methods.

SYSTEMS THEORY

STRENGTHS

Systems theory was specifically designed to be applied to chronic problems that were unresponsive to lesser methods. It achieves this through its breadth of view of the problem, its respect for participants by attributing responsibility to them for changes and through its hopeful orientation and use of humour and new solutions.

Breadth

A strength of systems theory is its breadth. If examining the interactions of the student and teacher does not lead to an improvement in the student's behaviour, then the teacher can look more and more widely, examining the student's interactions with peers or the school as a whole, and then looking at the family's relationship with the school and with other social agencies (Dowling, 1985). In so doing, it expands the options not only of the school personnel involved in finding a solution, but also of the student whose behaviour has been dysfunctional.

Respect for individuals

Like humanism, systems theory builds on individuals' strengths rather than diagnosing their deficiencies. This communicates respect for students, their parents and their teachers. It has the effect of normalising the stigmatised student by not blaming him but instead simply assuming that the complaint is a result of an unintentional mismatch between the problem and the attempts at its solution (Amatea, 1989).

Promoting the individual's motivation for change

The principle of neutrality is intended to ensure that the teacher does not negate the student's motivation for change.

Hopeful orientation

When students are behaving disruptively, staff lose confidence in themselves and appear to be at the mercy of students (Amatea, 1989). The staff's confidence is also undermined by diagnostic labels that define students as needing specialised expertise which staff believe they do not have (Dicocco et al., 1987). By avoiding labels, noticing individuals' strengths, cooperating with the perspective of all participants, and reinstating the teacher as leader in the group, systems principles offer hope and confidence that an improvement is possible.

Humour

Systems theory encourages creativity, light-heartedness and open-mindedness in the face of chronic problems (Molnar & Lindquist, 1989). This can make its approaches particularly attractive to children (Combrinck-Graham, 1991; Heins, 1988).

Facilitates new solutions

When a problem has become chronic, the participants become weary of their old solutions, although they cannot attempt new ones, since they believe strongly that their old solution is justified. Systems theory aims to motivate change by not displacing old ideas but simply by offering alternatives. This ensures participants do not feel criticised for their earlier attempts, and so increases their openness to new approaches.

Efficiency

Efficiency means being able to find a solution that frees both the student and school personnel to get on with the business of learning and teaching. Schools need speedy change when a student's behaviour is seriously disturbing; systems theory (especially brief strategic therapy) is tailored to work quickly (Dicocco et al., 1987). Systems theory promotes efficiency in many ways, say its proponents. First, success is promoted by the advice that only a small change is needed to effect a larger change that spreads through the system. Second, systems theory avoids the hopelessness that is engendered when home difficulties are thought to be the cause of school complaints. Changes at school are expected to spread to home, and thereby to remove some of the assumed cause of the school based problem.

Systems theory also achieves efficiency by not having to teach a new set of jargon to teachers or parents. Thus the theory can be used immediately by anyone willing to look at chronic problems in a new way. In accepting not only the language but also the beliefs of others, the worker is able to engage in a cooperative relationship with partici-pants, which is likely to lead to less resistance to suggested solutions and therefore to their greater efficiency (Murphy, 1992).

A fourth efficiency is the refusal to diagnose participants' deficiencies, and instead focus only on what is happening now and how those circumstances can be altered.

Fifth, it achieves efficiency by engaging children readily. Combrinck-Graham (1991) and Heins (1988) argue that many systemic techniques are active, imaginative, visual, fun and unpredictable, and so appeal to children. With their engagement comes a fund of information to which adults do not have access or which they may deny, and this information is useful in devising an intervention.

A final efficiency of systems theory is that techniques such as reframing and compression of time allow all the student's behaviours to be classified as belonging to a single pattern, and so to be dealt with by a single intervention.

Present focus

Focusing on the present is useful because school staff are looking for relief from present, not past, difficulties (Dicocco et al., 1987).

Social focus

Glasser would embrace systems theory's consideration of the student's social context, although he might argue that in refusing to diagnose causes, systems theory gives insufficient attention to the role of the school organisation and structure in provoking the disruptive behaviour of students.

Effectiveness of family therapy

Despite research difficulties, a growing body of studies has demonstrated some positive benefits of family therapy for a range of difficulties, including young people's behavioural difficulties (for instance, Seymour and Epston's (1989) study of family therapy for childhood stealing). Gains include cost savings (Thompson & Rudolph, 1992), improved marital satisfaction following resolution of children's behavioural difficulties

(Sayger, Horne & Glaser, 1993), and direct improvement in the presenting problem (Nicholson, 1989).

CRITICISMS

Individual interventions

The worker selects an individual intervention in each case (Dicocco et al., 1987). Interventions are not selected in a 'cookbook fashion' where a particular intervention is applied to a given type of problem (Murphy, 1992). While this makes the approach more powerful, it also makes family therapy a difficult theory to learn as it has few guidelines for specific practice. It also leaves room for harm to occur if assessment and planning are not carefully carried out with regard for the uniqueness of each individual's circumstances (Amatea, 1989).

Complexity

Some argue that systems concepts are difficult to grasp, and the way they are written about makes the theory especially inaccessible for the new practitioner. Furthermore, most school based systemic literature is written from the standpoint of a consultant to teachers. Teachers wishing to apply these ideas themselves must first translate the literature into their own circumstances, which can be difficult.

On the other hand, Amatea (1989) and Molnar and Lindquist (1989) contend that systems interventions do not require elaborate plans, and that they do not have to displace current practice. These writers conclude the ideas *are* accessible to teachers, and are able to be used by them without extensive training in the theory, while still retaining their own personal style.

Disregard for feelings

Critics say that by ignoring feelings and insight, systems theory lacks empathy for the clients (Amatea, 1989). Murphy (1992) addresses this criticism, first, by reporting that clients experience both humanist and systemic therapists as equally 'trustworthy and attractive'. Second, systems theory believes individuals feel emotions in response to their relationships and, when their relationships change, their feelings will too (Flaskas, 1989).

Also, many writers—for instance Kiser, Piercy and Lipchik (1993); Smith, Osman and Goding (1990)—observe that while the family therapy literature does not reflect a strong focus on feelings, clinical practice does. These writers point out three significant systemic practices that focus on feelings: cooperation, which is literally an emotional joining with the client and his frame of reference; using questions to probe feelings; and acknowledging feelings during goal setting and when checking progress.

Insincerity

Some writers have criticised systemic interventions for being insincere and covertly manipulative (Duncan, 1992; Murphy, 1992). Reframing is the frequent target of this criticism as some regard it as the deliberate distortion of information (Amatea, 1989). However, Molnar and Lindquist (1989) contend that there *are*, in fact, many different views of events, and the positive ones are just as likely to be correct as negative ones, and so there is nothing dishonest in selecting the most positive view on offer. Despite this justification, Molnar and Lindquist do caution the worker to use only those concepts with which she feels comfortable.

Potential for harm

In light of the potential for harm from therapeutic injunctions such as symptom prescription, many systemic writers—such as Amatea (1989) and Murphy (1992)—advise that a person using systemic interventions have access to ongoing supervision. Teachers may attend family therapy workshops or form a collegial group to provide support for their systemic work.

Lack of data on effectiveness

Much remains to be discovered about the effectiveness of brief strategic interventions with school related problems (Amatea, 1989). Evaluation of research studies into efficacy is made difficult by the wide range of definitions of family therapy, and how the research defines and then measures therapeutic effectiveness (Nicholson, 1989). Practitioners are also concerned about the intrusiveness of research on the family (Towns & Seymour, 1990). This gives rise to few studies, while many that are reported have methodological inadequacies and lack statistical rigour (Kirkby & Smyrnios, 1990; Smyrnios & Kirkby, 1989; Smyrnios, Kirkby & Smyrnios, 1988).

The school based practitioner needs to evaluate her interventions in a formal and systematic way, both to inform herself about what constitutes effective practice and to increase her own accountability to her employer and students.

CONCLUSION

The first part of this text has examined seven major theories about students' disruptive behaviour. Figure 9.2 shows the predominant focus of *intervention* expounded by each theory. The diagram illustrates that,

Figure 9.2   Primary focus of intervention for each theory of student behaviour management (Carey & Porter, personal communication, 1992)

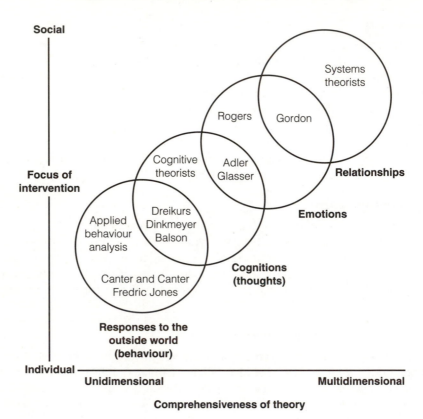

while a given theory may have many aspects, its priority for *intervention* is in the area indicated. This does not mean, however, that a theory ignores all other aspects of the student or his behaviour, but that additional aspects may be only a secondary focus. Those theories to the right, however, are more likely than those to the left to include more than a single dimension in their explanation of and intervention with student behaviour.

SUMMARY

The critique of each theory is summarised in table 9.3.

Table 9.3 Summary of strengths and weaknesses of each theory of student behaviour management

Theory	Strengths	Weaknesses
Limit-setting approaches	Practical recommendations Parent involvement Achieves order	Lack of efficacy data Not based on theory Contradicts other theories Teaches obedience Not comprehensive Authoritarian
Applied behaviour analysis	Precise methods Impartial behavioural observation Documented effectiveness	Authoritarian Lacks a preventive component Focus on superficial change Inefficient Disregard for students' motivation Uses complex jargon Less feasible for groups than individuals Time demands Trivial focus Negative effect on learning Maintenance of gains is doubtful User unfriendly Philosophical objections to determinism Ethical problems
Cognitive-behaviourism	Increased student motivation Improved educational and behavioural results Benefits for teachers Efficient Wide applicability Overcomes some ethical dilemmas of ABA	Has authoritarian undertones Vaguer than ABA Remedial, not preventive focus Continued reliance on behavioural methods Praise may not enhance self-esteem Diagnoses students' deficiencies Students may not be motivated to participate in self-management Requires advanced language skills Some interventions are long term
Neo-Adlerian theory	Democratic preventive methods Encouragement Clear prescriptions for action Parent training	Authoritarian interventive methods Unrealistic expectations of children Narrow list of emotional needs Reliance on diagnosis No evidence for behaviour goals Subjective diagnosis of goals Disrespect for students' self-knowledge Negative labelling of individuals Inequities between adults and children Use of logical consequences/punishments Criticism of parents Lack of social focus

Table 9.3 continued

Theory	Strengths	Weaknesses
Humanism	Preventive focus Promotes self-responsibility Enhanced learning Addresses real cause of student discontent Positive view of individuals Living democracy	Unscientific (Skinner, 1989) Lacks efficacy data No direct remedial teaching approaches Few immediate behavioural interventions Superficial focus on relationships Impure democracy Time demands Requires sophisticated communication skills on the part of the teacher Students may test the teacher's integrity Students need advanced verbal skills
Control theory	Self-responsibility Takes context into account Living democracy Removes heat from student–teacher conflicts Positive view of individuals Effective whole-of-school approach Wide applicability Adds direct interventions to the humanists approach	Teacher's thinking not examined Ten steps open to misuse as punishment Criticises schools and teachers Time demands Requires sophisticated communication skills on the part of the teacher Students need advanced verbal skills
Systems theory	Applied to chronic problems Breadth of focus Respect for individuals Promotes individuals' motivation for change Hopeful orientation Humour Facilitates new solutions Efficient Present focus Social focus Documented effectiveness	Individual interventions are difficult for a new practitioner to design Complex theory Disregard for feelings Open to insincerity Potential for harm Evaluation studies lack rigour

DISCUSSION QUESTIONS

Choose a theory that most interests you, or take each theory in turn, and address the following questions about it:

1. How well do the philosophical assumptions of the theory stand up to scrutiny from the standpoint of the other theories and from your own knowledge of child development?

2. To what extent is the theory's description of student behaviour comprehensive?
3. What does the theory offer for prevention of difficult behaviour?
4. To what extent are the recommended interventions comprehensive, valid, congruent with teaching goals, positive, ethical and 'user friendly'?
5. What strengths and weaknesses of the theory can you add to those presented in this chapter?
6. What blend of theories or approaches from other theories could you add for overcoming some of the shortcomings you have identified in the theory you have selected?
7. For instance, what would your blend of theories recommend for the case study of Adam, given in earlier chapters?
8. Do the combination of theories you have suggested share the same philosophical base?
9. Are the practical recommendations of the theories that form your blend compatible with each other?
10. In your opinion, is it possible to be eclectic about philosophy, theory or practice (see chapter 1)?

PART 2

PROACTIVE APPROACHES

10

CREATING A POSITIVE CLASSROOM CLIMATE

Children with positive self-concepts generally exhibit a number of positive characteristics: They enter new situations fearlessly, make friends easily, and experiment with new materials without hesitation. They trust their teacher even when the teacher is a stranger; cooperate and follow rules, and largely control their own behaviour: They are creative, imaginative, and free-thinking; talk freely and share experiences eagerly; and are independent and need minimal direction. Most important of all, they are happy. (Adler, Rosenfeld & Towne, 1992, p. 43)

KEY POINTS

- *The climate in the classroom is reflected in students' feelings about themselves, each other, the teacher, and the subject matter (Kindsvatter, Wilen & Ishler, 1992), in their engagement and achievement, and in the prevalence of behavioural difficulties.*

- *A warm climate is achieved when students can meet their needs most of the time.*

- *Physical needs in school are met by safeguarding students' physical safety, ensuring their physical comfort, and providing sufficient activity to balance inactive sessions.*

- *The need for a healthy self-esteem is met by teaching students to have realistic self-concepts, ensuring their standards for themselves are achievable, and accepting students. At the same time, the teacher himself needs to demonstrate a healthy self-esteem.*

- *Students' relationship needs are promoted when the classroom climate is warm and accepting, when relationships between the students and teacher are democratic, and when students feel that they belong in the classroom. The teacher can promote belonging by establishing a positive group purpose through cooperative learning teams and peer tutoring programs.*

- *Student autonomy is fostered when the teacher allows students to work independently of him, when expectations are clear and reasonable, when students are given genuine choices, and when the teacher demonstrates how to exercise self-control.*

- *Self-actualisation is promoted when individuals are permitted to be creative and are not required to conform to arbitrary expectations.*

- *Fun is needed to motivate learning and to balance the stressors which students face.*

INTRODUCTION

The term *climate* refers to the learning atmosphere and to the students' feelings about themselves, each other, the teacher, and the subject matter (Kindsvatter et al., 1992). Bill Rogers (1990) states that a positive classroom tone reflects the way the teacher organises the class to maximise students' self-esteem and learning. Jones and Jones (1995) agree, and conclude from a large body of research evidence that students behave more appropriately and learn more effectively when their basic needs are met in the classroom. These writers go further to say that, if schools can satisfy these needs, then a less than optimal home back-ground or cultural disadvantage can be offset. As an example, they report that Mortimore and Sammons' (1987) study (in Jones & Jones, 1995) found that school had six times more effect on reading progress than did the students' background. This offers a positive perspective on student behaviour, because rather than the teacher being at the mercy of students or their home background, he is instead acknowledged as a significant influence on students' academic and social learning. The teacher is particularly influential when he becomes a significant part of the students' lives and so can become a powerful role model.

HIERARCHY OF PERSONAL NEEDS

Human needs were first categorised in a hierarchy by Maslow (1968, in Jones & Jones, 1995), with earlier needs requiring satisfaction before later ones become a priority for the individual. These needs (adapted from Maslow's hierarchy) include: physical needs, self-esteem, relationship needs, and the needs for autonomy, self-actualisation and fun.

ASSESSING STUDENTS' NEEDS

The teacher can identify the unsatisfied needs of his students by consulting a list of needs such as the one given in this chapter, and making an educated guess about which need is likely to be unfulfilled. Or he could ask students what they need to enable them to learn; he could use systematic observation of how students behave in a range of situations (Jones & Jones, 1995); or administer questionnaires such as the Individualised Classroom Environment Questionnaire (see Burden & Fraser, 1993).

As well as responding to identified unmet needs, the teacher can prevent problems by structuring the classroom so that most students get most of their needs satisfied most of the time.

PHYSICAL NEEDS

Basic physical needs include the requirements for food, drink, rest and protection. This category also includes the needs for physical safety; activity (Lipsitz, 1984, in Jones & Jones, 1995); adequate lighting; limited background noise; safe touch; space to move; a visually attractive, comfortable, and warm environment; easy pace; and time to relax and reflect. Not only does the classroom environment come under consideration, but also the school's eating and play areas need attention. These need to offer respite so that students can equip themselves for the next learning session; if they do not, then the students' ability to learn will be reduced.

Teachers will need to note how much activity the school day offers students and supply enough activity for them to be able to operate quietly when necessary. Physical activity offers many benefits: it can give students confidence in their ability to control their bodies, exercises both the body and the brain (enhancing academic success), teaches children that they can meet physical challenges, and offers an outlet for stress, as long as it does not become another avenue for serious competition.

To promote student safety, teachers need to be present to supervise students at all times so that they are not at physical risk from injury or abuse (including bullying). Teachers will also need to be familiar with the signs of child abuse that may be occurring outside school, since they are legally obliged to report any suspicions to the local child welfare agency.

SELF-ESTEEM NEEDS

Erikson (1963) and Lipsitz (1984) (both in Jones & Jones, 1995) believe that children (especially in the primary school years) need to see themselves as competent, and to have this competence expanded and

Figure 10.1   Diagram of low self-esteem

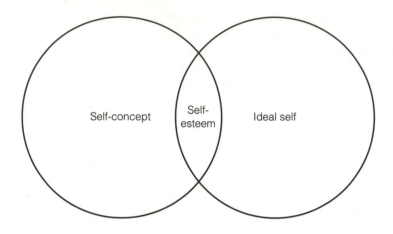

verified by other people who are important to them. In this way, self-esteem is learnt from other people's reactions. With this information, a child forms a picture of the type of person she is, and also creates a set of beliefs about how she 'should' be. She then judges how much she measures up to this ideal. Thus, MacMullin (personal communication) has described self-esteem as having three parts:

1. The self-concept: this is a set of beliefs we have about ourselves. It contains descriptions of our personal characteristics such as physique, clothing, health, possessions, relationships, abilities and talents at sport and academic pursuits, temperament, religious ideas, and ability to manage our lives.
2. The ideal self: this is a set of beliefs about what characteristics would be ideal.
3. Our self-esteem: this is how much we value ourselves. Our evaluation reflects the extent to which how we want to be matches up to how we are (as we see it).

A person with low self-esteem believes she has few of the characteristics she thinks are ideal (see figure 10.1).

A person with healthy self-esteem has a high degree of overlap between how she wants to be and how she thinks she is (see figure 10.2). (The two sets of beliefs will never overlap entirely, of course, otherwise the individual would have no ambitions or goals for which to strive.)

All three components can be addressed when aiming to improve students' self-esteem.

Figure 10.2   Diagram of high self-esteem

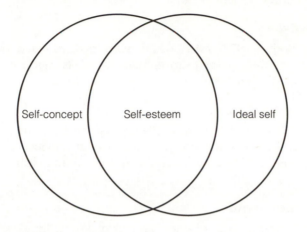

EXPANDED SELF-CONCEPT

One of the teacher's main functions is to arrange his teaching so that the maximum number of students are able to experience *genuine* success (Charles, 1996). Some methods of achieving this include: using clear goals which the students understand and feel confident about achieving; using a curriculum that progresses, so that new skills are built on skills they have already mastered; giving students feedback about their progress; using instructional materials to excite their interest; and developing group cohesion so that success is achieved within the group rather than within a competitive structure.

Acknowledge success

It is important to be honest with students and to allow them to recognise accurately when they are successful and when they are not (Charles, 1996). Jones and Jones (1995) report that teacher feedback is often too vague and does not specify success or failure accurately, and that instead teachers need to give verbal and written feedback that specifies exactly what the student has achieved. To promote a healthy self-concept, encouragement may be more suitable than praise, for the reasons put forward by the neo-Adlerians (see chapter 5).

Facilitate self-acknowledgment

Students can expand their self-concept by noticing their own successes through activities such as making lists of their skills and updating these lists regularly. They can also be guided in writing a personal record of their improvements in class, and in how to report their success to parents (Charles, 1996). Murals, class diaries, newsletters that document class progress, notes home to parents, and public performances can also give students acknowledgment of their successes.

Specific activities

Borba and Borba (1978, 1982) detail many activities that teachers can incorporate into their program to enhance students' sense of themselves and their special qualities.

Encourage risk taking

McGrath and Francey (1991) recommend that teachers allow students to take risks, set their own goals, organise their own activities, and negotiate learning contracts. Creativity is essential for positive learning (Knight, 1991).

Make activities useful

Students will cherish achievements that produce something useful (Knight, 1991).

Attribution training

Students need to be taught to attribute their success to their own effort, rather than to uncontrollable factors such as inability or luck. See chapter 4 for a fuller discussion of attribution training.

REALISTIC IDEALS

A description of how we 'should' be provides us with an internal comparison with how we believe we are.

Guide realistic standard setting

Teachers may expect too much of their students; some students may expect too much of themselves. To overcome this, teachers can guide students to have realistic ideals for themselves by helping them to evaluate whether their skills are appropriate for their age, rather than when compared to others.

Positive teacher expectations

On the other hand, students will perform down to low expectations, so teachers must communicate their faith in every student's ability to be successful and their expectation that all students will achieve high standards of work (Jones & Jones, 1995; Kindsvatter et al., 1992; Rogers, 1990).

Allow mistakes

Students need to know that no one has to get things right every time and that not all mistakes have to be corrected. Balson (1992) notes that most adults instruct children by focusing on their mistakes, in the erroneous belief that this will help them to learn. Instead, it discourages effort and contributes to continued failure by focusing on children's deficiencies and not noticing their strengths. Mistakes indicate a lack of skill, and skill is acquired only through practice, but discouraged children refuse to practise and so do not learn. Therefore, teachers could teach and live by the motto: 'Strive for excellence, not perfection'.

When the mistake is a behavioural one, it is important for the teacher to separate his judgment about what the student has done from his valuation of the student as a person. It is important that errors do not define the student's self-worth (Cangelosi, 1993).

ENHANCED SELF-ESTEEM

The teacher's main role in promoting a student's self-esteem is to enhance her *learning*, so she has some areas of competence to value in herself. The teacher can help a student make a plan for learning things that she nominates she would like to achieve (rather than the things she feels obliged to learn).

Allow students to share their feelings

McGrath and Francey (1991) observe that some students develop negative views of themselves because they believe that what they feel is wrong. When a teacher accepts a student's feelings and experiences, he communicates that feelings do not have to be judged by a standard. Also, discussing them with others may reveal that the child is not alone.

Respect and acceptance

A second central way to enhance students' self-esteem is by the respect a teacher conveys in the way he communicates with his students. This feeds students' self-esteem and fulfils their relationship needs. Steve Biddulph (1994) draws attention to how put-downs from adults become like seeds in a child's mind, teaching her how to think about herself and her capacities. This implies that teachers need to avoid using insults, sarcasm or emotional blackmail when talking with students. Bill Rogers (1990) qualifies the notion of respect by asserting that communicating respect does not mean teachers have to like every student or even to pretend they like them all, but that they behave in a professional manner with all students regardless of their personal feelings.

ACCEPT YOURSELF: TEACHER SELF-ESTEEM

Democracy is a two-way process. While accepting the rights of others, the teacher also needs to uphold his own rights. This has two effects: first, it signals to students that the teacher values everyone in the class, including himself and, second, it shows young people, through modelling, how to accept themselves.

Maples (1984) and the cognitivists attest to the importance of a teacher's healthy self-esteem in equipping him to cope with the challenges of a classroom. They suggest that a teacher who doubts his ability to respond appropriately to student behaviour may become defensive. This in turn will exacerbate management problems.

RELATIONSHIP NEEDS

The most basic relationship need is *emotional safety and protection*, both from peers and teachers while at school, and also on the way there and back. While the teacher can enhance the child's safety in the adult–child relationship by offering positive, supporting statements, Slee and Rigby (1994) observe that a school must also address how safe students feel among their peers by adopting a policy and practices that address school bullying (see chapter 12).

It is also important to give students work which they feel able to master, and to ensure they contribute to how that work will be assessed so that they can feel emotionally safe about the demands placed on them (Jones & Jones, 1995). A classroom that employs individual competition is likely to feel unsafe for many of its students.

Second in this category is a need for *personal involvement and trust* (Coopersmith, 1967; Lipsitz, 1984, in Jones & Jones, 1990). This includes the need for positive social interaction with peers and adults.

A third relationship need is love or *acceptance from others* and a feeling of *belonging*. Children of all ages are vulnerable to group rejection, while students with special needs or who are members of a minority group may be particularly at risk of feeling they do not belong in the mainstream classroom. Both peer and teacher messages about this are crucial.

Young people also need *flexibility in relationships* with adults, in line with their developing skills. Grossman (1995) contrasts flexibility with inconsistency, and concludes that the teacher needs to adapt to circumstances (be flexible) but he should not lower his standards just to avoid conflict.

WARM CLASSROOM CLIMATE

To create a positive tone in the classroom, teachers need to give students personal attention, they must be courteous and convey a positive attitude about all students and their abilities, they must be able to compliment them genuinely, be friendly, provide opportunities for personal discussions, and be willing to help students (Charles, 1996; Jones & Jones, 1995). On the other hand, while teachers must be friendly, they must also acknowledge that they are not their students' friends. It is important for students to see that their teachers have roles and lives that are different and separate from them and that the students themselves are aiming to achieve as adults (Jones & Jones, 1995; Tauber, 1990). Therefore, teachers should engage in appropriate, professional relationships with students whereby teachers share their reactions to school activities but limit sharing their feelings about their personal lives.

DEMOCRATIC STUDENT–TEACHER RELATIONSHIPS

The teacher has authority because of his expertise as a teacher (Gordon, 1991). His expertise gives him executive control of the classroom, and so he is a manager with a status equal to that of his students but with a different role. He can respond to students as a 'real' person rather than act out a role. These aspects comprise Carl Rogers' *facilitator* of student's learning (1983) and are the embodiment of democracy.

COMMUNICATION SKILLS

Chapter 6 detailed the communication skills of listening, assertiveness and collaborative problem solving, so these will not be repeated here. However, it is worth reminding ourselves that the decision about which set of skills to use depends on who is being inconvenienced by the behaviour—that is, whose rights are being violated. It will therefore be useful to consider teachers' and students' rights in the classroom. Rights are an expression of what we value and an expectation of how things ought to be (Rogers, 1989). They are not automatic but are granted, and they also carry a corresponding responsibility. These are summarised in table 10.1 (Knight, 1991; Lovegrove, Lewis & Burman, 1989; Rogers, 1989, 1990).

Bill Rogers (1990) believes that any rules that uphold rights for students, teachers or parents are 'fair'. Teachers therefore are justified in upholding these rights and responsibilities through assertive (but not hostile) messages.

Gordon (1974) gave 'I' messages as a formula for assertive messages, but this format may not be sufficient for all occasions. A range of assertive messages may be needed in addition to the 'When you . . . I feel . . . because . . .' formula. Jakubowski and Lange (1978) offer the alternatives of: 'I want' statements, mixed feeling statements, empathic assertion, and confrontive assertion.

Table 10.1   Rights and responsibilities of students, teachers and parents

Students' rights

To have physical and emotional safety
   and protection
To have access to materials and resources
To learn and to understand how school
   learning will help them live in the world
   now and as adults
To competent teaching that imparts vital
   knowledge
To receive teacher assistance
To enjoy learning, gaining pleasure,
   interest and confidence from learning
To feel important as people, who have the
   right to be individual and to express
   opinions
To be treated with dignity
To receive fair treatment
Protection from the abuses of authority
To participate in the schooling process
To specialist services as required
To privacy and confidentiality
To be free from unnecessary restrictions

Students' responsibilities

To care for themselves and others
To share equipment
To care for equipment and use it safely
Not demand teacher attention excessively
To be cooperative
To be considerate
To speak out
To listen and not obstruct the opinion of
   others
Not to dominate individuals or the group
Not to put other students down
To be accountable for one's actions

Teachers' rights

To defend optimal learning environments
   for all students
To be treated with courtesy
To expect students to cooperate with
   reasonable requests that will enhance
   their growth and respect teacher needs
To respond to disruptive behaviour
To express an opinion and be heard
To feel secure in the classroom, both
   emotionally and physically
To achieve job satisfaction
To support from school administration
To support from colleagues
To inservice training
To have access to consultants
To contribute to school policy

Teachers' responsibilities

To be competent
To provide an environment that is friendly,
   encouraging, supportive and positive
To assist students who need help
To model courteous behaviour
To have reasonable expectations of
   students, in line with the task demands
   and students' developmental levels
To protect students from harm, from
   themselves, other students and school
   personnel
To listen to students and colleagues
To be fair
To take responsibility for their own
   feelings, not blaming students for them
To provide forums for student participation
   in decision making
To take responsibility for their own actions
   that may detract from job satisfaction
   (e.g. stress management)
To support colleagues
To consult with colleagues and reach
   agreement
To make an effort to be involved

Parents' rights

To participate in their children's education
   through:

Parents' responsibilities

To ask for information when needed
To make the time to be involved

Table 10.1 continued

• information on school processes and curricula	To be open and willing to listen
• participation in decision making	To be willing to find workable solutions
• receiving and offering information about their children's learning and behaviour	
To expect consistent approaches by teachers	
To expect non-discriminatory practises	

'I want' statements

Stating one's wishes can often be misinterpreted as a demand, so the teacher can qualify his statement by asking if the other person is able to grant his request, by stating how strongly he feels it, or by limiting it in some way—for instance: 'I would like some quiet for a little while. Once you're ready, get started on your work alone but do interrupt me if you need help'.

Mixed feeling statements

With this assertion method, the teacher names more than one feeling and explains the origins of each. For example: 'I appreciate that you were working quietly for a while. It helped me to hear your individual reading. I'm disappointed now, though, that you're getting noisier because I still would like some quiet so that I can concentrate'.

Empathic assertion

This assertive message conveys understanding of the other person, while expressing the teacher's own needs. For example: 'I know that you're excited about the holidays and it's hard to work when they're so close. But we still have work to finish and I need you to settle yourselves down so that it can be done'.

Confrontive assertion

This is useful when the other person's behaviour violates an agreement about what she would do. The message has three parts:

1. a non-judgmental description of what was agreed to
2. a description of what the other person did
3. an expression of the teacher's wishes.

For example: 'We agreed that you could stay back to practise for the concert but that you'd clean up the hall afterwards. I see that you've left lots of gear out. I would like you to think about our agreement and decide if it still suits you'.

BELONGING

When students feel they belong in the class and are valued members of the school, their engagement and effort and subsequent success improves (Goodenow, 1993). Belonging refers to the extent to which students feel personally accepted, respected, included and supported by others (Goodenow, 1993).

Although personality factors play a part in a student's sense of school membership, situational factors influence this feeling greatly. Goodenow (1993) suggests that teachers administer a questionnaire such as the Psychological Sense of School Membership (PSSM) Scale to detect students who feel disengaged from school, with measures to increase their sense of belonging then directed at both the individual and organisational levels.

POSITIVE GROUP PURPOSE

When individual success is highlighted and rewarded, and failure disparaged by the teacher and the group, many children give up. Even the abler students may disrupt group processes by their arrogance. In contrast, establishing a cohesive group has been shown to have many advantages. Hill and Hill (1990) note that a sense of cohesiveness in the classroom motivates students so that they are willing to work within a structured collaborative setting. Cohesiveness requires that students feel they can trust other class members with their ideas and feelings, and that they accept others and are empathic.

Some key ways for developing a positive group purpose are through democratic class meetings (see chapter 7) and cooperative learning groups. Other strategies include holding open discussions about the barriers to inclusiveness, engaging the class in activities in which everyone participates (such as writing a class newsletter or staging a school play), and engaging in activities that encourage trust, including playing cooperative games (Hill & Hill, 1990; Orlick, 1982).

COOPERATIVE LEARNING

Many authors (such as Glasser, 1986; Johnson & Johnson, 1991; Johnson, Johnson & Holubec, 1990a) have observed that our schooling system has focused almost exclusively on the influence teachers have on students, and has neglected the positive and powerful influences peers have on each other's learning and socialisation. Cooperative learning aims to harness the many benefits that accrue when students work interdependently towards a shared goal. The purpose is for students to maximise their own and each other's learning since each member can achieve if, and only if, all other group members are successful and participate fully.

This is contrasted with competitive activity, in which the student's achievement is at the expense of others, and with independent tasks, in which the individual's achievement is independent of others (Hill & Reed, 1989; Johnson & Johnson, 1991; Johnson et al., 1990a).

Requirements for cooperative learning

Cooperation is not the same as having students sit or work together and neither does it necessarily imply harmony or compliance, but it may involve intellectual challenge. Cooperative groups will not just happen but will take practice on the part of teacher and students (Johnson & Johnson, 1991; Putnam, 1993), so teachers will need to know how to structure cooperative work.

Structuring cooperation in preschools

In preschool, the teacher can structure the environment and provide games that foster cooperation (Bay-Hinitz, Peterson & Quilitch, 1994; Hill & Reed, 1989; Orlick, 1982; Porter, 1996; Sapon-Shevin, 1995; Swetnam, Peterson & Clark, 1983). At the same time, the teacher will avoid competitive games since these increase aggressive behaviours and reduce cooperation (Bay-Hinitz et al., 1994).

Cooperative games

Competitive games are games where there are winners and losers, where the individual aims to win and to see her opponent fail. They may involve taunting or teasing (such as 'King of the castle'), grabbing or snatching at scarce toys (as in musical chairs), monopolising or excluding other children (for instance, the piggy in the middle game), or games involving physical force (such as tag ball) (Orlick, 1982; Sapon-Shevin, 1986). In contrast, cooperative games aim to involve otherwise isolated children and to foster sharing, turn-taking and touching other children gently. An example is the frozen bean bag game that requires children to move around with a small bean bag on their heads, freezing when it falls off and remaining still until another child helps by replacing the bean bag on their heads (Sapon-Shevin, 1986).

Cooperative games require coordinated effort by all members for them all to achieve success. They expand the pool of each child's potential friends and provide a non-threatening context for modelling and rehearsing social skills. They have been found to increase subsequent cooperative behaviour and decrease aggressiveness (Bay-Hinitz, et al., 1994). However, Sapon-Shevin (1986) observes that simply playing cooperative games will not ensure that the students generalise their skills to other activities, and so the teacher will need to supplement games with instruction that helps the students understand the process of interacting cooperatively.

Structuring cooperation in primary and secondary schools

The teacher structures cooperative learning by:

- providing clear objectives for the lesson
- making decisions, such as about group size and membership
- structuring the task so that cooperation is essential for success
- planning for group interdependence
- teaching basic concepts of cooperative learning
- monitoring group functioning
- evaluating both individual and group outcomes.

The teacher acts as technical expert, manages the classroom, and consults about group processes (Johnson & Johnson, 1986, 1991; Johnson et al., 1990a).

Objectives

Both an academic objective and the collaborative skills that will be emphasised in the lesson are specified at its outset.

Decisions

Group size

The teacher will decide on the size of the group, which usually ranges from two to six members. It is crucial that the group be small enough to foster interaction and for students to get to know each other socially. Small group size also enables feedback about each member's performance, and is useful when students are new to cooperative learning, when time is short, or when materials are scarce (Johnson & Johnson, 1986, 1991).

Group membership

Random assignment to groups is often effective in achieving heterogeneous group composition, which is thought to be optimal for cooperation. However, the teacher will still need to monitor group functioning to ensure that low-status students become fully included in their group (Johnson & Johnson, 1986, 1991).

Duration of group composition

Each student should work with every other one. Mostly, groups will change at the end of each unit of work to avoid rivalry building up between groups.

Room arrangement

Circles enable the best interaction and sharing of resources. The teacher will need to ensure he has easy access to every group, however.

Task structure

Students will need to share a sense of group purpose and cohesion. This is built up by structuring the task so that the group's purpose cannot be achieved without coordinated effort from all members. Tasks requiring creative thinking and problem solving are especially suited to cooperative work (Johnson & Johnson, 1991).

Group interdependence

Each group member's work must be indispensable to achieving the final outcome, and each person's contribution must be valued as unique, because of her personal resources or assigned role (Johnson et al., 1990a). This is termed *positive interdependence* (Johnson et al., 1990a). Many writers (Johnson & Johnson, 1991; Johnson et al., 1990a; Putnam, 1993) offer suggestions for promoting group interdependence: *goal* interdependence can involve students selecting one aspect of the topic for each member to study, and then combining all aspects to arrive at a complete product; *task* interdependence can be encouraged by division of labour; *resource* interdependence can be fostered by requiring group members to share resources; *role* interdependence can be fostered by assigning each member a complementary role which is essential for the group to function effectively (these roles may be the summariser, checker, accuracy coach, elaboration seeker, researcher, recorder, encourager or observer (Johnson et al., 1990a)); and *reward* interdependence is achieved by evaluating the group as a whole, rather than assessing individual achievement only.

Cooperative interpersonal skills

When first undertaking cooperative learning, teachers will need to teach social skills directly, beginning with enabling students to get to know each other. Students will need specific communication skills for the four tasks of: forming the team, working together, problem solving as a group, and managing differences (Hill & Hill, 1990). Teaching these and other social skills is the topic of chapter 12.

Individual accountability

The next step is to plan for individual accountability to the whole group for its achievements. To ensure that all students are contributing equally, the teacher needs:

- a way to assess both individual and group efforts
- to give feedback to groups and individuals
- to help groups avoid redundant effort by members
- to put in place methods to ensure that each member is responsible for the final product.

The teacher can ensure individual accountability by assessing individuals as well as the group, by choosing a group member at random and asking her to report on the material worked on together, by having each member sign the final document the group produces, or by having students fill out a self-evaluation questionnaire (Johnson & Johnson, 1991; Johnson et al., 1990a; Putnam, 1993). The group may produce a single product which each member signs to verify that: (a) she agrees with it and (b) she can explain how the answers were arrived at.

Evaluation

Evaluation needs to be criterion referenced, with the teacher explaining evaluation criteria at the outset (Johnson & Johnson, 1991). Both the teacher and the students themselves need ways to evaluate how their group is functioning and how successfully it is meeting its goals. Individual and group cooperative effort and academic performance can be assessed, with bonus points given to the group whose individual members all achieve satisfactorily on the academic and collaborative aspects of the task. Intergroup rivalry can be minimised by awarding all students bonus points (or other reward) if they all reach the criterion.

Advantages of cooperative learning

Johnson et al. (1990a) argue that the job market (and global conditions) require people to use their skills in interaction—not in competition—with others, and to do so without an authority figure standing over them. Therefore, schools need to teach not just the skill itself, but the use of that skill in cooperative relationships with others. Johnson et al. (1990a, p. 5) observe that, 'Cooperative learning should be used when we want students to learn more, like school better, like each other better, like themselves better, and learn more effective social skills'. These and other authors (such as Cole & Chan, 1990; Hill & Hill, 1990; Hill & Reed, 1989) elaborate on these advantages of cooperation.

Enhanced learning

Students taught in a cooperative framework achieve more highly than those in competitive or individual structures. Group exchange of ideas deepens understanding and contributes to the development of students' thinking and problem-solving skills.

Improved attitude to school

Students feel more positively about learning and about each other. They develop positive expectations about working with others.

More enjoyment and acceptance of each other

Because a basic human emotional need is to belong, learning

collaboratively with others is enjoyable, and offers challenges and rewards that working alone cannot. Cooperation promotes inclusion of others, and fosters care and respect for them. This is of particular benefit to children with disabilities who are included in regular classrooms.

Higher self-esteem

Compared with competition, cooperation provides healthier processes for obtaining feedback about oneself. Cooperative methods allow both high and low achievers to receive some acknowledgment of their efforts, and work tasks can be tailored to individual strengths so that each member comes to see herself as successful.

Improved interpersonal skills

Group learning allows children to practise constantly their group membership and leadership skills which help them now and as adults.

Prevention of later problems

Cooperation improves student sharing, strengthens peer relationships, decreases the need for teacher attention and reduces aggressiveness (Bay-Hinitz et al., 1994) which prevents later problems with student aggression.

Disadvantages of cooperative learning

Group rivalry

A major disadvantage of group learning, however, is the rivalry between groups. This may be dissipated if group membership changes regularly or for different tasks, so that an individual does not identify herself with just a few of her peers.

Gaining student involvement

The teacher may find that some students prefer competitive games to cooperative ones, and are reluctant at first to participate in cooperative activities or to touch other children if the game calls for it (Bay-Hinitz et al., 1994; Hill & Reed, 1989). However, children still benefit from even low participation rates (Bay-Hinitz et al., 1994) and can be encouraged to participate by attractive games and gentle persuasion (Hill & Reed, 1989).

Full inclusion

It is not certain that collaborative learning lives up to its promise of including children with disabilities fully into groups. The level of supports for teachers may be more crucial, as this affects their confidence in their ability to provide for all students (Cole & Chan, 1990; MacMullin, 1994;

MacMullin & Napper, 1993). Support needs to come from colleagues, the school deputy and principal and from specialists (MacMullin, 1994).

Balance with individual endeavour

Group work must still be matched to students' learning needs. As well as working cooperatively, students will need opportunities to compete for fun and to work independently when their interests and the task dictates (Johnson et al., 1990a).

Administrative issues

Cooperative learning can present administrative problems and requires a high degree of teacher management skills.

Conclusion: cooperative learning

Cole and Chan (1990, p. 348) conclude this discussion of the advantages and disadvantages of cooperative learning: 'Cooperative learning works best when it is well organised; when reinforcements encourage collaboration; when students and teachers agree on the value of overall goals; when class sizes are reasonably small; and when there are ample administrative support systems'. Their conclusion from the research evidence is that cooperative learning is more effective for teaching some subjects than is individual learning, but that it remains to be tested whether the social gains made by students are generalised to other settings or are maintained in the long term.

PEER TUTORING

Peer tutoring can involve either older or same-age students helping each other to learn. It fosters the notion that asking for and giving help are positive behaviours (Jones & Jones, 1995). At the emotional level, peer tutoring encourages cooperation and concern for peers, and enhances the confidence of the tutor. At an educational level, peer tutoring increases the academic knowledge of both tutor and learner.

The first step in establishing a formal peer tutoring scheme is to diagnose a given student's needs and establish explicit learning objectives. Next, the teacher selects a suitable tutor who can form a positive relationship with the learner and who shares similar interests. Appropriate materials are given to the tutor, who is trained in how to use them and how to deal with any problems that may arise. A suitable work area is designated and a practical work routine established. Finally, once the program is under way, the teacher will monitor the tutoring and give feedback about the process to the tutor and learner, about both the content learnt and the tutoring process, and will if necessary change a tutor if the relationship is not successful (Cole & Chan, 1990).

Jones and Jones (1995) offer a less formal peer tutoring method whereby students able to provide help during a particular activity place a green card on their desk, and those who need help signal that with a red card, for instance. Alternatively, the teacher can simply arrange desks into work groups with the instruction that students help each other. Informal support groups outside the classroom may be of benefit to secondary school students or to primary students who share a particular interest.

Advantages of peer tutoring

Peer tutoring delivers many of the advantages of learning offered by an expert tutor (Cole & Chan, 1990). These include improved motivation, social and academic gains, efficiency and a more democratic role for the teacher. These gains, however, occur only if the experiences are well planned and monitored by the teacher and carefully structured to match specific learning objectives (Cole & Chan, 1990).

Motivation

Children and adolescents can have more influence on each other than adults can (Cole & Chan, 1990). It is recognised that individuals are more likely to imitate a model whom they regard as being similar to themselves, so peer tutors can usually ensure a high level of learner participation. This awareness of modelling causes Schmuck and Schmuck (1988) to observe that it can be particularly beneficial for students from minority groups, for instance, to receive some tutoring from a person from their own culture.

Social gains

The tutor gains status and confidence from acting as a model to another student; the learner gains from being a 'friend' of a high-status peer or older student. Genuine affection can grow between tutor and learner, with none of the constraints of the formal teacher–student relationship (Topping, 1988), although one study found that acceptance of disliked students was not improved by their being a tutor or tutee (García-Vázquez & Ehly, 1992).

Academic gains

Children are often able to explain material to each other in more easily understood ways than adults can. Teaching improves the tutor's understanding of the processes of learning (Topping, 1988). The learner gains through individual guidance and personal care, with lessons tailored to meet her needs, and immediate feedback and correction (Cole & Chan, 1990; Kamps et al., 1994; Topping, 1988). These features of peer tutoring make learning more accurate and more fun.

Efficiency

In one study, teachers acknowledged that peer tutoring was simple to implement and to adapt to the classroom routine (Kamps et al., 1994). Once a peer tutoring program is in progress, the teacher is able to devote time to the neediest students (Cole & Chan 1990; Jones & Jones, 1995).

Democracy

Teachers can increasingly function as facilitators of learning, rather than as monopolisers of all wisdom. At the same time, the necessary monitoring of peer tutoring programs is more personal than monitoring a whole class (Topping, 1988).

Disadvantages of peer tutoring

Age of tutor

The tutor can become frustrated if she is not given the necessary interpersonal skills for assisting another student, while younger children in particular may become overbearing and dominant (Topping, 1988).

Choice of tutor

The responsibility of being a tutor may weigh heavily, especially on young children. Those children chosen to be tutors (or 'buddies' at young ages) may be those who believe that they must earn adult approval and that the only way they can do this is by helping others, even at the expense of their own needs. The selected tutor is often one who avoids peer relationships based on equality and instead can relate with others only if helping them. This constitutes what Berry (1988) calls a 'helpaholic' lifestyle, in which the individual's own needs are subdued in the interests of helping other people, which is likely to be unhealthy for both the helper and the helped.

Reciprocal helping relationships

Students who receive help also need an opportunity to provide help to others, lest the less able students come to feel inferior to their peers. Without reciprocity, some students may resent being one-down to those who are supposed to be their peers, may feel patronised, or may become overly dependent on the helping relationship. These difficulties may be less apparent with cross-age than with same-age tutoring.

STUDENT AUTONOMY

Coopersmith (1967) states that when people have autonomy and competence, they develop a healthy self-esteem; in contrast, when students are dependent on their teachers, they become hostile at this violation of their basic need to be self-determining (Ginott, 1972). Glasser (1986) identifies this need also and advocates that people be free from unnecessary restrictions, although their actions cannot infringe the rights of others.

PROMOTE INDEPENDENCE

A major benefit of democratic management methods is that they promote a student's self-reliance. Since being independent is such a basic human need, achievement of it will in turn enhance students' self-esteem. The teacher who can allow a student to work alone and to attempt tasks independently, and who can encourage emotional self-control, will be furthering that child's sense of competence and self-pride. Brown (1986, p. 26) notes that often our good intentions mean that we do things for children instead of allowing them to achieve things for themselves and feel good about themselves, and he goes on to say:

> Perhaps it is time to change our priorities from direct control aimed at stuffing the maximum possible amount of knowledge, skills and values into children to motivating them to manage their own lives—shifting the balance of our work with children from helping to enabling, from support to promoting self-reliance.

Self-reliance is of particular importance to children with disabilities, who may have restricted opportunities to be independent; any opportunity that remains must be capitalised on. All children will need increasing freedom to challenge their teachers about standards for student learning and behaviour.

CLARIFY EXPECTATIONS

It is important that students understand what is expected of them (Knight, 1991) so that they can remain in charge of their own behaviour.

INSIST ON APPROPRIATE BEHAVIOUR

Children who behave appropriately will be accepted by their peers; also, they gain self-esteem from being able to control themselves. Therefore, regardless of any label given to a student's behaviour, it is in the student's interests for the teacher to require acceptable behaviour.

PROVIDE CHOICE

Martin Seligman (1975) concluded that adults could 'inoculate' children against learning to be helpless, by giving them repeated experiences of control over even small aspects of their environment. Giving students some choice about their activities during lesson time also increases their engagement and reduces disruptive behaviour (Dunlap et al., 1994). Therefore, students must be offered choices at any opportunity. Even if they have no choice about doing an activity, they can be given a choice of how to go about it. On the other hand, it is also important not to offer fake choices, asking students if they want to do something when there is no option.

MODEL CONTROLLABILITY

The teacher will need to demonstrate being in control of himself so that students will copy this.

SELF-ACTUALISATION

Self-actualisation is each person's need to reach her potential and to express herself completely and creatively (Jones & Jones, 1990). This may include having the freedom not to conform to unnecessary group expectations without this being seen as noncompliance. Individuals need an opportunity to satisfy their curiosity and to understand their environment through exploration. This is the basis of Carl Rogers' philosophy on education (1983).

FUN

While Johnson et al. (1990a) contend that pressure to succeed must be matched with an equal level of social support, Glasser (1986) describes the need for all individuals, and young creatures in particular, to have fun. Elkind (1988) agrees and observes that we strip many childhood activities of fun by imposing a rigorous routine of lessons, tournaments, and competitions.

The needs for self-actualisation and fun are of a higher order than the other needs discussed in this chapter. I believe that they will be fulfilled when the lower order needs for physical well-being, self-esteem, belonging and autonomy are being satisfied. Much like the instruction to be spontaneous which itself violates spontaneity, self-actualisation and fun are not ends in themselves that can be programmed for, but are instead a natural outcome of the satisfaction of the lower order needs.

SUMMARY

A considerable body of research points to the value of meeting students' needs, both for the sake of their emotional and academic development and also as a means to prevent disruptive behaviour in schools (Grossman, 1995; Jones & Jones, 1995). The teacher can structure the interaction between himself and his students and among the student group, so that the students see themselves as part of a special group whose functioning depends on each and every member. Peers become a source of acceptance, people with whom to belong, and people from whom to learn positive social and academic skills. Kindsvatter et al. (1992) observe, however, that the strategies for creating a positive classroom climate remain insufficient by themselves: they must be supplemented by the teacher's wise and informed academic and social guidance within the present constraints.

DISCUSSION QUESTIONS

1. What can teachers do to enhance the self-esteem of students in the classroom?
2. What benefits to a student's self-esteem might you expect from offering encouragement instead of praise?
3. How does focusing on mistakes discourage student learning?
4. How does teacher self-esteem affect classroom management?
5. How would a teacher establish a warm climate in the classroom?
6. What do you believe is an 'appropriate professional relationship' (see p. 217) between teachers and their students?
7. Contrast assertive and hostile messages: what distinguishes them?
8. Give some disadvantages of competition in the classroom.
9. What are some advantages of cooperative learning?
10. In what ways would you seek to use peer tutoring in your classes?
11. Write your own charter of student and teacher rights and responsibilities. Would these differ from the rights and responsibilities listed in table 10.1? If so, what are your reasons for your inclusions and exclusions?

SUGGESTIONS FOR FURTHER READING

For detailed suggestions about class activities for fostering cooperation:

Hill, S. and Hill, T. 1990, *The collaborative classroom: A guide to cooperative learning*, Eleanor Curtin, Melbourne

Johnson, D.W. and Johnson, R.T. 1991, *Learning together and alone*, 3rd edn, Allyn & Bacon, Boston

Johnson, D.W., Johnson, R.T. and Holubec, E.J. 1990, *Circles of learning: cooperation in the classroom*, 3rd edn, Interaction Books, Minnesota

For activities for promoting students' self-esteem:

Borba, M. and Borba, C. 1978, *Self-esteem: a classroom affair. 101 ways to help children like themselves*, Winston Press, Minneapolis

——1982, *Self-esteem: a classroom affair. More ways to help children like themselves*, Winston Press, Minneapolis

McGrath, H. and Francey, S. 1991, *Friendly kids; friendly classrooms*, Longman Cheshire, Melbourne

For cooperative play activities for young children:

Sapon-Shevin, M. 1986, 'Teaching cooperation', *Teaching social skills to children: innovative approaches*, 2nd edn, G. Cartledge & J.F. Milburn (eds), Pergamon, New York

For cooperative play and instructional activities for children of all ages:

Orlick, T. 1982, *The second cooperative sports and games book*, Pantheon, New York

11

FACILITATING LEARNING

Being a spectator not only deprives one of participation but also leaves one's mind free for unrelated activity. If academic learning does not engage students, something else will. (Goodlad, 1983, in Jones & Jones, 1990, p. 163)

KEY POINTS

- *Effective classroom management includes how the teacher organises, delivers, monitors and communicates her instructional program (Charles, 1996).*

- *A strong beginning to the school year can set the tone for the rest of the year.*

- *The teacher will need to plan the physical space in the classroom so that the environment facilitates the type of work to be achieved there.*

- *Rules need to be established, taught and practised so that students can successfully observe the expectations for their behaviour and learning.*

- *Procedures are routines to negotiate potentially disruptive times. The teacher and class can establish procedures to use during direct instruction, individual seat work and group work.*

- *When delivering instruction, the teacher needs to enhance the students' motivation to participate by explaining the task, ensuring the work meets students' academic needs, employing an appropriate pace throughout the activity, catering to a variety of learning styles using a range of media, and being alert to and addressing problems as they arise.*

- *Some elements of the school environment may make it more difficult for students to achieve well in school; while the teacher may not be able to change some of these features, she can be alert to their effects on her students and adjust her demands when necessary.*

- *The teacher needs to exercise emotional and work-related self-discipline so that her own behaviour models the courteous behaviour she wishes her students to employ, and so she does not burden students with the task of meeting her personal needs.*

INTRODUCTION

Charles (1996) distinguishes three types of teacher: the well-liked teacher who, however, may not encourage the best work from students; the efficient teacher who excites good work but students do not enjoy being in her class and they behave well only because the structure demands it; and the master teacher. The aim of a master teacher is to present the instructional program in such a way that disruptive behaviour is minimised and student and teacher needs are met. The teacher assumes personal responsibility for her students' achievement; is personable; is positive with students; creates a good (positive or neutral) classroom atmosphere; provides clear structure, guidance, help and feedback to students; uses effective instructional and management methods from a wide repertoire of competencies; is efficient yet flexible in her organisation so that she is able to respond to circumstances; and not only knows what to do but also makes professional decisions about when and how to apply particular skills (Brophy & Good, 1986; Charles, 1996). The students behave well because they regard the teacher's standards as reasonable and because they want to please a teacher who likes and values them and who, when addressing transgressions, focuses on the act rather than criticises the actor.

Effective classroom management techniques include how the teacher organises, delivers, monitors and communicates her instructional program (Charles, 1996). Success in these endeavours depends on the teacher's knowledge, energy, motivation, and communication and decision-making skills (Brophy & Good, 1986).

BEGINNING THE SCHOOL YEAR

Effective managers are those who focus on issues of greatest concern to the students (Good & Brophy, 1994). While the first days in a school year must include passing out books and taking care of other administrative tasks, it is crucial that this time also be used to get to know the students and for them to renew their acquaintance with each other (Edwards, 1993). At its most basic this involves getting to know the students' names, although this is not sufficient. The teacher may use getting acquainted games, may demonstrate some of her own work (such as the art teacher showing her art work), and she may ask each student to write or talk about his family, his likes, and favourite activities in and out of school.

Next, the students will want to know the teacher's expectations for their class work. In the earliest days, activities should be familiar to allow all students to be successful—that is, to satisfy expectations—and not overload the students and teacher (Doyle, 1986). The activities can incorporate the information gained during the getting-to-know-you sessions (Emmer et al., 1994; Evertson et al., 1994).

PLANNING THE PHYSICAL SPACE

The physical arrangement of the classroom affects the amount that students working there can learn (Edwards, 1993). Gordon (1974) says that the classroom structure can not only make it difficult for students to stay motivated, but it can also provoke disruptive behaviour as a way of coping with an unconducive environment. Many issues relating to room arrangement may be considered (Edwards, 1993; Emmer et al., 1994; Evertson et al., 1994).

ARRANGE THE ROOM TO MAXIMISE THE INTENDED KIND OF LEARNING

The arrangement of the classroom will depend on how the teacher wants to use it. The teacher will need to consider the number of students using the room at one time, how close together they can be seated (depending on their age and behaviour patterns), whether she intends students to work mostly in groups, the kinds of activities the students will be doing, whether different kinds of activities will be occurring simultaneously, and whether she would like to have a quiet area for students who need to remove themselves temporarily from the bustle around them (Kerr & Nelson, 1989). Clusters or circles would be preferred for cooperative work; if the teacher wants to maximise on-task behaviour and individual learning with little student interaction, however, then desks should be arranged in rows. When desks are arranged in rows, the centre and front are where most activity happens and where students have most personal communication with the teacher (Doyle, 1986; Edwards, 1993; Good & Brophy, 1994); students on the periphery feel left out and receive mostly public communication. Therefore the teacher may want to move a withdrawn or distractable student or one with low self-esteem into the centre rows to ensure he becomes included fully. Also, moving around the room will ensure that communication with students who sit further away can be personal at times.

These and other decisions about room arrangements may need to be reviewed once the teacher has come to know the students both individually and as a group.

KEEP TRAFFIC MOVEMENT EFFICIENT

The room's organisation will need to promote efficient movement so that high traffic areas are free of congestion.

BE SURE STUDENTS ARE EASILY SEEN BY THE TEACHER

Most writers—for instance, Emmer et al. (1994); Evertson et al. (1994)—advise that if the teacher plans to work at her desk, then it should be in the front of the room so that all students are in view. However, Edwards (1993) advises that the teacher's desk should be in a corner or at the back so that she can work with individual students in relative privacy and is able to monitor students without being observed. The advice common to all writers is to ensure that all students are in view of the teacher at all times.

KEEP RESOURCES ACCESSIBLE

Bookcases and partitions can section off areas for specific purposes, offering privacy to students wishing to work alone, and ensuring easy access to materials needed for the activity occurring in the nearby area.

ENSURE STUDENTS CAN EASILY SEE INSTRUCTIONAL PRESENTATIONS

All students need to be able to read the blackboard, whiteboard, overhead projections, posters and so on, both during the presentation and for later reference if needed. This requirement refers both to the position and legibility of the presentations.

STRIVE FOR A FUNCTIONAL AND COMFORTABLE ENVIRONMENT

The room must not only be functional but also aesthetically pleasant and comfortable (Edwards, 1993; Rogers, 1990). The arrangements will need to be flexible as well, to enable a change of seating when the task requires it. Not only does floor space need to be considered, but also wall and ceiling displays can stimulate interest, as long as they do not distract students or inhibit free movement around the room.

The actual physical characteristics of the room—its size, lighting, warmth, storage space and so on—will constrain some decisions about furniture arrangement, although Rogers (1990) advises teachers to take whatever steps they can to improve ugly surroundings.

ESTABLISHING RULES

Rules are expectations of how individuals are to behave, and are in place to protect individuals' rights, and therefore by definition are 'fair' (Rogers, 1989, 1990). They may refer to student use of classroom space and facilities, to behaviour during whole-class activity, to small-group activity, to behaviour outside the classroom, and to specific times such as the beginning and end of the day or when a visitor arrives (Evertson & Emmer, 1982, in Jones & Jones, 1995). Rules will have one of four purposes (Cangelosi, 1993):

- to contribute to order to maximise on-task behaviour and minimise off-task behaviour, especially when it disrupts others
- to secure a safe and comfortable working environment
- to prevent activities of the class from disturbing its neighbours
- to maintain standards of courtesy among all school members, as long as these are not arbitrary, when the behaviour (such as wearing hats inside) has no detrimental effect on anyone else (Cangelosi, 1993).

The following are some guidelines for establishing rules (Doyle, 1986; Grossman, 1995; Jones & Jones, 1995; Lovegrove, Lewis & Burman, 1989; Rogers, 1989, 1990; Tauber, 1990).

CONCRETE RULES

Rules need to be concrete, specific, explicit and functional—that is, contribute to work accomplishment (Doyle, 1986). They should avoid vague terms such as requiring students to be 'polite'.

POSITIVE RULES

Rules should be expressed in positive terms, rather than stating what students must not do, although Grossman (1995) observes that a, 'Don't spit' rule is more credible than, 'Keep your saliva in your mouth'.

FEW RULES

The rules need to be few in number to maximise understanding and to avoid students feeling oppressed by a long list.

TEACH THE RULES

Effective managers integrate their rules and procedures into a workable system and teach this systematically to students (Doyle, 1986). Rules can be explained clearly and displayed prominently. Early in the year, the teacher will usher the system of rules along until students understand them (Doyle, 1986). Grossman (1995) observes that some students will take time to learn rules that differ greatly from their last school's or from their home environment. Therefore, he recommends that when these students have violated an agreed rule, teachers make them aware in specific terms about what they have done and that it infringed a rule, giving them opportunities to correct their behaviour. When they have improved, the teacher can give feedback about their behaviour but not rewards, because the problem is a learning not a motivational one. On the other hand, explanation is not necessary every time a student violates a rule (Grossman, 1995) because it is safe to assume that if the rule has been explained, then the student will know it, and is merely choosing not to observe it.

As well as teaching the rules, the teacher can teach a variety of nonverbal signals that remind students when a rule is being broken (Doyle, 1986).

STUDENT AGREEMENT

Students should agree with the rules (although even when an individual student does not agree, compliance is still required). Agreement implies that rules are seen to be reasonable and rational (Good & Brophy, 1994). If the teacher explains the cause-and-effect relationship between the rule and its outcome, students may be motivated to observe the standard. Jones and Jones (1995) also state that compliance is helped when peers and parents agree to and support the rules.

Some writers argue that students should participate in formulating rules and consequences to avoid provoking rebellion against externally imposed rules, to improve students' understanding of the rules and to promote their self-regulation of their observance (Tauber, 1990). Since students suggest similar rules to teachers, there is a potential for improved observance of rules with no compromise about standards. However, compliance to rules may be similar whether or not the students participate in formulating them (Grossman, 1995). While this may be true, the process of establishing the rules is educational and as an exercise in social problem solving it is valuable in itself.

One criticism of student participation is that school policy dictates some rules, and it is hypocritical of teachers to manipulate students into nominating or agreeing with these (Grossman, 1995). Perhaps, therefore, the teacher may present obligatory rules as a *fait accompli*, and discuss the rationale for them, and then negotiate remaining standards. A second criticism is that secondary teachers cannot operate with a different set of rules for each of their classes (Emmer et al., 1994; Grossman, 1995) and so will have to impose a common standard. Finally, Grossman (1995) observes that in a democracy we all have to abide by rules that have been decided by others, and that therefore this may not be detrimental for students.

MONITOR BEHAVIOUR

Student behaviour must be monitored continually and discussed frequently to check that it complies with the agreed rules.

ADMINISTER CONSEQUENCES

Students must be aware that their behaviour has consequences. Therefore when a rule is infringed, consequences must be enforced but in a dispassionate manner. Differing philosophies endorse natural, logical or contrived consequences, although all agree with Kerr and Nelson (1989) that consequences must be the least intrusive and restrictive of the available and effective methods.

REVIEW

Rules and consequences must be reviewed regularly.

CONCLUSION: RULE GUIDELINES

A system of rules is necessary but not sufficient for promoting order in a classroom. The teacher still needs to recognise when to act and how to improvise so that activities are not impeded by the students' behaviour (Doyle, 1986).

CONSISTENCY

Having established reasonable rules, the teacher will aim to be consistent in her application of them. Consistency refers to three aspects: first, maintaining constant expectations for appropriate and inappropriate behaviour; second, maintaining the same standards for all students; and third, applying consequences consistently if misdemeanours occur (Emmer et al., 1994; Evertson et al., 1994). At the same time, however, appropriate flexibility and informality increase the teacher's power as a decision maker

(Doyle, 1986). Inappropriate inconsistency will arise from three sources: first, when the rules are unreasonable, unworkable or inappropriate; second, when teachers are erratic in detecting misdeeds, leaving students who have been observed feeling disgruntled; and third, when the teacher does not feel strongly enough about the rule or procedure to enforce it. In these cases, the teacher can renegotiate the rules and their penalties with the class so that she is willing to enforce the new standards reliably.

The concept of consistency, however, is built upon the assumption of an external person (the teacher) enforcing standards of behaviour on others (the students). If this authoritarian concept is abandoned, then the need to be consistent abates. The teacher would simply express when her immediate needs were not being met by student behaviour or when a behavioural agreement were being violated. The democratic teacher would be consistent about upholding her needs, but the need itself (and resulting requests about student behaviour) may vary from day to day.

ENACTING PROCEDURES

Procedures are routines for students to follow when carrying out certain tasks (Grossman, 1995). These usually address potential disruption times and are aimed at ensuring the program runs smoothly. They allow students to know what is expected of them and so they cut down on confusion and wasted time.

DIRECT INSTRUCTION

Opening activities

It is usually best to have a short activity that students can begin as soon as they enter the room (Charles, 1996). Since a teacher must not begin until everyone is paying attention, Jones and Jones (1995) advise that she use some catchy phrase that the class have chosen to signal when it is time to start. (They give the example of using 'ho ho ho' in December.)

Distributing or using materials

Materials must be accessible, and when it is necessary to distribute materials, several students can assist.

Asking for teacher permission

Grossman (1995) advises that students should have the freedom, say, to go to the toilet, without having to gain permission each time, although if this is abused, a procedure may need to be enacted for students to attract teacher attention urgently but unobtrusively.

Transitions between activities

Knowing when to end an activity, and negotiating the transition to the next one, are both important for setting the tone of the activity that follows (Doyle, 1986; Grossman, 1995). Kounin (1970) observed two common mistakes with transitions: jerkiness and slowdowns. Jerkiness involves ending activities without warning, taking too long to set up materials for a new activity, redirecting student attention back to an activity that has already finished, and fragmenting the group so that students are moving along at a different pace or fragmenting the task into parts when it could be carried out as a single unit. Slowdowns involve spending too much time on detail, dwelling for too long on material the students have already understood, or spending too long preaching to students about their behaviour (Charles, 1996; Edwards, 1993; Grossman, 1995; Kounin, 1970).

Some ways of helping negotiate transitions include posting a schedule for the lesson or day, having material ready for the next activity, summarising the earlier task before beginning a new one, giving clear step-by-step instructions about the new activity, and reminding students of procedures associated with the new activity.

Ending the lesson

To avoid final instructions and summarising being accompanied by students packing up and beginning to move around, a procedure for ending lessons can be put in place. For instance, students can work until a few minutes before the lesson is due to end, with instructions then given during the final few minutes. This allows the lesson to end on time.

INDIVIDUAL WORK

Monitoring

Individual seatwork has two purposes: to give the students practice, and to give them and the teacher a measure of their progress (Jones & Jones, 1995). Therefore, a procedure is needed for the teacher to monitor the students' work and to give specific feedback, to ensure that the students are being successful rather than practising errors.

Students asking for help

Teachers can avoid students being unclear about what to do by explaining the task clearly, writing the steps on the board, circulating among students to check their progress, giving help briefly to students so that others are not waiting for help for a long time, and stopping the activity and reteaching the whole class if several students are unclear (Charles, 1996; Jones, 1987b). When students need help to complete their work, they will need a procedure for asking: they will not want to have their hand up for long periods, so instead they could place a cardboard sign on their desk, or write their name on the board, and be allowed to do something quietly while waiting for help (Grossman, 1995).

Giving help to students

Likewise, the teacher needs a procedure for giving help. Jones (1987b) observed that when helping, teachers usually remain for an average of five minutes with each student, which means only six students can be attended to during a 30 minute lesson, leaving others free to be off-task or disruptive. Instead, Jones advises teachers to give help in three steps: first, by offering specific *praise* about what the student has achieved so far, giving a brief *prompt* about what to do next, and then *leaving* before the student begins. This brief assistance conveys confidence in the student's ability to proceed and gives the teacher enough time to circulate among all students.

What to do with completed work

Students handing up work individually may create traffic and noise, so a procedure may be instituted for the teacher to collect all completed work at once (Charles, 1996).

What to do while waiting for others to finish

To avoid students waiting idly for others to finish, it may be necessary to sequence individual activities so that one follows another (Cangelosi, 1993). The teacher will also, however, want to avoid penalising students who finish early by giving them more to do, thus teaching them to work slowly to avoid extra work.

Contracts

Contracts can provide a way of monitoring students' work or directing their behavioural or academic improvement; however, they need to be reciprocal, specifying both what the student will achieve, and how the teacher will provide the necessary resources (Gurney, 1988).

GROUP WORK

As we saw in the previous chapter, students will need processes for developing team spirit, working together, problem solving and managing their differences. The teacher acts as a resource person in these processes, facilitating students to find their own solutions, but students will need procedures for seeking her help and clarification.

CONCLUSION: PROCEDURES

Teaching procedures alone may not be enough, especially for younger students, who may need demonstrations and opportunities to practise the routines (Grossman, 1995). And, like rules, procedures will need monitoring to ensure they are having their intended effect. On the other hand, too much routine and procedure (too much focus on order) can get in the way of educational aims (Doyle, 1986).

DELIVERING INSTRUCTION

When teachers run smooth lessons with few interruptions and engage students in the lessons and activities, students will work consistently and will not seek distractions (Brophy & Evertson, 1976, in Jones & Jones, 1995). Kounin (1970) found that effective teachers were those who scanned the classroom and dealt early with any difficulties, anticipated student needs, organised the classroom and the lesson to minimise disruptions, and effectively coped with multiple demands while teaching. These management skills both increase student learning and reduce disruptions, as one might expect. Research shows that some teacher skills that promote student engagement include: explaining the task, enhancing students' motivation, pacing, providing variety, and monitoring the group. Effective use of these skills conveys to students that the teacher is competent (Doyle, 1986).

EXPLAINING THE TASK

The teacher can summarise previous learning that will apply to the new task and state the goals for the new activity (Rosenshine & Stevens, 1986). Without overloading students with information, the teacher needs to give clear directions for beginning and completing the activity. The expected standard of the work and what to do with it when completed can also be useful parts of the instructions. Without this information, students will either interrupt with queries or will tune out. The teacher can complement verbal instructions with written instructions on the board, by asking students to write the instructions down themselves, by asking them to summarise the instructions verbally, or by calling for student questions about problems they anticipate. Once the students are clear about what they are doing, the teacher can ask them to indicate that they are committed to the activity.

It is important to give clear demonstrations of what students are to do, breaking the task down into small steps. Demonstrations need to be frequent, and the students' understanding checked in guided practice before they are asked to work independently (Rosenshine & Stevens, 1986). Guided practice involves giving prompts, feedback and corrective help early so that mistakes are not practised.

Once students begin independent practice (seatwork), their engagement will depend on how well they have been prepared by being guided through early practice items (Rosenshine & Stevens, 1986). Student engagement is also promoted when teachers have only short segments of seatwork, circulate among the students, and uphold routines such as those described above. Once independent practice is under way, the teacher must respond positively to students' questions so that they feel safe in the classroom. On the other hand, to safeguard students' self-concept and sense of autonomy, the teacher would be better to guide students' own problem solving, rather than to solve problems for them (Jones & Jones, 1995).

ENHANCING MOTIVATION

While some teaching may be aimed at meeting students' emotional needs directly, these emotional needs can also be satisfied indirectly through academic work (Jones & Jones, 1995). Motivating students to learn is important for the enhanced learning it promotes, for the fulfilment of students' emotional needs, and for the avoidance of disruptive behaviours that may fill in otherwise unoccupied time.

Teachers mainly attribute low academic performance to the students' lack of effort and so they engage in self-defeating interactions with low achieving students that involve lowered expectations of their work (Tollefson, Melvin & Thippavajjala, 1990). Instead, teachers need to consider the organisation of the learning environment and their own skills in helping students with a pattern of low achievement.

Teacher self-examination is facilitated by Jones and Jones' formula (1995) that describes three aspects of motivation: the student's expectation that he can be successful, his assessment of the benefits success will bring (including enjoyment, enhanced skill, or an increase in status because of increased skills), and the extent to which the emotional climate within the work environment meets his needs. Jones and Jones regard their formula as multiplicative, which implies that motivation requires all three components. Their formula is:

Motivation = Expectation of success × expected benefits of success × work climate

These writers report research findings that motivation is socialised rather than being inherent in students. This, therefore, gives teachers the power to promote student motivation rather than feeling powerless to influence it. A key way to motivate students is to ensure that academic learning meets their needs. The following list of academic needs is taken from Jones and Jones (1995).

The need to understand and value the learning goals

The teacher will need to outline the rationale for each and every activity, stating the purpose of each activity and how the skill it comprises will be useful to students now or in the future. In this way, students are taught three levels of content: fact, concept and value (Kindsvatter et al., 1992). If they do not understand the concept or value the task, they come to believe that learning is meaningless and full of traps which they cannot predict (Katz, 1988). They learn by rote instead of understanding the material, which will not work in the long run. And in turn their skills, interest in learning, and confidence in their abilities deteriorate.

The need to understand the learning process

The teacher will need to outline the reasons for a task or for going about it in a certain way. She will describe the intended learning outcomes. This informs the students as well as enabling the teacher to evaluate whether their learning outcomes meet her intended goals.

The need to be responsible for their own learning

As well as understanding the teacher's goals, students are more motivated when they can select their own goals. They need to study what interests them, rather than what they are told to study. Teachers will need to guide students to establish specific, short-term learning goals, as distinct from performance goals which are aimed at gaining a reward for completed work. Students' decisions may centre on what material to work on, when and how it will be completed, and on how to self-monitor the work (Jones & Jones, 1995).

The need for learning to be relevant to students' lives

Children remember information best when it is meaningful or relevant to them. More central than this, however, is the concept that if teachers want students to develop the skills needed for adult life, then they need to teach them to apply those skills in the present.

The need to experience success

Competence will breed confidence; on the other hand, repeated failure will cause students to alternate their attention between the task and their worries about failing and being criticised (Tobias, 1979, in Jones & Jones, 1995). This dual focus in itself will reduce their chances of success. Repeated failure will cause students to reject learning and the people involved with schooling.

The need for feedback

To enhance motivation, feedback about students' progress needs to be specific, immediate, genuine and constructive, especially for students who are concerned about possible failure. Feedback can take many forms. Students can be asked to summarise their own learning in a journal or display, through role plays (being a journalist who reports on events, for instance), or through presentations to others. Teachers can restate how the material relates to the students' lives and interests, can provide frequent review sessions, and can use tests as tools to help students summarise, as long as this information is acted on—that is, the teacher repeats lessons whose material needs to be covered again (Jones & Jones, 1995).

The need to receive benefits for achievement

It is hoped that many school tasks will be intrinsically reinforcing, although students may need some extrinsic reinforcers for tasks that are complex, difficult or tedious for them. External rewards have been repeatedly shown to diminish the power of intrinsic ones, however, and so should be used only as a last resort (Jones & Jones, 1995).

The need to find learning exciting

Teachers can convey their own excitement about the material and about solving the problems inherent in the tasks. They can also respond with interest and enthusiasm to students' comments.

The need for a safe, well-organised learning environment

Structure in the classroom provides clarity for students and can offset chaotic home backgrounds. On the other hand, the structure must be responsive to student needs, rather than the teacher being a slave to efficiency and procedures.

The need for time to integrate learning

Learning includes both acquisition of new skills and the consolidation of skills already gained. Without the chance to practise and consolidate their skills, students lose confidence in their grasp of the material, and in turn their motivation to continue to learn will be reduced.

The need for positive contact with peers

Cooperative learning has benefits for students' emotional well-being and learning outcomes, plus students' expectations of success (Johnson et al., 1990a).

The need for teaching that is matched to students' skill level

If teachers give the same activities to all students, then some will become frustrated and unmotivated, because the material is either too easy or too difficult for them. Obviously, knowing students' skill levels rests on assessing these both formally and informally. Therefore, schools will need policy, procedures and the physical and personnel resources to assist teachers to assess the academic skills of students, as long as the goal is to identify the resources a student needs to improve his skills, rather than to label and disenfranchise a student from learning (and excuse teachers from teaching).

As well as quantifiable differences in ability, students differ in their preferred mode for receiving information (verbally or visually), the pace at which they most comfortably learn, and the physical conditions (such as seating, noise, level of distractions and lighting) under which they learn best. Teachers can use inventories that ask students about their preferences and can observe the conditions that promote each student's learning, and then, where possible, incorporate these into the instructional program.

APPROPRIATE PACE

Lessons can lose momentum when teachers reiterate instructions, repeat material the students have already understood, or when they dwell on student behaviour. Jones and Jones (1995) recommend that the teacher videotape some of her lessons to assess whether her own tempo is too fast, slow, repetitive or unvaried. The teacher can also ask the students whether they have been given enough time to complete the work. She can teach them signals to tell her when she is going too fast or needs to wind up the pace, or can simply observe their natural nonverbal cues of restlessness and make adjustments based on her hunch about its causes, or ask the students themselves what the difficulty is.

The teacher can structure short breaks during long lessons, perhaps by giving students a moment to talk, stretch or play a short game, or by presenting a video that relates to the material.

VARIETY

Kounin (1970) believes that students need variety in order to maintain their attention. Teachers can vary the content, difficulty level, presentation method, materials used, study group configuration and instructional approaches (that is, direct instruction, individual work and group work) (Charles, 1996; Edwards, 1993). Individual work should be short in duration, and can be varied by providing cartoons or personalised questions on work sheets and by allowing students to work together (Jones & Jones, 1995).

OBSERVING THE CLASSROOM

Kounin (1970) coined the term *withitness* to refer to the need for teachers to remain vigilant about student behaviour, so that they notice the effects of their instruction. Teachers who can do this need to give only brief guidance to individuals later, since they have taken note and retaught when the group did not understand the task (Brophy & Good, 1986). In his research on the management approaches of successful versus less successful teachers, Kounin found that successful teachers conveyed their awareness of what was going on by being able to identify accurately who instigated a dispute between students (successful *targeting*) and by attending to serious matters while ignoring minor incidents. Timing is important too: the teacher cannot let a behaviour become too serious or spread to other students before intervening. Kounin also referred to a teacher's ability to monitor and attend to two issues at once or to maintain awareness of the whole class while attending to an individual, a skill he termed *overlapping*.

On the other hand, Good and Brophy (1994) warn of the dangers of selective perception when teachers observe and monitor the classroom. Bias and teacher anxiety are two of the many factors that can affect the accuracy of teachers' observations.

ADDRESSING SCHOOL CAUSED PROBLEMS

So far, our discussion in this chapter has focused on internal features of the classroom which the teacher can change to accommodate student needs. The school structure will also affect student attainment and behaviour. Some of these issues centre on the contrast between school and home (Grossman, 1995).

CROWDING

The sheer size of schools and classes gives an impersonality to the schooling process and may excite reactions to crowding (Grossman, 1995). It also may make school less attractive than home because students have very little private time either in the classroom or in play areas, whereas at home they are usually able to withdraw for privacy.

CONFLICT BETWEEN SCHOOL AND HOME

Contrasts and even conflicts between the values of school and home may leave students having to choose between them, with school less likely to win student loyalty.

FREEDOM OF CHOICE

Students' freedom of choice is likely to be more restricted at school than at home. At home they have the choice to do activities they enjoy and are competent at, whereas at school they must apply themselves to all endeavours.

PHYSICAL MOVEMENT

The constraints on their physical movement imposed by school is unnatural and restrictive, and students will vary in their ability to cope with this and in the time they take to adjust (Grossman, 1995).

LACKING READINESS SKILLS

The issue of matching teaching level to student skills has been discussed in the context of increasing student motivation. Teachers will need to be aware of the preparatory skills students will need for undertaking an activity, and ensure that they possess these as a foundation for new learning.

UNNECESSARY ANXIETY AND STRESS

While some challenge is necessary for exciting learning, once challenge turns into stress, learning is compromised. In Humphrey and Humphrey's study (1985), children reported that competition between classmates was the major cause of school stress. These writers identified three sources of anxiety in competitive activities: first, time pressure, which sets up demands for speed; second, humiliation, that is, public performance; and, third, emphasis on one right answer rather than on the process of problem solving. Grading students may exacerbate competition between them (Glasser, 1969; Jones & Jones, 1995). However, when a grading system has been imposed externally, the teacher can reduce students' stress by speaking with students in advance of assessments about the skills required to meet the standard, and afterwards giving individual feedback about which of those skills each student demonstrated, thereby focusing on positive accomplishments (Jones & Jones, 1995).

ADJUSTING TO ENVIRONMENTAL DISTRACTIONS

It will not always be possible to eliminate distractions in the environment (Grossman, 1995). If students have been unsettled by a recent event or announcement, for instance, the teacher may have to adjust the program to their mood. Adjusting to the students' feelings about events and about themselves is the essence of what Ginott (1972) calls *congruent communication*. This conveys an attitude of helpfulness and acceptance of their experience.

TEACHER SELF-DISCIPLINE

Ginott (1972) believes that the most important ingredient in classroom discipline is the teacher's self-discipline. This has two aspects: emotional discipline, and discipline about work. Central to emotional discipline is that teachers express their feelings appropriately and do not humiliate or denigrate students. That is, they use the courteous manners they wish their students to adopt. Teachers may still express anger and frustration, but should do so by stating their feelings rather than by blaming the student. Ginott believes that teachers cannot afford to make scenes, and should *never* use sarcasm. In the same vein, Bill Rogers (1990) observes that disciplining from emotion rather than reason is self-indulgent and unhelpful.

Emotional self-discipline will also involve the teacher in managing her own stress levels, leaving her private worries at home, ensuring that her students are not expected to supply her emotional or relationship needs, and feeling confident enough to enact good teaching procedures and to be emotionally warm with students.

Work discipline will require the teacher to be well-prepared and organised; capable in her teaching area and competent in delivering instruction; able to call on a sound and up-to-date theoretical base to guide her practice; open to feedback from students or colleagues; willing to engage in self-evaluation; and professionally accountable to students, parents, and the school as a whole.

SUMMARY

Students will learn best when they understand what is required of them, and when their active involvement and achievement is fostered by both the content and the process of delivery of the instructional program. The teacher can modify the classroom environment to be conducive to optimal learning, and can negotiate rules and procedures that promote the smooth functioning of the group. Student motivation can be enhanced by ensuring the learning tasks meet their academic needs, while clear, well-paced and varied instruction will promote on-task behaviour with a resulting improvement in student learning. The teacher will need to monitor the effects of her instruction, using awareness of the group's behaviour as a guide to its level of involvement, and will need to be prepared to be more professional and disciplined than she expects her students to be.

DISCUSSION QUESTIONS

1. Describe the characteristics of Charles' master teacher (1996). Contrast these qualities with the well-liked and the efficient teacher.

2. What considerations will inform the teacher's choice about the arrangement of the classroom?

3. What arguments can you give for and against student participation in rule making?

4. What procedures have you found necessary while you have been teaching? Which ones were successful, and which were less so? What differences distinguished successful from unsuccessful procedures?

5. List students' academic needs. Does your list coincide with the list of Jones and Jones (1995) given in this chapter? What are the differences, and what is your rationale for your inclusions and exclusions?

6. How do you motivate students? What benefits have you observed from your approaches?

7. What are the recommended components of clear instructions?

8. What is your conclusion on the debate about consistency? Does it fit with a democratic approach, and how does it compare with flexibility? Is it necessary for all students all of the time, for some students, or for none?

9. The teacher might begin addressing school caused behaviour problems by discriminating those things she can and those things she cannot change. How would you approach each type of cause?

10. What aspects of teacher self-discipline do you regard as most important?

SUGGESTIONS FOR FURTHER READING

For an overview of methods of promoting a warm classroom climate and of facilitating learning:

Charles, C.M. 1996, *Building classroom discipline: from models to practice*, 5th edn, Longman, New York

For detail about organising instruction in order to maximise learning and motivation:

Jones, V.F. and Jones, L.S. 1995, *Comprehensive classroom management: creating positive learning environments for all students*, 4th edn, Allyn & Bacon, Boston

For detailed discussion of many practical aspects of classroom management, with an eclectic theoretical base:

Good, T.L. and Brophy, J.E. 1994, *Looking in classrooms*, 6th edn, Harper Collins, New York

Grossman, H. 1995, *Classroom behavior management in a diverse society*, 2nd edn, Mayfield, California

Rogers, W.A. 1990, *'You know the fair rule'*, ACER, Melbourne

12

TEACHING SOCIAL SKILLS

When students have serious difficulties reading, they are referred to a specialist who works intensively with them for an extended period of time. Educators do not expect students to learn to read by being placed in time out or otherwise isolated from classmates . . . However, when students experience difficulties with their behavior, educators often isolate them, provide little or no instruction in how to behave appropriately, and expect one or two visits to a counselor or principal to resolve the problem . . . Instead educators must respond to unproductive student behavior by creating opportunities for students to develop much needed skills. (Jones & Jones, 1995, pp. 36–7)

KEY POINTS

- *Many children are isolated at school for a range of reasons, which can include their inappropriate behaviour.*

- *While lacking friends, they do not partake of the benefits friendships offer and do not have a social context within which to practise their social skills.*

- *Social skilfulness or competence comprises a complex set of cognitive and affective tasks that are carried out within an environment that influences the individual's competence.*

- *Teachers can assess their students' social competence using a range of measures, the most common of which is sociometric assessment.*

- *While social skills are mostly acquired naturally, they can also be taught. Once aware of students' social skill needs, the teacher can target individual students or offer social skills training to the whole class.*

- *Group programs comprise various modes of instruction and cover identification of and coping with one's own feelings, social problem solving skills and planning skills, with the exact components and the tasks covered in each section being influenced by the students' ages.*

* *Bullying is one form of aggressive, antisocial behaviour that benefits from a whole school approach at the levels of policy, procedures and skills training.*

INTRODUCTION

The rationale for teaching social skills to students is that some behave inappropriately because they lack the necessary skills to behave otherwise (Kerr & Nelson, 1989). In order to evaluate this proposition, this chapter will examine the different forms that isolation from peers can take, outline the benefits of friendships on which isolated children miss out, and then describe social competence, as a forerunner to outlining social skills training programs. Social competence will be examined from the standpoint that it is no different from other cognitively-based skills and therefore that what we know about cognitive training can be applied to the social skills domain (Asher & Renshaw, 1981; Dodge, 1985; Dweck, 1981; Ladd, 1985; Ladd & Mize, 1983). One added dimension to social skills, however, may be their emotive value to the student, in that social rejection will mean more to her than failure at some other, academic, task. Also, social learning may be more complex and may require more practice than other cognitive skills (Dweck, 1981).

ISOLATED CHILDREN

Many students are isolated from their peers at some time during their school life. Isolation can take three forms: neglect, rejection and mixed peer responses. At any one time, between 5% and 10% of primary school children are named as a friend by no one in their class (Asher & Renshaw, 1981). These youngsters are said to be *neglected*, which means that they are neither liked nor disliked by their peers. Neglected children may present as being withdrawn, although withdrawal may be the result rather than a cause of rejection (Coie et al., 1989) and so may not reflect a social skill deficit in the individual. Nevertheless, neglected children certainly lack the social opportunities to practise their skills and so their skilfulness may begin to lag behind their more practised peers.

Neglect is usually temporary and is not associated with long-term adjustment problems. Even so, temporary problems still cause pain for students and, therefore, intervention with neglected children is worthwhile (Schneider, 1989).

Whereas neglected students are neither liked nor disliked by their peers, *rejected* students are not liked and are highly disliked. There are four groups of rejected students: first, aggressive-rejected; second, physically unattractive children; third, rejected children who display strange behaviours; and fourth, students with none of these characteristics but who are nonetheless rejected (Coie et al., 1989). The most common reason for peer rejection is aggression, especially after the ages of seven or eight (Coie et al., 1989). Aggressive-rejected children may lack prosocial skills, or may have these skills but are not using them. As well as displaying few prosocial behaviours, they also act antisocially.

These children are not isolated out of choice, although despite this they were found to be no more lonely than popular children (Asher & Parker, 1989), which may mean only that they have hardened themselves to their rejected status.

A third group of students is the controversial children who are highly liked by some of their peers and highly disliked by others (Dodge, 1985).

All three types of students suffer isolation from their peer group, incurring the many damaging effects of a lack of friends. Therefore, all three groups are legitimate targets for social skills intervention, although the nature of this will differ according to their different needs and skill deficits.

EFFECTS OF ISOLATION

Low peer acceptance may have more damaging consequences than low academic achievement (Frosh, 1983). Children who are isolated miss out on the important benefits friendships offer, and are lonelier and less satisfied with those relationships they do have. Socially isolated children have more chance of dropping out of school, and have a higher incidence of school maladjustment and mental health problems as adults (Hartup, 1979; Hill & Hill, 1990; Hops & Lewin, 1984; LeCroy, 1983; Rose, 1983), especially if their low acceptance is due to their aggression rather than to shyness and withdrawal (Asher & Parker, 1989). Isolated children will have fewer supports for coping with the daily stresses of life, and less confidence in and experience at eliciting support from others, which will carry over into adult life (Asher & Parker, 1989).

However, we cannot conclude that isolation or a lack of friendships *cause* children's later emotional problems (Asher & Parker, 1989; Frosh, 1983; Ladd, 1985; Schneider, 1989). Early forms of what will develop into an adult emotional disorder may cause both peer rejection in childhood and the adult maladjustment. Nevertheless, isolated children will come to lack confidence in their skills, and even if their lack of confidence only maintains rather than causes their peer problems, remediation is still necessary (Ladd, 1985). Also, since peer rejection is correlated with adult difficulties, it can be a good measure to identify individuals who could benefit from special attention to their social needs.

BENEFITS OF FRIENDSHIPS

Friendship is a voluntary, ongoing bond between individuals who have a mutual preference for each other and who share emotional warmth. Friendships serve many important functions (Asher & Parker, 1989; Asher & Renshaw, 1981; Rubin, 1980).

SOCIAL SKILL DEVELOPMENT

Within peer relationships, children can experience affection; equality; validation of their interests, hopes and fears (Asher & Parker, 1989); self-worth; companionship; intimacy; negotiation; control of aggression (Hartup, 1979); cooperation; and consideration of others. Within a group, children learn humour (engage in pranks) (MacMullin, 1988), and complex forms of play (Asher & Renshaw, 1981).

By adolescence, peer relationships teach young adults about intimacy, empathy, compassion, loyalty, collaboration, altruism and self-disclosure, as well as give them support for their developing sexuality (Asher & Parker, 1989). Friendships play a role in teaching young people about management of their emotions (Asher & Parker, 1989), allowing them to express their feelings in a safe and playful context (Perry & Bussey, 1984).

SELF-ESTEEM

Peer acceptance feeds a child's self-concept. Comparing herself with peers gives her a realistic sense of her competencies and personal attributes (Asher & Parker, 1989).

EMOTIONAL SUPPORT

Friendships supply reassurance, enhance confidence in stressful situations, avoid loneliness, provide fun and foster individual happiness. Friends also offer practical and emotional support through giving information, advice and counsel.

COGNITIVE DEVELOPMENT

Young people pass on information, attitudes, values and skills to each other that they cannot obtain from adults (Johnson & Johnson, 1991). They provide practice at problem solving (Perry & Bussey, 1984) and can advance a young child's language skills (Kohler & Strain, 1993; Rubin, 1980). Play, a vehicle for development in all areas, is more extensive with friends than with non-friends (Asher & Renshaw, 1981). These cognitive and social benefits in turn enhance other skill domains as well (Swetnam et al., 1983).

SUPPLEMENTING HOME EXPERIENCES

Friendships can help children overcome negative home experiences (Rubin, 1980) or can supply experiences that simply are not available at home (Hartup, 1979). For example, unassertive parents will not be modelling conflict resolution skills to their child; instead she can learn these from her peers.

SOCIAL SKILLS AND SOCIAL COMPETENCE

Kerr and Nelson (1989) define social *skills* as specific social behaviours, whereas social *competence* refers to an individual's ability to use those skills in the right time and place. Social competence comprises the ability to transmit information and feelings (including making requests for another person to meet one's needs), the ability to achieve desired social responses from others without being harmful to them (Foster & Ritchley, 1979, cited by Rose, 1983; Peterson & Leigh, 1990), to evoke approving responses from others, and to respond to the demands of the adult world (Swetnam et al., 1983). In other words, the definition of social competence considers the influence of the social environment on the individual and the impact of the individual on her social environment (Peterson & Leigh, 1990).

It is likely that the subskills that form social competence change as children get older (Asher & Renshaw, 1981). Preschool-aged children need the specific social skills to establish and maintain contact, the language and communication skills for accurate exchange of information (past the age of 2 ½), and the motor skills to engage in favourite activities of the peer group (Finch & Hops, 1983), while ability to share feelings will be paramount at later ages. Also, the characteristics of the peer group itself may assume greater importance as children grow older (Dweck, 1981).

Figure 12.1   Components of social competence

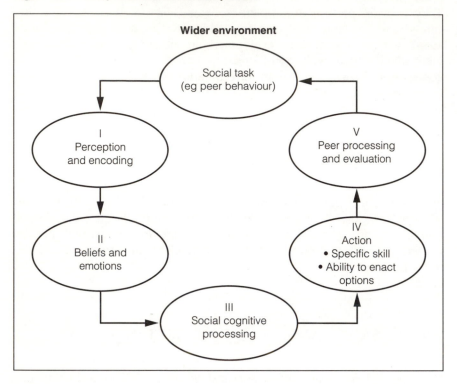

THE COGNITIVE VIEW OF SOCIAL COMPETENCE

The following model of social skills has been arrived at through an adaptation of the work of researchers into social skills (Asher & Renshaw, 1981; Dodge, 1985; Ladd, 1985; Ladd & Mize, 1983) and the cognitive theorists. It was introduced in chapter 4, and is described here in its application to social skills (see figure 12.1).

MODEL DESCRIPTION

The model in figure 12.1 describes a student responding within the wider social environment to a social stimulus such as another student's actions. She will need to interpret the task demands (phase I), following which she will call on her beliefs and attitudes about the task and her own abilities to negotiate it (phase II) in order to solve the dilemma. Social problem-solving skills (phase III) will be required, and her choice of action (phase IV) will be determined by her specific information about her behavioural options plus an ability to enact those options. In response to this behaviour, her peer will process and evaluate her action (phase V) using the same cognitive processes and will then respond, creating a new social task for the first student to negotiate. The peer's response will give the first student feedback about her behaviour and her status in the eyes of her peer, which in turn will affect her cognitive interpretation of the task, her feelings about it, her problem-solving processes . . . and so on in a cycle.

All these skills need to be coordinated: if any one subskill is deficient, the whole social problem-solving process goes awry.

THE WIDER ENVIRONMENT

Social skills problems reflect a mismatch between the individual and the environment (Schneider, 1989) or between the individual and the peer group. For instance, a gifted child may bore and be bored by her agemates and so may be rejected by them, not because of a deficit in the individual's social skills but because of a mismatch between her cognitive skills and interests and those of her peers. (Dweck, 1981).

The environment can affect the individual's acquisition of social knowledge (Bye & Jussim, 1993) or, even when the child's social processing skills are adequate, the environment can alter her actual performance (Dodge & Price, 1994). Given this dual effect, it may be more viable, relevant and benign to change the environment—in our case, the classroom or school structures—that may give rise to social problems than to attempt to change the individual through social skills training. Focusing on the context has many advantages compared with diagnosing individual deficiencies. First is that a student may not demonstrate a particular skill, not because of her inability to do so but because using the skill would be unsafe. This is illustrated by the example of teaching a student with a violent home environment to be assertive, when it would be more beneficial for her to develop a plan for keeping safe (Bye & Jussim, 1993). Second, since performance may be appropriate in one environment (say within the culture of home), but not in another (at school), then it becomes clear that the student who does not display a particular skill may not have a skills deficiency as such but merely a discrimination problem. Third, not only can environmental factors trigger social problems in the first place, but they can also inhibit generalisation of improvements gained in training sessions (Schneider, 1989). Therefore, with school based social problems, the school environment must be addressed before focusing on an individual's apparent social skill deficit.

THE SOCIAL TASK

The social tasks for which children and adolescents will need social skills include: gaining entry to the peer group, dealing with conflict constructively, responding to provocation such as teasing or bullying, controlling feelings, maintaining friendships (for example, tolerating differences in friends or dealing with each person's changing needs in the friendship) and terminating friendships amicably. A final social skill that students will need is dealing with people in authority.

PHASE I: PERCEPTION AND ENCODING

The first stage of social interaction requires perception of a social demand. This includes a sensitivity to the existence of problems or the potential for problems. The individual's perception is filtered by environmental factors as already mentioned, plus physiological factors such as tiredness, arousal level, attention, preoccupation with self, physical stamina and hearing and visual acuity (Bye & Jussim, 1993). These perceptual skills equip the individual to *detect and interpret available social cues.* Selective attention will limit the breadth of cues to which the individual attends (Bye & Jussim, 1993). For instance, aggressive children are more likely to misinterpret social cues and will attribute hostile intent to others when their behaviour is ambiguous (Ladd, 1985).

Having identified that a social task needs a response, the student needs knowledge *of general interaction principles,* such as cooperating, sharing, participating, and validating peers. Ladd (1985) reports that less popular children know less about friendship making than popular children.

PHASE II: BELIEFS AND EMOTIONS

In the model shown in figure 12.1, the second stage of a social response is the individual's beliefs that influence her feelings and motivation to interact prosocially. What the student believes about herself will ultimately affect what behaviour she attempts (Bye & Jussim, 1993). Her beliefs give rise to emotions that directly influence her recall of relevant social knowledge, her decision-making and problem-solving processes, and her actions. Some of the attitudinal and emotional aspects of cognition were detailed in chapter 4; some ideas that relate specifically to social skills are added here.

Self-efficacy and locus of control

Some children have difficulties with social skills because their responses to earlier difficulties have caused them to form a 'set' or preconceived notion about how likely they are to be successful (Dweck, 1981). Some children give up when faced with failure because they believe they are incompetent, while others interpret failure as a temporary setback that they have the skills to overcome. Since occasional failure in social situations is inevitable, the child's attributions about that will affect her future social interactions (Dweck, 1981).

Motivation

Motivation to exercise social skills is a crucial factor. Motivating and teaching a student to be less impulsive and to make rational decisions about her behaviour may be a bigger task than simply broadening her behavioural options (Schneider, 1989).

PHASE III: SOCIAL PROBLEM SOLVING

In the third stage of social interaction described in figure 12.1, the individual needs knowledge of specific social behaviours and their likely functions in interpersonal contexts. Students who display deficits in social skills may not necessarily have deep-seated emotional problems, but instead may simply lack the necessary social knowledge (Bye & Jussim, 1993). This includes knowledge about the goals of interaction, strategies that can achieve these goals, the contexts in which each strategy may be used appropriately (Ladd & Mize, 1983) and self-knowledge (Bye & Jussim, 1993). Generating specific behaviours requires *alternative* thinking (the ability to generate solutions), *means–end* thinking (planning steps needed to carry out a solution), and *consequential* thinking (consideration of the results before acting). Owing to a lack in these skills, unpopular children's strategies are often situationally inappropriate (Ladd, 1985).

PHASE IV: ACTION

Performing the social skill requires an ability to convert the information arrived at during the problem-solving phase into useful behaviours, and an ability to perform the actions skilfully. It also requires the ability to evaluate the outcomes of one's actions. This involves the ability to detect the effect of one's actions on others (using empathy) and to interpret success and failure in ways that encourage continued practice and skill refinement.

PHASE V: PEER EVALUATION

The child's actions are processed and evaluated by her peer who then formulates a response, which in turn is interpreted by the first child. It will then form one key emotional influence on the first child's next social response.

ASSESSING SOCIAL COMPETENCE

Social competence can best be measured by adults in the student's environment (Hops & Finch, 1985). The teacher can observe the social behaviour of students, and use any of the following seven measures of possible social difficulties:

1. the number of friends students can identify
2. the amount of time they spend playing with others
3. the type of play in which they engage
4. the degree of satisfaction or happiness they gain from their social interactions
5. teacher observation of persistent difficulties students have in handling particular types of social dilemmas
6. identification of the subskills that achieve success, and targeting of students who display fewer of these subskills
7. sociometric measures.

1. NUMBER OF FRIENDS

This is unlikely to be a good indicator of a student's social skills: the quality of relationships rather than their number will define the student's competence. Indeed, despite appearances to the contrary, especially during adolescence, it is the norm rather than the exception for individuals of all ages to have just one or two close friends (Porteous, 1979).

2. TIME SPENT WITH OTHERS

The amount of time spent with others may not be a good measure of social skilfulness. Some children may be very active socially but are aggressive or disruptive of others, while some children prefer solitude but are very competent and agreeable when they are with other students (Perry & Bussey, 1984).

Solitary play can be classified into three types: passive solitary play, reticence and active solitary play. The three types may appear to be a form of social withdrawal, although not all signal a social skills deficiency (Coplan et al., 1994). Passive solitary play or looking on (reticence) are appropriate and benign during early childhood, but by middle childhood they can indicate social withdrawal. Active solitary play among a group of peers is seen to be disruptive of their play and to signal impulsivity, and so indicates some potential or actual social difficulties.

3. TYPE OF PLAY IN WHICH STUDENTS ENGAGE

Young children engage in functional, repetitive play, and as they reach three to four years, their play becomes more constructive. Pretend or dramatic play is next to appear and finally games with rules begin appearing in the preschool years and continue until adolescence (Perry & Bussey, 1984). Not all children profit from the same types of play. However, a child may have social difficulties if she relies on simple play at an age when she should have mastered more sophisticated play (Frosh, 1983).

The two criteria—time spent with others and the type of play activity—combine to allow us to assess a child's social skilfulness. This is described by Perry and Bussey (1984, p. 305) who note:

> If children are wasting their time while alone—if they are unoccupied or are doing something that is better done in a group—then high rates of solitary play may be detrimental for the children's development. But if children are spending their time alone wisely, then solitary play may be beneficial.

4. PERSONAL SATISFACTION

The teacher could observe a student's interactions, and note whether she seems happy with her level of social contact, although this may miss identifying some students who appear to be accepted and to have friends but who are not satisfied with those relationships. Therefore, the teacher can ask students about their happiness or whether they have any social concerns.

5. DIRECT OBSERVATION

The teacher can observe the type of skills a student displays and typical difficulties she experiences. The type of social task that is an issue for one student may not be so for another, or may be a problem at one stage of development and not at another.

Since social skilfulness represents a match between the behaviour displayed and the context, direct observation allows observers to understand the sequence of social events and the conditions that led to them (Coie, Dodge & Kupersmidt, 1990), and to modify the environment rather than targeting an individual for training (Westwood, 1993). However, some behaviours—such as the stereotyped activity of a student with autism—are clearly inappropriate, while other skills are open to value judgments both about the behaviour and the context in which it is displayed. This introduces the potential for bias in teacher and peer observations (Dodge, 1985).

Another difficulty is that direct observation of social encounters may not be equally useful at identifying problems in all age groups. While overt behaviours (such as aggression or cooperative play) associated with social skilfulness in young children may be easily observable, the dimensions of friendship for older children (such as loyalty and companionship) will be harder to observe (Asher & Renshaw, 1981).

A further difficulty is that specific behaviours are only imperfectly correlated with group acceptance (Asher & Parker, 1989). This means that while the teacher could identify particular instances of a student's social ineptness, training in targeted skills may not in fact affect her social acceptance. This is not an issue if the teacher aims only to improve a student's social skilfulness but needs to be taken into account if he has a second aim of enhancing her group acceptance.

6. IDENTIFICATION OF SPECIFIC SUBSKILLS

One way around the dilemma of defining social competence separately from the biased social values of the observer, has been to observe the social skills of students already judged to be popular and unpopular, and identifying differences in the social skills the two groups display. This has identified aggressiveness, contentious statements and inappropriate solitary play as indices of social incompetence, although differences between popular and unpopular children on these indices are quite small (Dodge, 1985). Observations have focused on group entry and the sustaining phases of social interactions.

Entry skills

Entry skills provide a useful assessment of overall social competence (Putallaz & Wasserman, 1990). These skills include the ability to initiate contact or make new friends. Children need to recognise the appropriate time and place to initiate entry and use appropriate non-verbal messages to signal their wishes. Competent children are more adept at gaining entry to a group without being rejected (Perry & Bussey, 1984). These children typically follow a series of steps: they approach other children at play, quietly observe their game (hovering), wait for a natural break to occur, begin to behave in ways that relate to the group members' activity, and only then do they comment on the activity (Perry & Bussey, 1984; Putallaz & Wasserman, 1990). That is, they join the group's frame of reference and are unlikely to disrupt the game even if they do not conform to the group's activities (Putallaz & Wasserman, 1990). In contrast, less competent children disrupt the group process, perhaps by calling attention to themselves, criticising the way the children are playing, or introducing new games or topics of conversation.

Initial rejection is a very common response to requests to enter a group. Competent children have the confidence to persist despite early rejection, whereas less adept children appear to need to save face but in their attempts to do so behave in ways more likely to lead to repeated rejection (Putallaz & Wasserman, 1990).

Making new friends

Socially competent children initiate interactions more gracefully than their less competent and less popular counterparts (Perry & Bussey, 1984). They use greetings more often, ask about the other child (for example, 'What do you like to play?'), give more information about themselves ('I like climbing') and more often try to include the other child in their games.

Non-verbal messages

The socially competent child can use and comprehend non-verbal behaviour such as eye contact, facial expressions and body posture to send the message of cooperation and to discern social messages from other children. For example, she can assess whether her entry to a group would intrude at an awkward moment. In contrast, a boisterous child may be rejected simply because her activity level (non-verbal behaviour) is incongruent with the group's.

Sustaining skills

These include supportive actions, awareness of others, conflict management skills, language skills and moral reasoning.

Supportive actions

Once within the group, the child needs an ability to be supportive of her peers. Popular children are skilled at complementing, smiling at, complying with, imitating, cooperating with, helping, and sharing (both toys and their feelings) with their playmates, and by middle childhood can keep secrets. These behaviours signal that they are keen to cooperate and can be trusted. In contrast, 'Unpopular children not only reward their peers less often but also have unusual ideas about what constitutes helpful behaviour' (Perry & Bussey, 1984, p. 312).

Awareness of others

The socially competent child is sensitive to the other child's needs and wants. She can be tactful. She may moderate her behaviour to suit her playmates and respond to their friendly overtures.

Conflict management

When faced with a potential conflict, a child must have access to a repertoire of responses (non-assertion, assertion and aggression) and must be able to choose the appropriate time to use each. The competent child can use persuasiveness and assertiveness rather than bossiness when making suggestions about the group's play. She can obey social rules such as taking turns as group leader and using play materials, for example. She can solve disputes by citing a general rule of acceptable behaviour, and can offer alternative suggestions to a child whose actions have been disputed.

Language skills

A child will need sufficient verbal competence to ask for what she wants—such as requesting to enter the group—and then, having gained entry, she needs sufficient speech to sustain the play, elaborating on it at a similar level to her playmate, and to negotiate and listen to the other child (Rose, 1983; Rubin, 1980).

Moral reasoning

Socially competent children have a sophisticated understanding of right and wrong (Perry & Bussey, 1984). They are more likely to judge an action according to its effect on the welfare of others, rather than whether it attracts external reward or punishment.

Absence of antisocial behaviours

As well as possessing prosocial skills, the popular child is likely to lack a range of irritating behaviours that prevent acceptance by others. These antisocial behaviours include interrupting, disrupting games, impulsive and unpredictable behaviour, tantrums, abusive language and cheating at games (Westwood, 1993).

SOCIOMETRIC MEASURES

Sociometric measures have been the most frequently used formal measures of social relationships or social status (Hops & Lewin, 1984). They are of three types (Asher & Renshaw, 1981; Coie et al., 1989; Hops & Lewin, 1984; Westwood, 1993). The first is *peer nominations* of those classmates whom each student would most (or least) like to be friends with or to play or work with. Positive and negative nominations are not highly related because positive nominations measure popularity, whereas a lack of negative nominations indicates acceptance only. Measuring both scores will give a true indication of neglected students, these being the children who receive no negative or positive nominations (Hops & Lewin, 1984).

The second method, termed *peer ratings*, asks students to rate every member of the class on a likeability scale. These measures give an indication of acceptability or likeability, which is not the same as popularity. Peer ratings can be more sensitive than peer nominations to changes in a student's social status, and they overcome the problem of some students being forgotten or overlooked with a nomination approach (Hops & Lewin, 1984).

The third method is a *paired comparison* procedure in which each student is asked to choose the preferred child out of every possible pair in the class. This is sensitive to reciprocity in relationships, although it is lengthy to administer.

These measures can be adapted for preschool children, for instance by using photographs of classmates instead of written lists of their names in a peer rating scale, and by having the scales administered verbally (Hops & Lewin, 1984).

CONCLUSION: MEASURES OF PEER RELATIONS

Peer relationship measures are quite accurate in identifying rejected children (who receive significant negative nominations) (Asher & Parker, 1989; Asher & Renshaw, 1981; Hops & Lewin, 1984). At the same time, however, they identify many students who do not have a greater risk of later adjustment difficulties. If, on the basis of the measures, particular individuals are targeted for intervention, then some are stigmatised unnecessarily; on the other hand, it would be inefficient to focus on the whole group when not all members need extra skills training.

A second issue is that positive nominations on sociometric measures do not closely reflect students' actual friendships and may instead represent the peers with whom they would wish to play (Hops & Lewin, 1984). Also the measures seldom acknowledge reciprocity of choices, which must form the basis of a friendship.

A third issue is that peer ratings give little information about the specific behaviours that have excited rejection or neglect of particular students (Johnson, Jason & Betts, 1990b) and therefore what skills to include in a social skills program (Kerr & Nelson, 1989). More information can be gained by combining nomination and rating measures to distinguish acceptance from friendship. Children who score low on both measures appear less skilled socially than those low only on the friendship measure, and both are less skilled than students who are high on both measures.

HELPING STUDENTS DEVELOP SOCIAL SKILLS

OPPORTUNITY

Social skills are learnt in a social context. The role of teachers in encouraging students' social skills, therefore, is to provide a context and to give students some freedom and the confidence to practise prosocial skills.

TEACH DEVELOPMENTAL SKILLS

Because children's play centres around doing things, it helps social interaction for the child to have similar abilities to her peers. Thus, young children need the chance to practise physical games, such as ball skills, skipping, hopscotch or whatever active pursuit their peers presently enjoy.

RESPOND TO INAPPROPRIATE BEHAVIOUR

As already stated, the most common reason for children to be rejected is aggression, especially after the ages of seven or eight (Coie et al., 1989). The teacher will need to respond to a student's aggressive and other antisocial behaviours—first, to protect the other students and, second, to protect the aggressor from being shunned by her peers.

SOCIAL SKILLS TRAINING

Training in social skills can be justified by the following reasoning:

1. Children and adults need social skills.
2. Children experiencing peer relations problems are unhappy in the present, and some show adjustment problems as adults.
3. Social competence can be, but is not necessarily, acquired through natural learning.
4. Natural learning can be supplemented by specific training.
5. Children's peer relations improve in response to increased skilfulness (Ladd, 1985; Rose, 1983).
6. Children's peer group acceptance is relatively stable over time (Asher & Parker, 1989; Hill & Hill, 1990) which means that social skill deficits, and aggressive behaviour in particular, are unlikely to disappear spontaneously (Schneider, 1989). Therefore training is not only useful but necessary.

A rationale for social skills training is that students who lack the social skills to form relationships in turn lack the relationships in which to practise social skills. What may have begun merely as a lack of opportunity or a delay in skill acquisition may become a significant problem for the student unless she is given both the opportunity and the guidance to practise social skills.

A second rationale is invoked for students with intellectual disabilities. The key factor affecting their inclusion in regular classes is not their academic level as might be expected, but instead their social skills, including their responsiveness to the classroom procedures that the other students observe (MacMullin, 1988; Salend & Lutz, 1984, in Cole & Chan, 1990). Therefore, where social skills deficits are apparent, training will improve the student's chances of successful inclusion in mainstream schooling.

RATIONALE FOR GROUP TRAINING

Rose (1983) makes the point that students with social skills difficulties cannot be treated individually because of time constraints. Therefore the whole class group can be instructed in social skills. As well as being more cost-effective, group instruction also teaches the skills more effectively. It is more relevant to teach peer relationship skills with the peers with whom the student is relating, group training can help break the ice between group members, gains are more likely to generalise from training sessions to the peer group in natural settings, the group offers a variety of relationships, and group training can incorporate peer tutoring (Rose, 1983).

PROGRAM FOCUS

The type of program offered will depend on whether it is aimed at *preventing* social difficulties before they are displayed, *intervening* with students already displaying a few deficits, or *rehabilitating* students, perhaps with disabilities, whose social skills deficits are pronounced (Rose, 1983).

Students for whom social skills training is most suitable include impulsive or hyperactive children (who need to mediate their impulses and think before they act), and aggressive or destructive students (who need alternative forms of behaviour). Also to benefit are socially withdrawn students who exhibit a low rate of social behaviour, and those who are isolated from (neglected by) or are rejected by their peer group. These groups each lack particular skills and therefore intervention would differ for the various groups (Coie et al., 1989; Dodge, 1985).

GOAL FOR SOCIAL SKILLS TRAINING

Weissberg (1989, p. 335) reports that the goal of social skills training programs is: '. . . to train a combination of behavioral, cognitive, and/or affective skills that will enhance individuals' capacities to interact effectively with others and to handle social tasks adaptively'. The goal implicit in Weissberg's statement is that students will become less isolated and consequently better adjusted. Because some students are rejected because of home background and other features they cannot control, improving their social skills will not necessarily improve their friendship rate, but is still likely to increase their acceptance by the group (Cillessen & Ferguson, 1989). This is still an achievement because while activity partners may not become close friends, they still offer companionship which is valuable in itself (Oden, 1988).

COMPONENTS OF TRAINING

We have established that it is not entirely certain that children who display social skills difficulties lack skills as such: they may have the skills but are not using them because of: their peer group status (Asher & Renshaw, 1981; Cillessen & Ferguson, 1989), external factors such as the lack of a true peer group (Dweck, 1981) or class size (Frosh, 1983), emotional reasons (Dodge, 1985), an inability to process social experiences and information (Oden, 1988), or an inability or unwillingness to enact behavioural options. That is, a student may not have a *skills* deficit but a *performance* deficit (Schneider, 1989). However, without a way as yet to assess the relative importance of each factor, social skills training must address them all. The categories of skills taught will be similar across the age groups, while the actual skill taught will differ according to the students' ages.

TRAINING METHODS

Programs need four components: design, implementation, evaluation and institutionalisation (Weissberg, 1989). This last refers to putting in place practices at the class and school level which support and maintain the skills being taught in the social skills program.

Training methods include (Ladd & Mize, 1983; Rose, 1983):

1. Direct instruction, which involves verbal or modelled instruction about what constitutes social competence and about social goals and behaviours that might meet those goals. This can be teacher-led or can involve group problem solving.
2. Rehearsal (verbal, covert or overt), such as through role-playing.
3. Feedback, which can be self-administered or informative.
4. Reinforcement of appropriate behaviour, which at first may be socially delivered, although can become self-administered.
5. Many opportunities to practise.

No single intervention technique will be suitable for students of all ages. Modelling techniques are most effective with preschoolers, while the more complex packages using a variety of techniques are more suited to older students (Schneider, 1989). Nevertheless, researchers (such as

Gesten et al., 1979) recommend using little direct instruction and offering maximum opportunities for students of all ages to participate actively in the learning process.

PRESCHOOL AND RECEPTION-AGED CHILDREN

Early childhood is an ideal time to intervene with social difficulties, for three reasons. First, social skills naturally receive considerable attention during the preschool years (Mize & Ladd, 1990). Second, the flexibility of young children and the repetitive nature of directions by teachers or care workers make preschoolers responsive to adult direction (Swetnam et al., 1983). Third, intervention during the early years avoids a child's difficulties becoming entrenched and leading to rejection which in turn aggravates the child's social skill deficits (Mize & Ladd, 1990; Swetnam et al., 1983).

Care or teaching staff can use the child's numerous social interactions to shape her social skills, which are reinforced by the responses of her playmates. While a remedial program may not be necessary at young ages, the teacher can intervene with the whole group through structuring the environment to foster appropriate interaction skills, through informal or incidental teaching, and by providing cooperative games (see chapter 10).

Formal training involves similar methods as for older ages, such as explanation of the principles of social interaction and generation of social goals, coaching in translating these goals into effective action, and monitoring that the action worked (Mize & Ladd, 1990). The skills to be taught include entry and sustaining skills. (For an example, see Kohler & Strain, 1993.)

Whom to target for intervention during the preschool years is an issue, since neglect at this age may not lead to later adjustment problems and aggressive-rejected children may lack skills or may simply find that aggression works and so are not motivated to change their behaviour (Mize & Ladd, 1990).

Naturally, very young children have some cognitive limitations compared with older students. They may be more difficult to engage in training, they do not filter out distractions as automatically as older children (Mize & Ladd, 1990), and they do not respond as well as older children to self-instruction and other cognitive approaches (Finch & Hops, 1983). In addition, special provisions to foster generalisation may be necessary at the younger ages (Swetnam et al., 1983)—for instance, fading out instructor support and helping the child develop self-efficacy (Mize & Ladd, 1990). These limitations can be eased with adult guidance and appropriate task structure—for example, by teaching skills during sociodramatic play and extending rehearsals to contexts that are as near to real life as possible (Mize & Ladd, 1990).

PRIMARY SCHOOL STUDENTS

One single-term program for primary school students (MacMullin et al., 1992) involves a social problem-solving approach. This program offers a similar curriculum to that described by Gesten et al. (1979) and begins by discussing *feelings*, since interpersonal problems frequently excite strong emotions. First, the students identify their own array of feelings, and then reflect on how to identify another child's feelings by looking, listening and asking. The next units address *interpersonal problems*, with the goal of teaching children to solve problems. Role plays and other activities allow students to generate solutions to social problems and to evaluate their consequences.

A second, full-year, primary school program includes a wider range of interpersonal skills (McGrath & Francey, 1991). These include playing games well (including being fair, and winning and losing gracefully), being positive (about yourself, other people and experiences), taking risks, cooperating, being interesting, and standing up for yourself. Skill mastery (that is, competence) is promoted by having the teacher and group generate a rationale for learning each skill, examining how to perform the skill, and practising it. The second part of the program involves setting up a positive classroom with class meetings, rules and procedures for solving problems. The self-esteem of students is also addressed.

Petersen and Ganoni (1989) also predicate their 'Stop Think Do' program on good communication skills between students and the teacher, followed by separate training programs for primary and secondary students. As the program's title implies, social problem solving comprises the steps: stop, think, do, with the issues addressed being similar to the MacMullin et al. (1992) program. The key differences between the 'Stop, Think, Do' programs for primary versus secondary students are the activities used and the degree of sophistication of the social tasks. The program also incorporates a teacher training component whose theory base for the behaviour management section is neo-Adlerian (see chapter 5) in its identification of the goals of student behaviour.

Bash and Camp (1986) used Meichenbaum and Goodman's steps (see chapter 4) for teaching primary school students to think through the steps involved in solving problems. Soon after they become familiar with these steps for academic tasks, they are instructed in consequential thinking and then both sets of skills are applied to social problems.

SECONDARY SCHOOL STUDENTS

Even if earlier training is successful at preventing social skills problems during the primary school years, the personal and relationship changes that occur during adolescence (Bloom, 1990) can provoke new challenges which the individual may struggle to deal with appropriately. At the same time, however, adolescents have increased ability to learn new coping responses, and therefore skills training in these years is useful (Johnson et al., 1990b).

Social skills in adolescents fall into five categories: scholastic competence (as this affects social acceptance), behaviour, peer acceptance, friendships and romantic appeal (Johnson et al., 1990b). All high school students—not just those experiencing social difficulties—can be taught these skills. Social problems may be prevented at a school-wide level by encouraging student participation in the organisation of the school and by establishing buddy systems, class discussions, peer tutoring programs and cooperative study groups for all high school students (Johnson et al., 1990b). These can prevent problems by helping adolescents feel less alone, and can increase their motivation to participate in skills training sessions since they are more open to trusting each other. Adolescents can also have more influence on each other than adults can (Caplan & Weissberg, 1989; Schneider, 1989).

Less proactively, only those students displaying social difficulties might be targeted for intervention. Two types of social difficulties have been identified in adolescents: the individual's interpersonal style that might provoke acceptance or rejection, and her problem-solving skills that may result in poor resolution of social problems (Johnson et al., 1990b). These problems may be evidenced in three behaviour patterns: aggression, withdrawal and immaturity (Goldstein et al., 1986). These three patterns of behaviour are characterised by the presence of antisocial behaviours and the absence of particular prosocial skills, with the clusters of skills needed to be trained being different for the three groups.

Targeted programs for adolescents have comprised training in *social task* skills such as establishing relationships with same- and opposite-gender peers, resisting peer pressure to take dangerous risks, responding to teacher expectations, gaining independence from adult authority, and giving and receiving both positive and negative feedback. A second component comprises skills for dealing with *feelings*, such as anger, frustration, stress, embarrassment, responding to success and failure, and dealing with provocation. A third component is self-management or *planning* skills, such as goal setting, gathering information, making decisions about alternative behaviours, problem-solving and negotiating skills (Caplan & Weissberg, 1989; Goldstein et al., 1986; LeCroy, 1983).

Improving the social skills of adolescents does not necessarily lead to reduced antisocial behaviour (Johnson et al., 1990b). If social skills training is to be effective with adolescents, the participants themselves must choose their goals, rather than having them selected by teachers and other adults (LeCroy, 1983). Their own belief systems must be tapped into and their ability to handle emotions such as frustration and anxiety must be addressed (Caplan & Weissberg, 1989). Adolescents' self-esteem may be fragile, so it will be crucial to improve their self-concept and acknowledge their successes. They need repeated practice and a school environment that promotes the display of prosocial skills, plus inclusion of social skills in other curricular areas (Johnson et al., 1990b).

Designing programs for this age group is made difficult by the group's social diversity. A year or two's difference in development which in earlier ages could be accommodated in social settings makes for both qualitative and quantitative differences in adolescents' social skills. Programs must be tailored to individual needs (Goldstein et al., 1986) and yet this is difficult in secondary schools. Subject based instruction leaves little time for nonacademic activities and makes it difficult to nominate one teacher or one subject area that should be responsible for social skills training. This difficulty is exacerbated by the fact that the changing needs of individuals throughout the adolescent period mean that programs must be maintained and topped up throughout secondary school, rather than being a one-off course (Caplan & Weissberg, 1989).

ISSUES FOR SOCIAL SKILLS TRAINING

Generalisation

Generalisation of skills is not guaranteed. Social competence is complex, and requires sophisticated decision making and problem solving. These affect the individual's ability to transfer skills taught in sessions to less structured social occasions. Generalisation is likely to be improved when the target behaviours are functional, when training uses a variety of methods (prompting, feedback and reinforcement) and when the program lasts for some months (Chandler, Lubeck & Fowler, 1992). It is also important for teachers to incorporate the social skills concepts throughout their teaching methodology and in other curriculum areas, not just in the social skills training sessions. The social skills package must not become an insulated part of the curriculum to which little reference is made outside the lesson time.

Competence versus skill

Individuals need to discriminate the appropriate setting in which to display a particular social skill. This discrimination ability distinguishes social skill from social competence. It is easier to teach skills than it is to impart competence, however.

Emotional variables need addressing

Direct instruction approaches are based on the assumption that a student not displaying a given social skill does not possess it. Instead, as already mentioned, she may possess it but is unwilling to use it. In this instance, more instruction in specific skills will not help: motivation and self-efficacy will need addressing. Goldstein et al. (1986) believe that motivation unfolds with the development of the teacher–student relationship, with selecting relevant skills to target for training, and when training sessions are held at times and places that suit the students. Supportive and accepting group dynamics would also foster participation.

Environmental assessment

The context may not provide appropriate opportunities for enacting social skills. The environment needs to be arranged so that prosocial interaction with peers serves a purpose. Cooperative teaching and peer tutoring may assist this. Another important factor is that the environment may not be a safe place for making mistakes (Bye & Jussim, 1993). For these reasons, the environment needs assessing, in addition to deficits within individuals being identified.

Training the trainer

The teacher's philosophy may need to change if he is to carry out social skills training packages. His *interpersonal* skills must enable him to deal with students' feelings, to observe and listen within a sound knowledge base of child and adolescent development and to give feedback sensi- tively (Goldstein et al., 1986). His *teaching methods* must allow students to discover their own answers to social dilemmas, rather than giving them the right response. The teacher will need to withhold judgment of students' work, instead allowing them to evaluate themselves. He will also need to tolerate noise as a sign of constructive activity (Bash & Camp, 1986), be willing to use little verbal instruction in favour of more interactive teaching methods (Schneider, 1989), and he must have the confidence to initiate and sustain activities such as role-playing (Goldstein et al., 1986). Finally, the teacher's *thinking processes* may need refining. Like his students, the teacher needs to emphasise the process rather than the end product, to generate and accept alternative solutions, and predict obstacles and generate several possible ways to overcome them (Bash & Camp, 1986).

One program that prepares teachers for offering social skills training to students is Bash and Camp's teacher training program (1986) which aims to enhance the teacher attributes just listed.

EFFICACY OF SOCIAL SKILLS TRAINING

Most authors (including Asher & Renshaw, 1981; Schneider, 1989) report many short-term benefits of social skills training, especially in the cognitive and motor aspects of social skills, with less reliable data about long-term effectiveness. The most effective training programs have taught students to link their actions with their social outcomes, which directly impacts on the students' perception of control (Dweck, 1981). Other writers (for instance, Hops & Lewin, 1984) observe that programs may be successful with the majority of the class but less successful with the most socially at risk students. Some of the lack of success may be due to an error in assuming that students who display inappropriate skills lack more prosocial alternatives. If they already know the skill, then teaching it to them again could be expected to produce limited change. Also, more information is needed about which aspects of social skills should be included in training programs for particular groups of students.

BULLYING

Tattum (1993a, p. 3) does not mince words when he calls bullying 'the most malicious and malevolent form of antisocial behaviour practised in our schools'. Bullying occurs in most schools and, while prevalent throughout the history of schooling, has until recently received only minimal attention. This may be because victims usually keep quiet about it and, because the bullying occurs in private, it can go undetected (Smith & Sharp, 1994; Tattum, 1993a). Tattum, however, says that it is crucial to intervene with school bullying, since ignoring it does not make it go away and, despite views to the contrary, it is not inevitable and it does not teach children to look after themselves.

While some intervention is directed at the individuals involved, bullying is a complex problem that is embedded in systems (family, classroom and school) that inadvertently model, maintain and reinforce domination and intimidation (Pepler et al., 1993; Tattum, 1993c), and therefore, any intervention needs to address the wider context. An instance of the importance of social mores is the sexual harassment of female students and teachers, arising from boys being taught to be competitive, dominant, forceful, tough, uncaring about others, ambitious and opposite to females (Tattum, 1993c).

DESCRIPTION OF BULLYING

Definition

Bullying is a subtype of aggressive behaviour, comprising an unjustified and deliberate intent to inflict hurt by repeatedly taking advantage of one's own superior physical or psychological strength (Slee & Rigby, 1994; Slee, 1995a, 1995b). It is the systematic (deliberate, planned and repeated) abuse of power (Smith & Sharp, 1994). The use of the word *repeated* in this definition signals that the duration of the bullying influences its cumulative effects on the victim. Bullying can range in duration from a few days to many months (Slee & Rigby, 1994; Slee, 1995a), with longer durations being typical for upper primary students (Slee, 1995b).

Types of bullying

Bullying comprises direct physical attacks; direct verbal attacks such as taunting; extortion; and indirect methods such as spreading vicious rumours or excluding someone from the social group (Smith & Sharp, 1994; Tattum, 1993a). Sexual harassment as a form of bullying involves verbal comments (which is the most common form in single-sex girls' schools), physical touch and visual harassment such as using pornography or defacing school posters of women to embarrass or intimidate girls (Drouet, 1993). Girls may be required to perform favours (not necessarily sexual) at the threat of rumours affecting their sexual reputation being circulated, and they may feel obliged to avoid areas in which males congregate.

Half of bullying occurs in a one-to-one relationship and half involves a larger group (Smith & Sharp, 1994). This gives rise to Pikas's assertion that the word *bullying* should be replaced with *mobbing* to emphasise the group dynamics involved in many instances (Roland, 1993).

Prevalence

Bullying can occur in any social group, although groups comprising members with large differences in status and who receive low supervision are particularly susceptible to bullying. At least 10% of students at any one time are subject to bullying, around 5% of students are bullies and around 6% are both bully and victim, with over one-third of students reporting that they feel unsafe because of bullying (Slee, 1994b; Smith & Sharp, 1994; Tattum, 1993a). Half of all school students may be subjected to bullying during their school life (Pepler et al., 1993). Bullying is most prevalent in the middle years of primary school (Slee, 1994b) and peaks again in the first two years of high school (Slee, 1994a). Students with disabilities and members of minority racial groups are especially vulnerable to being bullied (Smith & Sharp, 1994; Whitney, Smith & Thompson, 1994; Tattum, 1993a).

Sex differences

Sex differences in the prevalence of bullying are not large, although teachers and peers usually under-identify girls as victims (Cowie & Sharp, 1994). Male bullies may be more directly aggressive while girls employ less direct approaches such as exclusion from the peer group (Slee, 1995b), which may make girls' bullying less easy to detect (Smith & Sharp, 1994). It is nonetheless intense and distressing to its victims (Slee, 1994b). There is a higher incidence of bullying in single-sex schools, although as might be expected, there is a higher incidence of sexual harassment, another form of bullying, in co-educational schools (Rigby, 1993).

EFFECTS OF BULLYING

Continued or severe bullying leads to unhappiness at the time as well as long-term adjustment problems (Smith & Sharp, 1994). Bullying can compound the violence that students suffer at home (House of Representatives Standing Committee on Employment, Education and Training, 1994). It causes absenteeism from school, psychosomatic health complaints, impaired capacity to relate to others, low self-esteem—although low self-esteem may also occasion bullying (Slee & Rigby, 1994)—depressive tendencies, and feelings of isolation, unhappiness and loneliness in victims (Slee & Rigby, 1994; Slee, 1995a). It can lead to peer rejection and low peer acceptance during school, and to poor self-esteem and depressive tendencies as adults (Smith & Sharp, 1994). As might be expected, the victim becomes intimidated and lacks confidence and so is unlikely to report the abuse. At the same time, the victim's learning suffers.

The bullies themselves, contrary to myth, are usually outgoing and confident, with little anxiety or remorse owing to a lack of empathy for others. They are impulsive and they believe in dominance and in being violent to gain status (Smith & Sharp, 1994; Tattum, 1993a). They may lack social skills, although many are socially skilful and are choosing not to use their skills prosocially, so social skills training is not useful for them. There are links between persistent school bullying and later delinquency (Smith & Sharp, 1994; Tattum, 1993c), and between bullying and aggression towards teachers, school property and siblings (Tattum, 1993a).

The third group affected is peers. Some collaborate with the bullying because of group pressure or to avoid becoming victims themselves, while peers who are not involved but who observe bullying experience distress and anxiety (Pepler et al., 1993).

ROLE OF THE SCHOOL

Whole-school policy

A core intervention with bullying is to create a whole-school policy on bullying as part of an overall policy about aggression and discipline (Roland, 1993; Sharp & Thompson, 1994). This involves both statements of philosophy and enunciation of procedures for intervening with bullying. It needs to be established through consultation with staff at all levels of the school, and with students and their parents. Those schools that engage in the widest consultation in developing policy show greatest improvement in bullying (Sharp & Thompson, 1994). Parent support for policy and action is crucial, as is support for the school from consultants (Smith & Sharp, 1994).

In its attempts to reduce bullying, the school philosophy can address student behaviour at two levels. At the first level is an attitude to student welfare and general behaviour. This may comprise establishing a warm, positive school environment that de-emphasises competition and maximises cooperation, setting limits on unacceptable behaviour and enacting nonhostile sanctions when these limits are violated (Smith & Sharp, 1994; Tattum, 1993b). At the second level, the school policy can address bullying directly. The policy needs to describe a moral climate in which bullying is not tolerated, so that uninvolved students can support those being bullied (Smith & Sharp, 1994).

Slee and Rigby (1994) propose an anti-bullying program for schools which they describe by the acronym PEACE:

P   is for a school *policy* against bullying that is part of the school policy on behaviour management in general. It includes a philosophy statement and clear grievance procedures.
E   stands for *education* about what is meant by bullying and how to enact the policy at all levels of the school.
A   means *action* at all levels, involving close supervision in the yard, class discussions, and individual talks with bullies and victims, backed up with clear sanctions that the students play a part in determining.
C   stands for helping victims and bullies *cope* with their difficulties, which may for instance include a social skills training program.
E   stands for *evaluation* of the effectiveness of the program, with adaptation to policy and procedures carried out accordingly.

Curricula

When the school includes issues of bullying in its overall curricula, changes are most marked and long lasting (Cowie & Sharp, 1994). Just as with policy, curricular issues can be addressed at two levels. The first is the preventive approach of enhancing cooperative learning with its focus on shared goals, empathy, acceptance of others and collaborative problem solving (Cowie & Sharp, 1994). The second level is direct intervention by including antibullying issues within traditional subject areas. Drama, role-playing, videos and general discourses about bullying can be included within many subjects. Discussion needs to focus both on the content and on the affective aspects of bullying and being bullied (Tattum, 1993b) and on how it affects both individuals and the group (Herbert, 1993). While the content of lessons is important to prevent and address bullying, the interpersonal processes between teachers and students and among the students are also crucial (Roland, 1993).

Staff training

The school will need a commitment to providing ongoing inservice staff training on discipline in general and bullying in particular. Preservice teacher training courses give inadequate preparation and single, one-off workshops for teachers are insufficient (House of Representatives Standing Committee on Employment, Education and Training, 1994).

Increased supervision

Most bullying in schools occurs in playgrounds, which may be due to the low levels of supervision there compared with other areas of the school (Boulton, 1994). One disturbing feature of bullying is the perception by a quarter of students that teachers seldom act to protect them from bullying (Slee, 1994a), so intervention with aggressive behaviour is necessary for students to feel physically and emotionally safe at school. Since it is unlikely that more supervisors will be appointed to playground duty, then supervisors need to be more effective (Boulton, 1994). This requires training in detecting and then responding to bullying. Detection includes the ability to discriminate aggression from normal rough and tumble play, and real from mock aggression (Boulton, 1994), as well as the ability to identify sexual harassment as a form of bullying (Drouet, 1993). Teachers would also benefit from differentiating between idle tale-telling and reports of aggression (Tattum, 1993a).

As a preventive approach, teachers may organise cooperative play activities that give students something prosocial to do, or they might join in the children's games, while enriching the playground can also help avoid antisocial play (Boulton, 1994; Whitney et al., 1994).

Mobilising peers

Targeting bystanders is crucial in the light of reports that almost half of students report that they would not come to the aid of a victim (Pepler et al., 1993; Slee & Rigby, 1994) which, we must also remember, means that half would (Rigby & Slee, 1993). While older children (aged eight to fifteen years) have an increased capacity for empathy, they are also subjected to greater normative pressures and so are more likely to reject victims and to condone bullying (Rigby & Slee, 1993). The teacher can capitalise on the empathy of the majority of students to impart the belief that bullying is everyone's responsibility and that bullies are not to be admired (Boulton, 1994). The aim of such discussions is to encourage those not involved to help victims, and to discourage peers from joining in the bullying (Pepler et al., 1993).

Direct intervention

Victims are frequently advised either to ignore the bullying, or to stand up for themselves, although without being given any specific information about how to do so (Sharp & Cowie, 1994). Ignoring does not reduce the recurrence of the bullying and is likely to make its victim feel powerless. Therefore, teachers will need to take action but at the same time will need to avoid the temptation to meet bullying with aggression since this will reinforce dominance (Boulton, 1994). They need to employ a hierarchy of sanctions which bullies accept as reasonable; otherwise they may exact revenge on their victim. Alternatives to punishment can include collaborative problem solving and training victims to use a range of assertive messages (as long as being assertive does not put them at risk of physical harm), counselling the bullies to enable them to stop their behaviour, and mediating between the victim and bully (Sharp & Cowie, 1994). Mediation between bully and victim involves defining the problem, how the victim feels about it, what she would like to happen, and what could be done (Sharp & Cowie, 1994).

At younger ages (below nine years), and for individual rather than gang bullying, the teacher might simply tell the bully to stop (Smith, Cowie & Sharp, 1994). For students over the age of nine, and those bullying in gangs, some recommend Pikas's method of shared concern or Maines and Robinson's non-blame approach (Smith et al., 1994; Tattum, 1993b). These approaches are built on the concept that some members of the gang go along with the bullying because of peer pressure and because diffusion of responsibility allows them to evade awareness of their part in causing the victim's distress. The steps involved in the two methods differ in their sequence although, in essence, the teacher listens to the victim, and conveys these feelings to the bullies, either individually or as a group. The teacher describes nonjudgmentally that the victim is in a bad situation, without accusing the bullies or asking for an admission of guilt. Each student is invited to participate in finding a solution and is asked for a commitment to the agreed option. A follow-up meeting checks whether the solution is working. A group meeting could be extended to include a discussion of bullying in general, so that the group does not switch its bullying to another victim.

Schools will need a commitment to the shared concern method so that teacher time is allocated for this purpose. This commitment is best reflected in the method's inclusion in the school bullying policy.

It is useful to collaborate with parents also (Roland, 1993; Smith et al., 1994), although they too may need to be counselled not to punish the bullies. Coordination with the community and social service agencies (including the police) is also crucial (House of Representatives Standing Committee on Employment, Education and Training, 1994).

SUMMARY

Friendships have many benefits, including the obvious salve against loneliness. Children who are isolated do not partake of the benefits of friendships and so are at risk of unhappiness in the present and later adjustment difficulties (although we must remember that this link is not necessarily causal). It has been postulated that isolated children lack the social skills for forming close relationships and, while this may not always be so, feeling neglected or rejected is likely to lower their confidence in the skills they do possess.

Social competence is more than mere knowledge of skills. It requires insight into the right time and place to use a skill, based on awareness of the social context and the needs of others. Therefore, social skills training requires more than instruction in a wider repertoire of behaviours: it involves enhancing emotional and cognitive skills as well. Training methods differ for students of different ages, although in the main they involve instruction, rehearsal, feedback, reinforcement of appropriate behaviour, and repeated opportunities to practise social skills.

The teacher also has a responsibility to modify the demands of the social environment to maximise the chances of social success for students. This includes giving students opportunity, skills and reason to interact prosocially, as well as satisfying their emotional and academic needs so that frustration of these does not lead to antisocial behaviour.

DISCUSSION QUESTIONS

1. From the list given in this chapter, what in your view is the most crucial benefit that friendships provide for children?
2. Why isn't it possible to argue that rejection as a child causes adult maladjustment?
3. Think about schools in which you have taught or that you attended as a student. In what ways does their wider environment shape the social skills of their students?

4. Think about students in the age group you teach. With which social tasks do they have the most difficulty?
5. How could impulsive students be instructed in social-cognitive problem-solving skills? Which aspect (emotional, cognitive, behavioural, or environmental) would you expect to be the most crucial for changing their social behaviour?
6. With which measures of social skills deficits are you familiar? Which seemed (or do you expect to be) the most useful to you as a teacher?
7. How could you go about teaching a social skills program to students in the age group in which you specialise?
8. What steps might you follow to institute an antibullying program in a school?

SUGGESTIONS FOR FURTHER READING

For discussion of issues of social skills training:

Cartledge, G. and Milburn, J.F. (eds) 1986, *Teaching social skills to children: innovative approaches*, 2nd edn, Pergamon, New York

For programs for social skill training in schools:

MacMullin, C., Aistrope, D., Brown, J.L., Hannaford, D., and Martin, M. 1992, *The Sheidow Park social problem solving program*, Flinders University, Adelaide

McGrath, H. and Francey, S. 1991, *Friendly kids: friendly classrooms*, Longman Cheshire, Melbourne

Petersen, L. and Ganoni, A. 1989, *Teacher's manual for training social skills while managing student behaviour*, ACER, Melbourne.

For descriptions of cooperative games in early childhood settings:

Sapon-Shevin, M. 1986, 'Teaching cooperation', *Teaching social skills to children: innovative approaches*, 2nd edn, G. Cartledge & J.F. Milburn (eds), Pergamon, New York

For cooperative activities for all age groups:

Orlick, T. 1982, *The second cooperative sports and games book*, Pantheon, New York

For details of school approaches to bullying:

Rigby, K. and Slee, P. 1992, *Bullying in schools: a video with instructional manual*, Institute of Social Research, University of South Australia, Adelaide

Sharp, S. and Smith, P.K. (eds) 1994, *Tackling bullying in your school: a practical handbook for teachers*, Routledge, London

13

DEVELOPING A SCHOOL
DISCIPLINE POLICY

Where members of a school community have worked together to develop their policy, we have observed that parents, teachers and students have a much better understanding of the school rules; parents have confidence that the school has a positive sense of direction; teachers know they have the consistent backing of other staff in handling students; there is more cooperation among the students themselves and a greater sense of responsibility. (Cowin, Freeman, Farmer, James, Drent & Arthur, 1990, p. xiii)

KEY POINTS

- *A school discipline policy provides accountability for students and parents, and it offers staff documented support for their actions.*

- *The policy will take into account departmental policy, the school's own philosophy on student welfare, discipline and teacher satisfaction, its goals and how it aims to achieve those goals.*

- *The practical aspects of the policy will comprise the school rules and procedures to enforce the rules.*

- *Administrative structures to support these policy dimensions will include student and parent participation in policy construction and refinement.*

- *Special procedures—such as using consultants and responding to suspected child abuse or bullying—will also be enunciated in the comprehensive policy.*

- *A method for reviewing the policy will be detailed.*

- *Policy development can follow a series of steps, with wide consultation at each stage to promote widest acceptance of the final policy statement.*

INTRODUCTION

A school-wide policy on discipline expresses how school members are expected to behave towards each other so that they can work productively together (Cowin et al., 1990). It offers students, teachers and parents safeguards and clear expectations of their roles, rights and responsibilities.

The policy document will need to reflect the philosophy and policy of the employing body—namely, the Education Department or the board of an independent school. The policy will comprise statements about: the school's philosophy, its goals, how to achieve its goals, school rules, procedures to enforce rules, policy on parent involvement and procedures for evaluating the effectiveness of policy and procedures. It may also address special issues such as child abuse, harassment and bullying.

SCHOOL PHILOSOPHY

Discipline is a process for helping students to learn and to gain personal skills: it is not an end in itself (Jones & Jones, 1995). Therefore, a policy statement about student behaviour will include more than a direct focus on intervening with disruptive behaviour. Rather, it can encompass three aspects: student discipline, student welfare, and teachers' job satisfaction. The Education Department of South Australia—now titled the Department for Education and Children's Services—(1989) enunciates the following underlying principles:

- Schools must be safe, caring, orderly learning environments in which the rights of all students to learn and all teachers to teach are supported and protected.
- Schools will be oriented to success, giving students support and opportunities to experience academic, social and physical success.
- Schools will develop a partnership between staff, students and their families in order to establish expectations and consequences related to student behaviour.

DISCIPLINE

The purpose of discipline will be enunciated. Definitions of responsible behaviour will be developed, in the context of society's democratic values and the policy of the employer. The managerial and three educational functions of discipline will need to be considered as potential aims for the school.

STUDENT WELFARE

The whole school environment should be conducive to appropriate behaviour, rather than individual breaches being focused upon exclusively. Bill Rogers (1989) says the policy must intentionally aim to minimise embarrassment and hostility, maximise students' choices about their behaviour, develop and maintain respect, maintain a sense of humour, and ensure follow-up and follow-through.

With the aim of promoting students' emotional welfare and preventing behavioural difficulties, the policy might include the following statements (Edwards, 1993; Gurney, 1988):

- The school will provide a caring community that supports both students and teachers.
- It will provide a sound pastoral care system. This may comprise methods for integrating new students into the school to enable them to develop friendships, to become familiar with procedures and expectations, and to get academic help as required (Jones & Jones, 1995).
- The school will foster cooperation between students and encourage students to help each other.
- The school will be committed to the responsible and self-directed behaviour of all students—that is, it will provide for student autonomy.
- Students will be taught how to evaluate their own learning and behaviour.
- Teachers will develop warm, yet professional, relationships with students.
- Rules will correspond to the instructional program.
- Rules and procedures will help students achieve consistency between their intentions and their behaviour.
- The school will maintain respectful, ongoing and positive contact with parents.
- It will offer a wide range of extracurricular activities.
- Its organisational structure will not intrude abrasively on students and staff.
- Students and staff will be protected from the abuse of power from above (Knight, 1991) and from other students (as in bullying).
- The school will be accountable to its consumers (Knight, 1991).

TEACHER SATISFACTION

As well as meeting student needs, a school policy must establish a system for meeting teachers' needs (Good & Brophy, 1986; McCaslin & Good, 1992). These needs fall into two areas: possessing the skill to motivate and manage students so that teachers experience success and job satisfaction, and receiving personal and professional support (Jones & Jones, 1995).

Teacher skill

Staff need to understand the range of theories available for the effective management of student behaviour and need opportunities and support to use the skills recommended by these theories.

Professional support

Bill Rogers (1990) observes that teachers are isolated within a sea of children for most of their day, and so it is important that they can add to their personal resources by seeking support from colleagues in planning programs and sharing ideas and work. While decreasing teacher stress and feelings of isolation, regular meetings with peers give teachers an increased sense of professionalism, Rogers contends. This support should be seen to be normative, rather than being a favour to a teacher who is experiencing difficulties (Rogers, 1994). It will involve emotional or moral support, structural help (such as releasing the teacher to work with a difficult student individually) and problem-solving help (such as in team planning meetings). These are built on a recognition that behaviour problems need a team approach, rather than isolating a teacher who is having problems.

Other resources needed for teachers to maintain their professional skills include inservice opportunities and consultation with specialists about classroom management and approaches for dealing with particular behaviours (Jones & Jones, 1995).

SCHOOL GOALS

Enunciating goals requires awareness of sound educational theory and principle (Knight, 1991). A school discipline policy will express the aim of fostering a well-disciplined school in which teachers can work and students can learn. This will produce a working definition of personal and social development in schools (Herbert, 1993). This larger goal may be achieved through subgoals such as the following (Wayson et al., 1982, in Cowin et al., 1990):

- To improve the way in which people in the school work together to solve problems. Having a positive attitude to problems will prevent disruptive behaviour.
- To develop rules and disciplinary procedures that will promote self-discipline.

- To improve curriculum and instructional practices in order to reach more students.
- To deal with personal problems that affect life within the school. This can uncover the cause of behaviour problems, or can relieve stress on staff and students, enabling more effective participation in learning and teaching.
- To improve the physical facilities and organisational structure of the school to reinforce its other goals. A school environment which is pleasant, conducive to the tasks being carried out there, and sensitive to the culture and values of its students, will promote appropriate behaviour.

STATEMENT ABOUT HOW TO ACHIEVE GOALS

The policy will detail positive programs the school will adopt to achieve these goals. It should describe the responsibilities of students, teachers and administrators. This will include describing who is responsible for acting in particular situations, what the procedure will be, and what school and other resources can be called on to support the action that is taken.

SCHOOL RULES

The policy statement will contain clear school rules that are communicated systematically to students, parents and staff. It cannot be assumed that everyone will naturally understand these. Rules will have one of four purposes, as discussed in chapter 10—namely, to maximise learning, ensure safety, prevent disruption of others, and maintain courtesy (Cangelosi, 1993). The humanists simplify this list by upholding rules that safeguard anyone's rights (Gordon, 1991; Knight, 1991).

The school discipline policy should avoid unnecessary rules. At the school-wide level, the list of rules may include only those behaviours prohibited at school, such as drug use. It is likely that this brief set of mandatory rules will be imposed on students without negotiation, while the policy may direct teachers to formulate classroom rules in collaboration with the students.

PROCEDURES TO ENFORCE RULES

Procedures provide a framework in which systematic action can be taken. Procedures will focus on how the school and teaching can be organised so that most behaviour difficulties are prevented and those that do occur receive a constructive response (Cowin et al., 1990). They must give attention to both prevention and intervention, and must offer some guidance on the ethical issues surrounding interventions. A formal policy has the advantages of ensuring some consistency between teachers while ideally still allowing them some autonomy (Cangelosi, 1993; Good & Brophy, 1986).

PREVENTION

Because chronic behaviour difficulties have serious consequences for students, teachers must avoid exacerbating problems and instead give responsible behaviour far greater attention than infractions of the rules. Appropriate behaviour may abate if it is insufficiently acknowledged. Also, as we have seen in part 2 of this text, the teacher needs to be a skilful communicator to avoid provoking or escalating problems.

The preventive statement will focus on establishing a positive school climate and enacting positive consequences for responsible behaviour.

INTERVENTION

Irresponsible behaviour requires a response which protects the rights of students to learn, supports the rights of teachers to teach and offers the student involved a chance to learn how to make a more responsible choice in the future. Therefore, a policy should include a clear statement about consequences for infringing school rules. These procedures need to ensure consistent, fair (nonarbitrary) and nonpunitive responses to behaviour that is disruptive or which violates a prior agreement. While ensuring that the student takes responsibility for his actions, it is also important that he be granted due process (Knight, 1991). By due process, Knight means not being abused by those in power, being presumed innocent until proven guilty, and being permitted to state his side of events.

There must be a progressive or graded response to misdemeanours. The first intervention will involve the teacher's adjusting the instructional program and implementing classroom management approaches that reduce disruptiveness and increase motivation. This step is based on addressing the cause, rather than the expression, of discipline problems and is directed at the whole class (Cowin et al., 1990).

The next interventive step would involve teachers handling discipline problems themselves, in a one-to-one intervention with the student concerned.

At the last stage of intervention the teacher will consult senior school staff, the student's parents and specialists both from within the school and from outside it to formulate a suitable response to the student's behaviour.

STUDENT PARTICIPATION

Students will be empowered to participate in school decision making about their behaviour and learning. Their rights and responsibilities will be specified, including affording students due process (Knight, 1991) and channels of appeal against what they may perceive to be injustices.

PARENT INVOLVEMENT

A partnership between staff, students and their families is necessary for successfully developing the responsible behaviour of students and advancing their academic achievement. A strong cooperative bond between school and home promotes parental support of the school and reduces the likelihood of parents and teachers undermining each other's efforts. Moreover, students may not be convinced to change their behaviour unless they see that their teachers and parents are working in partnership together (Grossman, 1995).

The policy should include a systematic procedure for involving parents in academic and behavioural issues (both positive and negative). At its most basic, the policy tells the community about the school's aims, and what the community can expect of the school. More than this, though, the policy may specify procedures for making three types of contact with parents: early introductions, ongoing routine communication, and problem-solving meetings. The early contacts provide a positive basis for later routine or problem-focused meetings (Jones & Jones, 1995; Simpson, 1990). Some guidance might be offered about providing positive information while also not hiding a student's real behavioural or academic difficulties, since frank diagnosis followed by a plan for intervening shows more compassion for parents than obscuring their child's problem. The policy may convey an expectation that verbal communication will be followed up in writing, especially for sensitive material such as when conveying a diagnosis of a student's learning or other difficulties (Turnbull & Turnbull, 1990).

REFERRAL TO CONSULTANTS

It would be useful to include in the policy a statement about how the school can use consultants, how and to whom to refer students for help, and in which circumstances a student might be referred. Child abuse creates the necessity for such referrals; teachers will be empowered to refer other academic and behavioural issues best dealt with by specialists if they have clear procedures for doing so and if the procedures are uncluttered by bureaucracy.

SPECIAL ISSUES

It may be useful for the school policy to mention specific issues such as bullying (see chapter 12), sexual harassment procedures, and child abuse. Teachers are legally obliged to report any suspicions of child abuse to the local child welfare agency. Advising parents of this obligation and detailing issues surrounding child abuse may raise awareness of the issue, which in turn may prevent some abuse, or at least can set a foundation for some constructive intervention by school staff if abuse is suspected.

EVALUATION

Evaluation of the policy is necessary for assessing its effects. The criteria for evaluating the policy will be specified and may include such measures as the number of student absentees or referrals for disciplinary intervention, record of negative consequences, location of most behaviour problems (the class, school grounds, toilets, for example) and the source of most referrals.

The policy also needs to mention how it can be adapted to meet individual circumstances.

COMMUNITY CONSULTATION

When writing a school policy, consultation within and outside the school aims to reduce authority and status differences among all persons in the school, and so increase all members' sense of belonging to the school. It aims to ensure that each school member will be committed to acting responsibly and dealing with behavioural issues. As the opening quote to this chapter reported, when the school formulates its policy in consultation with parents and students, they have a better understanding of and increased confidence in the school rules, and at the same time teachers have confidence in parental support when consequences for infractions must be invoked (Cowin et al., 1990).

STEPS FOR POLICY DEVELOPMENT

The following steps for developing a policy were suggested by Cowin et al. (1990).

PHASE A: DECIDING WHETHER TO START

The first step of this phase is to examine whether discipline is a current issue for the school community, what resources may be necessary for reviewing the policy, and, having created interest in the issue, making a decision whether to review current policy. A decision not to go ahead at this time may be due to the adequate functioning of the present policy, a lack of resources for conducting the review, or the timing may be wrong (for instance, being towards the end of a school year). This phase is about motivation: when staff are unified in their concern, they will make policy development a high priority and will ensure that consultation and action are not just superficial (Sharp & Thompson, 1994).

PHASE B: PLANNING

An individual or small coordinating group needs to be appointed to oversee the next stages of the process of developing a policy. It will need to be decided how decisions will be reached (such as by consensus, majority vote or by the principal), and actions to be carried out will be specified. Next, the planning group will seek the involvement of all parties whom the policy will affect, both to gain their input and also to ensure their support, which is unlikely to be given if they have been excluded from the policy development process. This invitation to be involved will need to outline the decisions made thus far and how those being consulted can contribute to the development of the policy.

PHASE C: DATA GATHERING

This phase begins with a description of present policy and practice, followed by canvassing the opinions of teachers, students and parents about these. This allows decisions to be made about which aspects of the current policy the school will wish to preserve and which it will want to abandon. Next, official documents, such as Education Department policy, that dictate the parameters of the school's policy need to be gathered.

Identifying the practices needs further expansion, since what staff say they do, and what actually happens, may differ. Data can be obtained by observation of classes, by interviews with students, through activities such as students' story writing or sentence completion, and by questionnaires (Cowin et al., 1990). Consultation can occur during regular class times and through using existing school committees (Sharp & Thompson, 1994). The issues highlighted by these methods can then be circulated, with questions asked about how well the present policy has been communicated to and accepted by students. Next, an evaluation is made about what action is suggested by the findings. If none is implied—that is, if the policy is working and has been well accepted by the school community—then the review process may lapse at this point.

If, however, issues are raised thus far, then next the school must clarify the community's expectations of its discipline approach. Parents can be surveyed to outline this.

PHASE D: POLICY CONSTRUCTION

The first issue to address is which areas the policy will cover. This decision will be guided by awareness of the shortcomings of the present policy, which have been highlighted by the process carried out so far, and by familiarity with the aspects described in this chapter.

Next, information about a range of theories and practices must be gathered in order to inform the group on how to achieve school goals. Proactive approaches, school organisation, and intervention with behaviour problems, must all be considered.

Once informed through reading, staff development, and visits to model schools, the policy group can then select acceptable options for action, taking into consideration the following questions (adapted from Cowin et al., 1990; Sharp & Thompson, 1994):

- Are recommended practices realistic?
- Will staff be willing to carry them out?
- Do they have the skills to do so?
- If not, how could they be equipped with the required skills?
- What advantages do the endorsed practices bring?
- What shortcomings do they have?
- Are the endorsed practices consistent with the school's philosophy, aims and objectives, with the stated aims of the discipline policy, and with Education Department regulations?
- What supports can be put in place to support the change process and the ongoing commitment to the policy and procedures? Support will need to come from senior staff in the school and from external consultants.
- How can the school manage the fact that change will take some two to three years to take hold (Sharp & Thompson, 1994)?
- How can a secondary school deal with its special problems of size and organisation, compared with the usually smaller and more tightly organised primary school?

- How can the policy development team safeguard the policy development process from changes in team membership and in key personnel in the school? How can it bring new staff up to date with the policy?

Having addressed these issues, the planning group needs to produce a draft document for comment by all other parties, and to gain their agreement on putting it into practice for a specified trial period.

PHASE E: IMPLEMENTATION AND REVIEW

A plan needs to be formulated for equipping all school staff with the skills needed to enact the policy and its procedures. Also, the policy will need to specify performance indicators that will demonstrate the effects of the procedures (Whitney et al., 1994). At the end of a trial period, the effects of the policy are evaluated by survey or documentation, and any necessary changes are made.

The next step is to plan how to inform students, teachers and parents of the now formalised policy. This will need to be an ongoing process to accommodate staff and student changes and evolution of community attitudes, and to maintain the profile of the policy so that it is kept alive in the school's awareness and practices.

Finally, periodic reviews of the policy will need to be completed, following many of the steps involved in its initial evolution.

SUMMARY

Because student behaviour affects everyone in the school, management is most effective if everyone in the school agrees on procedures. This can be promoted if the school enunciates a policy that has been arrived at through wide consultation and is supported at the highest level of the school and by the parent group. However, policy alone is not enough. It must be carried to the next stage of detailing procedures that will uphold it and that are consistent with its philosophy.

Success in enacting a school policy will in part depend on the school staff's belief in their school and its students, the principal playing a key role in policy and the day-to-day workings of the school, teamwork in the school being led by the principal and others with leadership qualities, and the school having strong ties with parents and the wider community, including being open to critical review from these groups (Cowin et al., 1990).

The successful school policy on student discipline and welfare will underpin the choices individual teachers make about their own practice. While schools with an overall policy do not have better results in terms of student behaviour than when teachers are left to formulate their own approach, a school-wide policy does help those teachers who have been experiencing discipline problems with their classes (Charles, 1996). A policy arrived at through school-wide and community consultation offers teachers support for their discipline approach, both from their peers within the school and from the wider community. In turn, the community can also respond positively to the increased accountability that a written policy can offer.

DISCUSSION QUESTIONS

1. What advantages and disadvantages can you identify of having a school-wide policy on discipline?
2. What is the policy of your employer or potential employer (an Education Department or independent school)?
3. What goals would you seek to include in your school's discipline policy?
4. What would its philosophy statement comprise?
5. What procedures would you set in place to uphold that policy?
6. Discuss ways to collaborate with parents. If you have used successful approaches in past or present teaching, what helped make those approaches work for you? For the parents? For the students?
7. If your school (or a school you attended on placement) adopted the policy you espouse, what changes would occur in its prevention of, and intervention with, student behaviour?
8. What constraints can you identify that would impede implementation of a policy such as the one you have enunciated?

14

FORMULATING A PERSONAL DISCIPLINE PLAN

Any intervention can be misused and abused if the person using it lacks an ethical system of personal and professional values. Practitioners must never forget that knowledge is power and that with power comes the responsibility to apply that power for the benefit of all persons. (Walker & Shea, 1995, p. 14)

KEY POINTS

- *The aim of understanding theory is to empower the teacher with a wide repertoire of responses to students' behaviour difficulties and to enable him to give a clear rationale for his selected approach.*

- *The teacher's personal philosophy might begin with a statement of his needs, as distinct from his educational goals for his students.*

- *His philosophical statement will comprise his formal and informal beliefs about children and how they learn, the purpose of discipline, the causes of inappropriate behaviour, the power status of students in comparison with teachers, and the teacher's role in guiding students' behaviour.*

- *Proactive measures will be given most emphasis in the teacher's policy because prevention of problems is more powerful than intervention.*

- *When choosing to intervene, the teacher will consider the seriousness of the behaviour and whether the conditions at the time are conducive to dealing with it.*

- *The teacher's personal policy will be constrained by factors such as the school's policy, his own personality, the type of activity in which students are engaged at the time, the students' ages and ability levels,*

> *how stable the group is, the teacher's tenure, and the teacher's stress or comfort levels at the time.*

INTRODUCTION

It is fitting that this text both begins and ends with a discussion of a teacher's personal discipline plan, since enabling teachers to formulate such a plan was the purpose of this text. The advantages of a personal plan were outlined in chapter 1—namely, that the teacher can remain in control of his own feelings and actions, rather than being subjected to the moods of his students. A plan can reduce teacher frustration, increase accountability, and improve management since the teacher is able to respond more appropriately and in a more considered way. A formal plan will contain all the elements of a school discipline plan although each component will be more specific.

NEEDS

The first step in designing a personal discipline plan is for the teacher to examine his own personal needs, as distinct from his professional goals (Charles, 1996). These might include the need for:

- a pleasant physical environment in which to work
- a measure of order in the classroom
- courteous behaviour between all members of the class
- job satisfaction
- parental and school support

Later steps will be designed to meet these personal needs as well as the teacher's educational goals for his students.

PHILOSOPHY

A personal philosophy of discipline is part of, and should be consistent with, the teacher's philosophy of education and of life (Edwards, 1993). The teacher will identify his own beliefs about children and how they learn, the purpose of discipline, the reasons for inappropriate behaviour, the status of teachers compared with students, and the role of the teacher in guiding appropriate behaviour. These are the philosophical dimensions by which this text classified each of the theories of student behaviour management. With a knowledge of the theories, the teacher can draw on a range of formal beliefs on each dimension: in addition, he may include his own less formal statements on these issues.

BELIEFS ABOUT THE PURPOSE OF DISCIPLINE

The teacher may believe that discipline serves mainly a managerial function of promoting order. Or, he may uphold any or all of the three educational functions (self-discipline, group cooperation and responsible citizenship). If, for instance, the teacher equates discipline with the managerial function alone, then he is more likely to plan to intervene with a wider range of behaviours, and more likely to use interventions from the authoritarian theories.

BELIEFS ABOUT THE MOTIVATION OF BEHAVIOUR

This text has compared and contrasted the seven theories' views about students' motivation for their behaviour. As well as these formal views, if the teacher usually believes that a student's action was deliberate, he is more likely to respond to it than if he believes it was unintentional (Lewis, 1991).

BELIEFS ABOUT THE TEACHER'S ROLE

Teaching is a challenging job (Brophy & Good, 1986) and, in my opinion, one that needs no expansion. The teacher is not a nurse, nor a psychologist, nor counsellor for students and families, nor welfare officer, nor even a friend (since friends are unpaid) although he will be *friendly*. I believe that teachers cannot expect themselves to conduct therapy with students (unless that is within a special job description), since they will lack supports from their administration and because the roles of teacher and counsellor can conflict.

On the other hand, the teacher is in an ideal position to identify at risk children and adolescents and, like the general practitioner in medicine, to refer distressed young people to a specialist. Meanwhile, even once a sympathetic consultant is engaged, the teacher still must deal with a disturbed student at school and so must be familiar with a range of discipline options and some specialist interventions, either to carry parts of them out at school where these fit within the teaching role, or not to undo the specialist's interventions through ignorance.

Thus, the teacher needs a clear concept of his role and needs to adopt only those practices that will be supported by the school admin-istration. The teacher has a right to feel confident and competent in his area of expertise, and not to apologise that it is not all-encompassing, since no professional's role is. All professionals need to realise what they do not know, and should allow themselves to focus their efforts on their own area of expertise while referring on those problems that are outside their domain.

THEORY TO GUIDE PRACTICE

Having increased his awareness of his philosophical beliefs, the teacher will select a theory or theories that share these beliefs. He will assess their assumptions and practices on criteria such as those introduced in chapter 1.

PRACTICE

The third aspect of a discipline plan is its recommended practices. The teacher will choose a theory that offers a comprehensive range of preventive and interventive measures. He might supplement the recommendations of his chosen theory with other congruent practices chosen from complementary theories that share a similar philosophical base to his selected theory.

PROACTIVE MEASURES

Prevention is far more powerful than intervention (Doyle, 1986). The main focus of a personal discipline plan is the teacher's endeavours to meet goals that he wants his students to realise as members of the classroom and members of the wider society (McCaslin & Good, 1992). He may plan to establish a physical and emotional environment in the classroom aimed at satisfying students' emotional needs; facilitate their learning through a worthwhile and enjoyable curriculum (Charles, 1996); promote prosocial behaviour through instruction, peer collaboration and fair rules that protect individuals' rights; recognise students' achievements; empower them to participate in decisions that affect them; and give them strategies for coping with stress. Efficient, self-sustaining rules and procedures for achieving all these aims will need to be detailed, with ways to include students in formulating and managing them. A plan for ongoing contact with parents is also integral to prevention.

The teacher will need to consider what type of positive behaviours he would wish to encourage, and what positive consequences they will attract. This system of acknowledgments will need to be compatible with curriculum goals: for instance, if the teacher favours self-discipline for students, then external rewards are incompatible with that goal (McCaslin & Good, 1992).

At the same time, the teacher will need a plan for continual professional self-development to help him in these aims (McCaslin & Good, 1992).

INTERVENTION

Target behaviours

The teacher will need to specify those behaviours that he plans to discourage, such as those that disrupt the learning activity. However, he will need to develop his thinking further than this general guideline. He might examine behaviours in categories, including those that pose no real problem, minor difficulties and more serious problems.

The first category of student behaviour, *non-problem* behaviour, reflects the fact that students cannot control all their behaviour all the time, any more than adults can. This category includes brief periods of inattention or inactivity prior to getting started and brief chats between students (Emmer et al., 1994; Evertson et al., 1994). Another form of natural behaviour is when students give vent to strong feelings. While these behaviours will be inconvenient at times, even angering the teacher, Grossman (1995) advises that teachers will cope better when they can adjust and accommodate to the nature of young people, accepting that at times their behaviour is 'par for the course' given their age and stage of development.

This means that the teacher will decide to leave alone examples of normal childhood exuberance, minor or accidental infractions, transgressions that have extenuating circumstances, behaviours that arise because of unrealistic expectations, and temporary set-backs in an overall improving trend (Grossman, 1995).

A second category of behaviour is *minor problems* which involve just one or two students, for brief periods only, and infrequently. These behaviours require monitoring and intervention if: they become more frequent; are likely to spread to other students; or are intrinsically rewarding to the student.

Persistent problems require immediate intervention, especially if the behaviour is dangerous or destructive. Serious problems include: behaviour that is harmful or distracting to the student himself or others, persistent behaviour, and violations of a behavioural agreement (Grossman, 1995).

Priority of the behaviour

Having thought about classes of behaviour in general, the teacher can then ask some of the following questions about the significance of a given behaviour:

1. How serious or threatening—to the student or to others—is the behaviour?
2. Would an improvement in the target behaviour be important in its own right and, if not, would improvement benefit the student in other ways? For example, dealing with disruptive behaviour may appear to be simply for the teacher's convenience, but if it allows the student to be accepted by her peers, then it can have vital benefits for her self-esteem and social skills.
3. If this behaviour decreased, would it affect the student negatively? For example, would limiting an autistic student's twirling of toys discourage her from playing altogether? Or would the focus necessary to produce a change cause the student to become self-conscious and lower her self-esteem?
4. Is the behaviour actually a problem which needs action? It may instead be:

    *   the student's problem, not the teacher's
    *   a difficulty, not a problem
    *   a conflict of values, in which case the difference has no material impact on the teacher, and so the student cannot be asked to change her behaviour.

5. Would other students copy the uncorrected behaviour, creating management problems if a number of students became involved?
6. Is the environment conducive to appropriate behaviour? That is, should the conditions be changed rather than focusing on the individual?
7. Is a decision to intervene based on hearsay, the 'halo' effect, foreknowledge about the student from previous teachers, or from previous interactions with her? Is this biasing the teacher's decision?
8. Are the rights of the individual being subordinated to the rights of the group? Is this justifiable?

EXERCISE

The ripple effect demonstrated in Figure 14.1 is adapted from Evans and Meyer (1985). Use it as an example to identify the positive effects of altering a behaviour which is or has been an issue for you in the classroom.

Contextual factors

A plan for intervening with a behaviour will be influenced by contextual factors such as when the behaviour occurs and who is present at the time (Lewis, 1991). For instance, safety reasons may suggest prompt intervention during a science experiment, while the same behaviour could

Figure 14.1   Example of the positive ripple effect following behavioural intervention (adapted from Evans & Meyer, 1985)

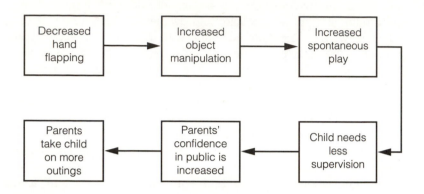

be tolerated in another class. The teacher's own personal resources and available time may also influence his decision and action.

The teacher must also consider whether contextual factors are provoking the student's behaviour and whether alteration of these would prevent its recurrence.

Risks of intervention

While it is recognised that some behaviours disrupt learning, intervention can be even more disruptive (Doyle, 1986). The risks mean that a teacher will be cautious about intervening. When debating whether to do so, he will make complex judgments about the act itself, the individual student's history, and the circumstances in the classroom at the time (Doyle, 1986). It can be better to delay reacting to behaviour about which the teacher does not have all the facts, when there is not enough time to resolve the issue right then, when it would have to be dealt with in public, or when the student is too upset to respond rationally at the time (Grossman, 1995).

The teacher will formulate a series of graded responses to misdemeanours, which are enforceable, fair and effective. In choosing a particular intervention, the teacher will consider whether it would be unduly restrictive (controlling) or intrusive (impinging on the educational process) and whether a potential intervention would be ethical. He will ask whether all information about intervention options has been sought. Kerr and Nelson (1989) advocate that the teacher should choose an intervention that will do the least damage to the student: they call this the *least dangerous assumption*. Again the teacher's management aims must be congruent with the wider curriculum goals, since students will not learn exploration and risk taking if they are trained to be obedient (McCaslin & Good, 1992).

Ethics

Chapter 3 presented some ethical guidelines for the teacher who is addressing an individual's behaviour. These guidelines include: ensuring the environment is conducive to appropriate behaviour and is physically and psychologically safe for students, that interventions benefit the student by teaching functional skills, that the teacher be competent and use the most effective treatment, that he gain the student's or parents' voluntary and informed consent to the intervention, and that all matters pertaining to that student remain confidential (Alberto & Troutman, 1995; Geldard, 1993; Martin & Pear, 1992; Rekers, 1984).

CONSTRAINTS ON THE TEACHER'S PERSONAL PLAN

While formulating his plan, the teacher will be aware that he cannot necessarily act as he would wish. Some constraints limit his options.

SCHOOL AND EMPLOYER POLICIES

School and employer policies (and parents' views) will dictate teacher behaviours to some extent, although for day-to-day decisions the teacher will have a certain amount of autonomy and must rely on a comprehensive repertoire of skills that is unlikely to be described in detail in a policy document.

THE TEACHER'S PERSONALITY

The teacher's personality will affect what behaviour he chooses to intervene with, and how (Grossman, 1995; Lewis, 1991). Teachers vary in the amount of movement and noise they tolerate, what activities they allow students to do without asking for teacher permission, their emphasis on interpersonal skill development (process) versus knowledge acquisition (content), the types of instruction they use, the extent to which they allow students to participate in the development of classroom rules, their status with respect to students, their emphasis on intrinsic versus extrinsic motivation, and their emphasis on cooperation versus competition (Grossman, 1995).

Nevertheless, the teacher's expectations of students need to be realistic, taking into account their abilties and the demands of the task at hand.

ACTIVITY TYPE

Regardless of their personal preferences, teachers will vary their managing role according to the type of activity being performed—direct instruction, individual seatwork or group work (Doyle, 1986). As might be expected, the more complex the social and academic demands, the more likely it is that students will be disruptive and the harder it will be to retain a focus on the activity itself. This means that teachers will respond more often to behaviour during complex tasks than during simpler tasks, so that order can be restored, enabling students to regain their focus on the activity (Doyle, 1986).

THE STUDENTS' ABILITY LEVELS

Highly motivated and achieving students are likely to be task focused and are less likely to be distracted when teachers issue behavioural reminders to other students, even when these interrupt the flow of the activity; on the other hand, low-achieving students are more easily distracted and so the teacher may avoid reprimanding them for rule violations in order to maintain their focus on the lesson content (Doyle, 1986).

THE STUDENTS' AGES

Kohlberg (in Grossman, 1995) described three main stages of moral development in young people, with children up to the ages of six to eight being motivated to do what is expected of them because adults have the power to reward or punish them. In the second stage (from seven to eleven years) children are more able to understand why rules are necessary and will observe rules that make sense. During adolescence, young people's decisions about right and wrong hinge on what feels right, and they exercise judgment accordingly. Some writers (for instance, Grossman, 1995; Lewis, 1991) suggest adjusting the management method to the students' age and related stage of moral reasoning, because younger children cannot respond to self-directive approaches of management.

However, six arguments rebut this suggestion. First, there is very little research verifying the effectiveness of adjusting the teacher's management approach to the students' stage of moral reasoning (Grossman, 1995).

Second, older students who are suddenly expected to exercise self-discipline may find the experience uncomfortable, and therefore need earlier opportunities to practise self-regulation (Lewis, 1991).

Third, once students have reached the legal age for leaving school, there are few threats that schools can carry out to ensure the compliance of unwilling students. If procedures for self-direction are enacted before students become alienated from school, behavioural problems in this senior group can be prevented.

Fourth, it is worth remembering that, for instance, while four-year-olds have only four-year-old social problem-solving abilities, they usually only have four-year-old problems to solve, and so they can be guided to apply their skills to age-appropriate problems.

Fifth, preschools successfully teach self-management and yet older students are given fewer opportunities to direct themselves (McCaslin & Good, 1992). The success of preschools may be due to their child-centred focus in contrast with schools, whose organisation is more hierarchical and authoritarian. If this is so, it suggests that it is the context, not the students' ages, that dictates management style.

Finally, Kohlberg's stages of moral reasoning may result from the typical ways in which we discipline children at various ages. Rather than creating the need for that discipline style, the stages may be a result of it. Knowledge of the stages may cause teachers to underestimate student skill, which then becomes a self-fulfilling prophecy.

GROUP PROCESSES

The intervention a teacher chooses may be dictated to some extent by the stage of development of the group. This does not refer to the age of its members but to the length of time the group has been a cohesive unit. If it has existed intact for some time, its rules and roles will be more firmly established, and it will probably be functioning more smoothly than a group which has formed recently.

Napier and Gershenfeld (1993) note that successful leaders will be able to adapt their behaviour to the needs of the group. They postulate that early in a group's functioning, it will need high task orientation with little focus on individual relationships. The second stage of group development requires that the leader offer high support for individuals, while maintaining a high task focus. The leader during the group's third phase does not need to direct the task as closely but still maintains high support, until finally the leader can withdraw direct leadership and allow the group to function relatively autonomously.

THE TEACHER'S TENURE

A teacher whose relationship with the students is a short-term one, such as when relief teaching, may be obliged to adopt the approaches used by the class's regular teacher. The longer the relationship is anticipated to last, the less this becomes an issue, as students can adjust to different expectations from a range of teachers, although McCaslin and Good

(1992) caution against a series of changes from democratic to authoritarian management styles and back again.

THE TEACHER'S STRESS LEVELS

Many teachers find that, while they believe in fostering student autonomy, they sometimes instead find themselves responding to students in authoritarian ways (Lewis, 1991). Lewis reports that new teachers begin with concerns about their own needs and their suitability for the role of teacher, then with experience they become focused on the teaching process, and finally they are able to address how to meet student needs. When stressed, however, even experienced teachers can regress to being concerned about their own survival and may revert to authoritarian discipline. Some reasons for this include:

1. Teachers may know the authoritarian methods best because as children they were subjected to them themselves, and so when they feel stressed, they resort to controlling methods as if by reflex.
2. When individuals feel out of control, their natural tendency is to try harder to exert control, both over themselves and others, which means using authoritarian methods.
3. Teachers receive varying degrees of training in how to respond to student behaviours. What they do receive is often authoritarian in nature and so they are obliged to use these approaches by default, even when their personal philosophy is more democratic.
4. Students will at times push a teacher to see if he will use punitive methods under pressure. It is as if they are testing his integrity and commitment to the more democratic philosophies, and are searching for any sign of hypocrisy.
5. Schools are organised hierarchically, with teachers subjected to external discipline themselves. Within this environment, it is natural that they apply this control downwards to students.
6. The teacher's thinking can be counter-productive, as examined in chapter 4. He might attribute blame to students, which in turn causes him to feel personally threatened (Glasser, 1992; Lewis, 1991) and to respond emotionally instead of rationally.

Despite these temptations to revert to dysfunctional management methods, Rogers (1989) reminds us that, while an old dog cannot learn new tricks, with effort and support, *people* can. Teachers *can* develop a plan for their practice that while not a panacea, offers some guidelines. They *can* seek out a colleague who will discuss issues with them, and they *can* use their feelings to inform, not deform, their practice.

EVALUATION OF THE PLAN

The teacher's personal plan will need some modification once he becomes familiar with the specific needs of his students, or when the plan seems to be ineffective. The teacher might modify it on his own initiative, in collaboration with students or in consultation with colleagues or specialists, in line with Glasser's (1976) advice that: 'If something isn't working, stop doing it'. Even so, the teacher will need to remember that there are no guarantees: there are times when certain students do not respond to even the best planned, most sophisticated and best executed approach. Their motivation does not reflect any deficiency on their part, but a social problem: we raise students' expectations that hard work will be rewarded with good jobs, when they have neither the supports (such as nutrition, health and safety) to continue to work hard at school nor the likelihood of work when they leave (McCaslin & Good, 1992). Some who come to realise this grow disillusioned and refuse to work within a system that has let them down.

CONCLUSION

The approach to discipline that we use with young people is not selected in a vacuum, but within the context of a society that has endorsed and justified a power imbalance between adults and children (and other devalued groups). Thus, interpersonal interactions within the classroom cannot be divorced from their sociological basis: justice becomes a criterion for assessing the worth of any theory.

However, effectiveness must be a criterion also. The democratic writers contend that democracy is both ethical and effective: they believe that in addition to the moral imperative to equalise status between adults and children, failure to do so is also ineffective. Thus, their position is both a moral and a pragmatic one. You, the reader, are invited to decide for yourself whether the democratic approaches meet the criterion of effectiveness, and whether the authoritarian approaches meet the criterion of achieving justice.

DISCUSSION QUESTIONS

1. What are your beliefs about the purpose of discipline? How are these influenced by your understanding of childhood and how children learn, the reasons for inappropriate behaviour, and the status of teachers with respect to students? What do these imply for the role of the teacher?

2. Which theory (or blend of theories) of discipline is consistent with your beliefs?
3. Are the theories that form your blend consistent with each other?
4. What practices would you consider ideal in your present or intended teaching context?
5. What constraints can you identify that may affect the use or success of those practices?
6. Would these factors require you to use approaches whose underlying philosophy differs from your own?
7. If so, how would you manage the inconsistencies inherent in using an approach you do not fully endorse?

SUGGESTIONS FOR FURTHER READING

For a succinct overview of the range of theories and practices outlined in this text, you could consult:

Edwards, C. 1993, *Classroom discipline and management*, Macmillan, New York
Lewis, R. 1991, *The discipline dilemma*, ACER, Melbourne

For a description of personal discipline plans, you might refer to:

Charles, C.M. 1996, *Building classroom discipline: from models to practice*, 5th edn, Longman, New York

BIBLIOGRAPHY

Adler, A. 1954, *Understanding human nature*, Fawcett, Connecticut

Adler, R., Rosenfeld, L. and Towne, N. 1992, *Interplay: the process of interpersonal communication*, 5th edn, Holt, Rinehart & Winston, New York

Alberto, P.A. and Troutman, A.C. 1995, *Applied behaviour analysis for teachers*, 4th edn, Merrill, Columbus, Ohio

Amatea, E.S. 1988, 'Brief strategic intervention with school behavior problems: A case of temper tantrums', *Psychology in the Schools*, vol. 25, no. 2, pp. 174–83

——1989, *Brief strategic intervention for school behavior problems*, Jossey-Bass, San Francisco

Ansbacher, H.L. and Ansbacher, R.R. 1956, *The individual psychology of Alfred Adler*, Basic Books, New York

Asher, S.R. and Parker, J.G. 1989, 'Significance of peer relationship problems in childhood', *Social competence in developmental perspective*, eds B.H. Schneider, G. Attili, J. Nadel & R.P. Weissberg, Kluwer Academic Publishers, Dordrecht

Asher, S.R. and Renshaw, P.D. 1981, 'Children without friends: social knowledge and social-skill training', *The development of children's friendships*, eds S.R. Asher & J.M. Gottman, Cambridge University Press, Cambridge

Ashman, A. and Conway, R. 1989, *Cognitive strategies for special education*, Routledge, London

Axelrod, S. 1977, *Behaviour modification for the classroom teacher*, McGraw Hill, New York

Bailey, J. and Pyles, D. 1989, 'Behavioral diagnostics', *The treatment of severe behavior disorders: Behavior analysis approaches*, ed E. Cipani, The American Association on Mental Retardation, Washington, DC

Bailey, J.S. 1991, 'Marketing behavior analysis requires different talk', *Journal of Applied Behavior Analysis*, vol. 24 , no. 3, pp. 445–8

——1992, 'Gentle teaching: trying to win friends and influence people with euphemism, metaphor, smoke, and mirrors', *Journal of Applied Behavior Analysis*, vol. 25, no. 4, pp. 879–83

Balson, M. 1992, *Understanding classroom behaviour*, 3rd edn, ACER, Melbourne
——1994, *Becoming better parents*, 4th edn, ACER, Melbourne
Bandura, A. 1986, *Social foundations of thought and action*, Prentice Hall, Englewood Cliffs, New Jersey
Bash, M.A.S. and Camp, B.W. 1986, 'Teacher training in the think aloud classroom program', *Teaching social skills to children: innovative approaches*, 2nd edn, eds. G. Cartledge & J.F. Milburn, Pergamon, New York
Bay-Hinitz, A.K., Peterson, R.F. and Quilitch, R. 1994, 'Cooperative games: a way to modify aggressive and cooperative behaviors in young children', *Journal of Applied Behavior Analysis*, vol. 27, no. 3, pp. 435–46
Benes, K.M. and Kramer, J.J. 1989, 'The behavioral tradition in schools (and miles to go before we sleep)', *Cognitive-behavioral Psychology in the Schools*, eds J.N. Hughes & R.J. Hall, Guilford, New York
Benson, A.J. and Presbury, J.H. 1989, 'The cognitive tradition in schools', *Cognitive-behavioral Psychology in the Schools*, eds J.N. Hughes & R.J. Hall, Guilford, New York
Berg, I.K. and de Shazer, S. 1989, *Four useful questions in solution construction*, Brief family therapy center, Milwaukee
Bernard, M.E. 1986, *Becoming rational in an irrational world: Albert Ellis and rational-emotive therapy*, McCulloch, Melbourne
Berry, C.R. 1988, *When helping you is hurting me*, Harper & Row, San Francisco
Biddulph, S. 1994, *The Secret of Happy Children*, rev edn, Bay Books, Sydney
Biederman, G.B., Davey, V.A., Ryder, C. and Franchi, D. 1994, 'The negative effects of positive reinforcement in teaching children with developmental delay', *Exceptional Children*, vol. 60, no. 5, pp. 458–65
Bloom, M. 1990, 'The psychological constructs of social competency', *Developing social competency in adolescence*, eds T.P. Gullotta, G.R. Adams & R. Montemayor, Sage, Newbury Park, CA
Bolton, R. 1987, *People skills*, Simon and Schuster, Sydney
Borba, M. and Borba, C. 1978, *Self-esteem: a classroom affair. 101 ways to help children like themselves*, Winston Press, Minneapolis
——1982, *Self-esteem: a classroom affair. More ways to help children like themselves*, Winston Press, Minneapolis
Boulton, M.J. 1994, 'Understanding and preventing bullying in the junior school playground', *School bullying: insights and perspectives*, eds P.K. Smith & S. Sharp, Routledge, London
Brophy, J. and Good, T.L. 1986, 'Teacher behavior and student achievement, *Handbook of research on teaching*, 3rd edn, ed M.C. Wittrock, Macmillan, New York
Brown, B. 1986, 'We can help children to be self-reliant', *Children Today*, Jan-Feb 1986, pp. 26–8
Burden, R.L. and Fraser, B.J. 1993, 'Classroom environment assessments', *Psychology in the Schools*, vol. 30, no. 3, pp. 232–40
Bye, L. and Jussim, L. 1993, 'A proposed model for the acquisition of social

knowledge and social competence', *Psychology in the Schools*, vol. 30, no. 2, pp. 143–61

Camp, B. and Bash, M.A. 1980, 'Developing self-control through training in problem solving: "The Think Aloud" program', *Social competence: interventions for children and adolescents*, eds D.P. Rathjen & J.P. Foreyt, Pergamon, New York

Cangelosi, J.S. 1993, *Classroom management strategies: gaining and maintaining students' cooperation*, 2nd edn, Longman, New York

Canter, L. and Canter, M. 1976, *Assertive discipline: a take charge approach for today's educator*, Lee Canter and associates, Los Angeles, California

——1992, *Assertive discipline: Positive behavior management for today's classroom*, Lee Canter and Associates, Santa Monica, California

Caplan, M.Z. and Weissberg, R.P. 1989, 'Promoting social competence in early adolescence', *Social competence in developmental perspective*, eds B.H. Schneider, G. Attili, J. Nadel & R.P. Weissberg, Kluwer Academic Publishers, Dordrecht

Carlson, C. 1992, 'Models and strategies of family-school assessment and intervention', *The handbook of family-school intervention: a systems perspective*, eds M. Fine & C. Carlson, Allyn & Bacon, Boston

Carter, F. and Cheesman, P. 1988, *Anxiety in childhood and adolescence: encouraging self-help through relaxation training*, Croom Helm, New York

Cartledge, G. and Milburn, J.F. (eds) 1986, *Teaching social skills to children: innovative approaches*, 2nd edn, Pergamon, New York

Chandler, L.K., Lubeck, R.C. and Fowler, S.A. 1992, 'Generalisation and maintenance of preschool children's social skills: a critical review and analysis', *Journal of Applied Behavior Analysis*, vol. 25, no. 2, pp. 415–28

Chang, J. and Phillips, M. 1993, 'Michael White and Steve de Shazer: new directions in family therapy', *Therapeutic conversations*, eds S. Gilligan & R. Price, W.W. Norton & Co, New York

Charles, C.M. 1992, *Building classroom discipline: from models to practice*, 4th edn, Longman, New York

——1996, *Building classroom discipline: from models to practice*, 5th edn, Longman, New York

Cillessen, T. and Ferguson, T.J. 1989, 'Self-perpetuation processes in children's peer relationships', *Social competence in developmental perspective*, eds B.H. Schneider, G. Attili, J. Nadel & R.P. Weissberg, Kluwer Academic Publishers, Dordrecht

Coie, J.D., Christopoulos, C., Terry, R., Dodge, K.A. and Lochman, J.E. 1989, 'Types of aggressive relationships, peer rejection, and developmental consequences', *Social competence in developmental perspective*, eds B.H. Schneider, G. Attili, J. Nadel & R.P. Weissberg, Kluwer Academic Publishers, Dordrecht

Coie, J.D., Dodge, K.A. and Kupersmidt, J.B. 1990, 'Peer group behavior and social status', *Peer rejection in childhood*, eds S.R. Asher & J.D. Coie, Cambridge University Press, Cambridge

Cole, P. and Chan, L. 1990, *Methods and strategies for special education*, Prentice Hall, New York

Combrinck-Graham, L. 1991, 'On technique with children in family therapy: how calculated should it be?', *Journal of Marital and Family Therapy*, vol. 18, no. 4, pp. 373–7

Conoley, J.C. 1989, 'Cognitive-behavioral approaches and prevention in the schools', *Cognitive-behavioral psychology in the schools*, eds J.N. Hughes & R.J. Hall, Guilford, New York

Conway, R. and Gow, L. 1990, 'Moderate to mild disability: teaching and learning strategies to improve generalisation', *The exceptional child*, ed S. Butler, Harcourt Brace Jovanovich, Sydney

Coopersmith, S. 1967, *The antecedents of self-esteem*, W.H. Freeman, San Francisco

Coplan, R.J., Rubin, K.H., Fox, N.A., Calkins, S.D. and Stewart, S.L., 1994, 'Being alone, playing alone, and acting alone: distinguishing among reticence and passive and active solitude in young children', *Child Development*, vol. 65, no. 1, pp. 129–37

Corey, G. 1991, *Theory and practice of counseling and psychotherapy*, 4th edn edn, Brooks/Cole, Monterey, CA

Corno, L. 1989, 'Self-regulated learning: a volitional analysis', *Self-regulated learning and academic achievement: theory, research, and practice*, eds B.J. Zimmerman & D.H. Schunk, Springer-Verlag, New York

Cowie, H. and Sharp, S. 1994, 'Tackling bullying through the curriculum', *School bullying: insights and perspectives*, eds P.K. Smith & S. Sharp, Routledge, London

Cowin, M., Freeman, L., Farmer, A., James, M., Drent, A. and Arthur, R. 1990, *Positive school discipline: a practical guide to developing policy*, rev. edn, Narbethong Publications, Boronia, Victoria

Davis, C.A., Brady, M.P., Williams, R.E. & Hamilton, R. 1992, 'Effects of high-probability requests on the acquisition and generalization of responses to requests in young children with behavior disorders', *Journal of Applied Behavior Analysis*, vol. 25, no. 4, pp. 905–16

de Shazer, S. 1982, *Patterns of brief therapy*, Guilford, New York

——1993, 'Creative misunderstanding: there is no escape from language,' *Therapeutic conversations*, eds S. Gilligan & R. Price, W.W. Norton and Co, New York

de Shazer, S., Berg, I.K., Lipchik, E., Nunnally, E., Molnar, A., Gingerich, W. and Weiner-Davis, M. 1986, 'Brief therapy: focused solution development', *Family Process*, vol. 25, no. 2, pp. 207–22

de Shazer, S. and Molnar, A. 1984, 'Four useful interventions in brief family therapy', *Journal of Marital and Family Therapy*, vol. 10, no. 3, pp. 297–304

Dicocco, N.E., Chalfin, S.R. and Olson, J.M. 1987, 'Systemic family therapy goes to school', *Social Work in Education*, vol. 9, no. 4, pp. 209–21

Dinkmeyer, D. and Dreikurs, R. 1963, *Encouraging children to learn: the encouragement process*, Prentice Hall, Englewood Cliffs, NJ

Dinkmeyer, D. and McKay, G. 1989, *Systematic training for effective parenting*, 3rd edn, American Guidance Service, Minnesota

Dinkmeyer, D., McKay, G. and Dinkmeyer, D. 1980, *Systematic training for effective teaching*, American Guidance Service, Minnesota

Dobson, J. 1970, *Dare to discipline*, Bantam, Toronto

Dobson, K.S. and Pusch, D. 1993, 'Towards a definition of the conceptual and empirical boundaries of cognitive therapy', *Australian Psychologist*, vol. 28, no. 3, pp. 137–44

Dodge, K.A. 1985, 'Facets of social interaction and the assessment of social competence in children', *Children's peer relations: issues in assessment and intervention*, eds B.H. Schneider, K.H. Rubin & J.E. Ledingham, Springer-Verlag, New York

Dodge, K.A. and Price, J.M. 1994, 'On the relation between social information processing and socially competent behavior in early school-aged children', *Child Development*, vol. 65, no. 5, pp. 1385–97

Dowling, E. 1985, 'Theoretical approach—a joint systems approach to educational problems with children', *The family and the school*, eds E. Dowling and E. Osborne, Routledge and Kegan Paul, London

Doyle, W. 1986, 'Classroom organization and management', *Handbook of research on teaching*, 3rd edn, ed M.C. Wittrock, Macmillan, New York

Dreikurs, R. and Cassell, P. 1990, *Discipline without tears*, 2nd edn, Dutton, New York

Drouet, D. 1993, 'Adolescent female bullying and sexual harassment', *Understanding and managing bullying*, ed D. Tattum, Heinemann Educational, Oxford

Duke, D.L. and Meckel, A.M. 1984, *Teacher's guide to classroom management*, Random House, New York

Duncan, B.L. 1992, 'Strategic therapy, eclecticism, and the therapeutic relationship', *Journal of Marital and Family Therapy*, vol. 18, no. 1, pp. 17–24

Dunlap, G., dePerczel, M., Clarke, S., Wilson, D., Wrights, S., White, R. and Gomez, A. 1994, 'Choice making to promote adaptive behavior for students with emotional and behavioral challenges', *Journal of Applied Behavior Analysis*, vol. 27, no. 3, pp. 505–18

Dweck, C.S. 1981, 'Social-cognitive processes in children's friendships', *The development of children's friendships*, eds S.R. Asher & J.M. Gottman, Cambridge University Press, Cambridge

Dyck, M.J. 1993, 'New directions in cognitive-behaviour therapy', *Australian Psychologist*, vol. 28, no. 3, pp. 133–6

Education Department of South Australia, 1989, *School discipline: the management of student behaviour: policy and guidelines for practice*, Government Printer, South Australia

Edwards, C.H. 1993, *Classroom discipline and management*, Macmillan, New York

Elkind, D. 1988, *The hurried child: growing up too fast too soon*, rev edn, Addison-Wesley, Massachusetts

Ellis, A. 1962, *Reason and emotion in psychotherapy*, Lyle Stuart, Secaucus, New Jersey

——1973, *Humanistic psychotherapy*, McGraw-Hill, New York

——1977, *Handbook of rational-emotive therapy*, Springer Publishing, New York

Emmer, E.T., Evertson, C.M., Clements, B.T. and Worsham, M.E. 1994, *Classroom management for secondary teachers*, 3rd edn, Allyn & Bacon, Boston

Evans, I. and Meyer, L. 1985, *An educative approach to behaviour problems*, Paul H. Brookes, Baltimore

Evertson, C.M., Emmer, E.T., Clements, B.T. and Worsham, M.E. 1994, *Classroom management for elementary teachers*, 3rd edn, Allyn & Bacon, Boston

Fawcett, S.B. 1991, 'Some values guiding community research and action', *Journal of Applied Behavior Analysis*, vol. 24, no. 4, pp. 621–36

Feindler, E.L. 1991, 'Cognitive strategies in anger control interventions for children and adolescents', *Child and adolescent therapy: Cognitive-behavioral procedures*, ed P. Kendall, Guilford, New York

Finch, M. and Hops, H. 1983, 'Remediation of social withdrawal in young children: considerations for the practitioner', *Social skills training for children and youth*, ed C.W. LeCroy, Haworth Press, New York

Fine, M. 1992, 'A systems-ecological perspective on home-school intervention', *The handbook of family-school intervention: a systems perspective*, eds M. Fine & C. Carlson, Allyn & Bacon, Boston

Fine, M. and Holt, P. 1983, 'Intervention with school problems: a family systems perspective', *Psychology in the Schools*, vol. 20, no. 1, pp. 59–66

Fisch, R., Weakland, J.H. and Segal, L. 1982, *The tactics of change: doing therapy briefly*, Jossey-Bass, San Francisco

Flaskas, C. 1989, 'Thinking about the emotional interaction of therapist and family', *Australian and New Zealand Journal of Family Therapy*, vol. 10, no. 1, pp. 1–6

Fontana, D. 1985, *Classroom control*, British Psychological Society & Methuen Publishers, London

Foxx, R. 1982, *Decreasing behaviors of severely retarded and autistic persons*, Research Press, Illinois

Frey, J. 1984, 'A family/systems approach to illness-maintaining behaviours in chronically ill adolescents', *Family Process*, vol. 23, no. 2, pp. 251–60

Frosh, S. 1983, 'Children and teachers in schools', *Developments in social skills training*, eds S. Spence & G. Shepherd, Academic Press, London

García-Vázquez, E. and Ehly, S.W. 1992, 'Peer tutoring effects on students who are perceived as not socially accepted', *Psychology in the Schools*, vol. 29, no. 3, pp. 256–66

Geldard, D. 1993, *Basic personal counselling*, 2nd edn, Prentice Hall, New York

Gesten, E.L., De Apodaca, R.F., Rains, M., Weissberg, R.P. and Cowen, E.L. 1979, 'Promoting peer-related social competence in schools', *Social competence in children*, eds M.W. Kent & J.E. Rolf, University Press of New England, Hanover, New Hampshire

Ginott, H.G. undated, *Between parent and teenager*, Cookery Book Club, London

——1969, *Between parent and child*, Crosby Lockwood Staples, London

——1972, *Teacher and child*, Macmillan, New York

Glasser, W. 1969, *Schools without failure*, Harper & Row, New York

——1976, *The ten step discipline program*, videotape, USA

——1977, 'Ten steps to good discipline', *Today's Education*, vol. 66, pp. 61–3

——1984, 'Reality therapy', *Current psychotherapies*, 3rd edn, ed R.J. Corsini, Peacock, Illinois

——1986, *Control theory in the classroom*, Harper & Row, New York

——1992, *The quality school*, 2nd edn, Harper Perennial, New York

Glasser, W. and Zunin, L. 1979, 'Reality therapy', *Current psychotherapies*, 2nd edn, ed R.J. Corsini, Peacock, Illinois

Goldstein, A.P., Sprafkin, R.P., Gershaw, N.J., and Klein, P. 1986, 'The adolescent: social skills training through structured learning', *Teaching social skills to children: innovative approaches*, 2nd edn, eds G. Cartledge & J.F. Milburn, Pergamon, New York

Good, T.L. and Brophy, J.E. 1986, 'School effects', *Handbook of research on teaching*, 3rd edn, ed M.C. Wittrock, Macmillan, New York

——1994, *Looking in classrooms*, 6th edn, Harper Collins, New York

Goodenow, C. 1993, 'The psychological sense of school membership among adolescents: scale development and educational correlates', *Psychology in the Schools*, vol. 30, no. 1, pp. 79–90

Gordon, T. 1970, *Parent effectiveness training*, Plume, New York

——1974, *Teacher effectiveness training*, Peter H. Wyden, New York

——1991, *Teaching children self-discipline at home and at school*, Random House, Sydney

Grossman, H. 1995, *Classroom behavior management in a diverse society*, 2nd edn, Mayfield, California

Guess, D. and Siegel-Causey, E. 1985, 'Behavioral control and education of severely handicapped students: who's doing what to whom? and why?', *Severe mental retardation: from theory to practice*, eds D. Bricker & J. Filler, Division on Mental Retardation, Council for Exceptional Children, Virginia

Gurney, P. 1988, *Self-esteem in children with special educational needs*, Routledge, London

Haley, J. 1973, *Uncommon therapy: the psychiatric techniques of Milton H. Erickson, M.D.*, W.W. Norton, New York

——1980, *Leaving home: the therapy of disturbed young people*, McGraw-Hill, New York

——1984, *Ordeal therapy*, Jossey-Bass, San Francisco

Hall, R.J. and Hughes, J.N. 1989, 'Cognitive-behavioral approaches in the school: an overview', *Cognitive-behavioral psychology in the schools*, eds J.N. Hughes & R.J. Hall, Guilford, New York

Hammel, B. 1989, 'So good at acting bad', *Control theory in the practice of reality therapy*, ed N. Glasser, Harper & Row, New York

Harrison, J. 1991, *Understanding children: towards responsive relationships*, ACER, Melbourne

Hartup, W.W. 1979, 'Peer relations and social competence', *Social competence in children*, eds M.W. Kent & J.E. Rolf, University Press of New England, Hanover, New Hampshire

Hayes, H. 1991, 'A re-introduction to family therapy: clarification of three schools', *Australian and New Zealand Journal of Family Therapy*, vol. 12, no. 1, pp. 27–43

Heins, T. 1988, 'Relearning childthink', *Australian and New Zealand Journal of Family Therapy*, vol. 9, no. 3, pp. 143–9

Herbert, G. 1993, 'Changing children's attitudes through the curriculum', *Understanding and managing bullying*, ed D. Tattum, Heinemann Educational, Oxford

Herbert, M. 1987, *Behavioural treatment of children with problems: a practice manual*, 2nd edn, Academic Press, London

Heward, W. and Cooper, J. 1987, 'Definition and characteristics of applied behaviour analysis', *Applied behaviour analysis*, eds J. Cooper, T. Heron & W. Heward, Merrill, Columbus, Ohio

Hill, S. and Hill, T. 1990, *The collaborative classroom: a guide to cooperative learning*, Eleanor Curtin, Melbourne

Hill, S. and Reed, K. 1989, 'Promoting social competence at preschool: the implementation of a cooperative games programme', *Australian Journal of Early Childhood*, vol. 14, no. 4, pp. 25–31

Hinshaw, S.P. and Erhardt, D. 1991, 'Attention-deficit hyperactivity disorder', *Child and adolescent therapy: cognitive-behavioral procedures*, ed P. Kendall, Guilford, New York

Hitz, R. and Driscoll, A. 1988, 'Praise or encouragement? New insights into praise: implications for early childhood teachers', *Young Children*, July 1988, pp. 6–13

Holmes, S. 1982, 'Failure to learn: a system view', *Australian Journal of Family Therapy*, vol. 4, no. 1, pp. 27–36

Hops, H. and Finch, M. 1985, 'Social competence and skill: a reassessment', *Children's peer relations: issues in assessment and intervention*, eds B.H. Schneider, K.H. Rubin & J.E. Ledingham, Springer-Verlag, New York

Hops, H. and Lewin, L. 1984, 'Peer sociometric forms', *Child behavioral assessment*, eds T.H. Ollendick & M. Hersen, Pergamon, New York

Horner, R.H. 1994, 'Functional assessment: contributions and future directions', *Journal of Applied Behavior Analysis*, vol. 27, no. 2, pp. 401–4

House of Representatives Standing Committee on Employment, Education and Training, 1994, *Sticks and stones: report on violence in Australian schools*, Australian Government Publishing Service, Canberra

Hsia, H. 1984, 'Structural and strategic approach to school phobia/school refusal', *Psychology in the Schools*, vol. 21, no. 3, pp. 360–7

Humphrey, J.H. and Humphrey, J.N. 1985, *Controlling stress in children*, Charles C. Thomas, Illinois

Iwata, B.A., Pace, G.M., Cowdery, G.E. and Miltenberger, R.G. 1994, 'What makes extinction work: an analysis of procedural form and function', *Journal of Applied Behavior Analysis*, vol. 27, no. 1, pp. 131–44

Jakubowski, P. and Lange, A. 1978, *The assertive option: your rights and responsibilities*, Research Press, Illinois

James, J.E. 1993, 'Cognitive-behavioural theory: an alternative conception', *Australian Psychologist*, vol. 28, no. 3, pp. 151–5

Johnson, D.W. and Johnson, R.T. 1986, 'Mainstreaming and cooperative learning strategies', *Exceptional Children*, vol. 52, no. 6, pp. 553–61

——1991, *Learning together and alone*, 3rd edn, Allyn & Bacon, Boston

Johnson, D.W., Johnson, R.T. and Holubec, E.J. 1990a, *Circles of learning: cooperation in the classroom*, 3rd edn, Interaction Books, Minnesota

Johnson, J.H., Jason, L.A. and Betts, D.M. 1990b, 'Promoting social competencies through educational efforts', *Developing social competency in adolescence*, eds T.P. Gullotta, G.R. Adams & R. Montemayor, Sage, Newbury Park, CA

Jones, F.H. 1987a, *Positive classroom discipline*, McGraw-Hill, New York

——1987b, *Positive classroom instruction*, McGraw-Hill, New York

Jones, V.F. and Jones, L.S. 1990, *Comprehensive classroom management: motivating and managing students*, 3rd edn, Allyn & Bacon, Boston

——1995, *Comprehensive classroom management: creating positive learning environments for all students*, 4th edn, Allyn & Bacon, Boston

Kamps, D.M., Barbetta, P.M., Leonard, B.R. and Delquadri, J. 1994, 'Classwide peer tutoring: an integration strategy to improve reading skills and promote peer interactions among students with autism and general education peers', *Journal of Applied Behavior Analysis*, vol. 27, no. 1, pp. 49–61

Kaplan, J.S. and Drainville, B. 1991, *Beyond behavior modification: a cognitive-behavioral approach to behavior management in the school*, 2nd edn, Pro-Ed, Austin, Texas

Katz, L. 1988, 'What should children be doing?', *Rattler*, Spring 1988, pp. 4–6

Kendall, P.C. (ed.) 1991, *Child and adolescent therapy: cognitive-behavioral procedures*, Guilford, New York

Kerr, M. and Nelson, M. 1989, *Strategies for managing behavior problems in the classroom*, 2nd edn, Merrill, Columbus, Ohio

Kindsvatter, R., Wilen, W. and Ishler, M. 1992, *Dynamics of effective teaching*, 2nd edn, Longman, New York

Kirkby, R.J. and Smyrnios, K.X. 1990, 'Child-oriented family therapy outcome research: comparisons between brief family therapy and an alternative treatment', *Australian and New Zealand Journal of Family Therapy*, vol. 11, no. 2, pp. 75–84

Kiser, D.J., Piercy, F.P. and Lipchik, E. 1993, 'The integration of emotion in solution-focused therapy', *Journal of Marital and Family Therapy*, vol. 19, no. 3, pp. 233–42

Knight, T. 1991, 'Democratic schooling: basis for a school code of behaviour,' *Classroom discipline*, eds M.N. Lovegrove & R. Lewis, Longman Cheshire, Melbourne

Kohler, F.W. and Strain, P.S. 1993, 'The early childhood social skills program', *Teaching Exceptional Children*, vol. 25, no. 2, pp. 41–2

Kounin, J.S. 1970, *Discipline and group management in classrooms*, Holt, Rinehart & Winston, New York

Kral, R. 1988, *Strategies that work: techniques for solution in the schools*, Brief family therapy center, Milwaukee

——1992, 'Solution-focused brief therapy: applications in schools', *The handbook of family-school intervention: a systems perspective*, eds M. Fine & C. Carlson, Allyn & Bacon, Boston

Kutsick, K.A., Gutkin, T.B. and Witt, J.C. 1991, 'The impact of treatment development process, intervention type, and problem severity on treatment acceptability as judged by classroom teachers', *Psychology in the Schools*, vol. 28, no. 4, pp. 325–31

Ladd, G.W. 1985, 'Documenting the effects of social skill training with children: process and outcome assessment' *Children's peer relations: issues in assessment and intervention*, eds B.H. Schneider, K.H. Rubin & J.E. Ledingham, Springer-Verlag, New York

Ladd, G.W. and Mize, J. 1983, 'Social skills training and assessment with children: a cognitive-social learning approach', *Social skills training for children and youth*, ed C.W. LeCroy, Haworth Press, New York

Lalli, J.S., Browder, D.M., Mace, F.C. and Brown, D.K. 1993, 'Teacher use of descriptive analysis data to implement interventions to decrease students' problem behaviors', *Journal of Applied Behavior Analysis*, vol. 26, no. 2, pp. 227–38

Lang, T. and Lang, M. 1986, *Corrupting the young and other stories of a family therapist*, Rene Gordon, North Balwyn, Victoria

LeCroy, C.W. 1983, 'Social skills training with adolescents: a review', *Social skills training for children and youth*, ed C.W. LeCroy, Haworth Press, New York

Lee, C. 1993, 'Cognitive theory and therapy: distinguishing psychology from ideology', *Australian Psychologist*, vol. 28, no. 3, pp. 156–60

Lewis, R. 1991, *The discipline dilemma*, ACER, Melbourne

Lindquist, B., Molnar, A. and Brauchmann, L. 1987, 'Working with school related problems without going to school: considerations for systemic practice', *Journal of Strategic and Systemic Therapies*, vol. 6, no. 4, pp. 44–50

Lochman, J.E., White, K.J. and Wayland, K.K. 1991, 'Cognitive-behavioral assessment and treatment with aggressive children', *Child and adolescent therapy: cognitive-behavioral procedures*, ed P. Kendall, Guilford, New York

Lovegrove, M.N., Lewis, R. and Burman, E. 1989, *You can't make me! Developing effective classroom discipline*, La Trobe University Press, Melbourne

Lusterman, D. 1985, 'An ecosystemic approach to family-school problems', *The American Journal of Family Therapy*, vol. 13, no. 1, pp. 22–30

Maag, J.W., Reid, R. and DiGangi, S.A. 1993, 'Differential effects of self-monitoring attention, accuracy and productivity', *Journal of Applied Behavior Analysis*, vol. 26, no. 3, pp. 329–44

Maag, J.W., Rutherford, R.B. and DiGangi, S.A. 1992, 'Effects of self-monitoring and contingent reinforcement on on-task behavior and academic productivity of learning-disabled students: a social validation study', *Psychology in the Schools*, vol. 29, no. 2, pp. 157–72

Mace, F.C. and Wacker, D.P. 1994, 'Toward greater integration of basic and applied behavioral research: an introduction', *Journal of Applied Behavior Analysis*, vol. 27, no. 4, pp. 569–74

MacMullin, C.E. 1988, Assessment of children's social skills: identifying social situations that are problematic for children at school, unpublished doctoral dissertation, University of Connecticut

MacMullin, C., Aistrope, D., Brown, J.L., Hannaford, D., and Martin, M. 1992, *The Sheidow Park social problem solving program*, Flinders University, Adelaide

MacMullin, C. and Napper, M. 1993, *Teachers and inclusion of students with disabilities: attitude, confidence or encouragement?*, paper presented to Australian Early Intervention Association (SA Chapter) Conference, Adelaide, June 1993

MacMullin, C. 1994, *Inclusion: an overview*, paper presented to Education Support Principals' Conference, Perth, March 1994

Maples, M. 1984, 'Self-concept, locus of control, and self-discipline: valuable constructs for effective classroom management', *Journal of Humanistic Education and Development*, vol. 23, no. 2, pp. 80–7

Martin, G. and Pear, J. 1992, *Behaviour modification: what it is and how to do it*, 4th edn, Prentice Hall, Englewood Cliffs, New Jersey

McCaslin, M. and Good, T.L. 1992, 'Compliant cognition: the misalliance of management and instructional goals in current school reform', *Educational Researcher*, vol. 21, no. 3, pp. 4–17

McGrath, H. and Francey, S. 1991, *Friendly kids; friendly classrooms*, Longman Cheshire, Melbourne

McLeod, W. 1989, 'Minor miracles or logical processes? Therapeutic interventions and techniques', *Journal of Family Therapy*, vol. 11, pp. 257–80

Meyers, A.W., Cohen, R. and Schleser, R. 1989, 'A cognitive-behavioral approach to education: adopting a broad-based perspective', *Cognitive-behavioral psychology in the schools*, eds J.N. Hughes & R.J. Hall, Guilford, New York

Miller, L.K. 1991, 'Avoiding the countercontrol of applied behavior analysis', *Journal of Applied Behavior Analysis*, vol. 24, no. 4, pp. 645–7

Mize, J. and Ladd, G.W. 1990, 'Toward the development of successful social skills training for preschool children', *Peer rejection in childhood*, eds S.R. Asher & J.D. Coie, Cambridge University Press, Cambridge

Molnar, A. 1986, 'A systemic perspective on solving problems in the school', *NASSP Bulletin*, vol. 70, no. 493, pp. 32–40

Molnar, A. and Lindquist, B. 1989, *Changing problem behaviour in schools*, Jossey-Bass, San Francisco

Murphy, J. 1992, 'Brief strategic family intervention for school-related problems', *Family Therapy Case Studies*, vol. 7, no. 1, pp. 59–71

Napier, R. and Gershenfeld, M. 1993, *Groups: Theory and experience*, 5th edn, Houghton & Mifflin, Boston

Neef, N.A., Mace, F.C. and Shade, D. 1993, 'Impulsivity in students with serious emotional disturbance: the interactive effects of reinforcer rate, delay, and quality', *Journal of Applied Behavior Analysis*, vol. 26, no. 1, pp. 37–52

Nicholson, S. 1989, 'Outcome evaluation of therapeutic effectiveness', *Australian and New Zealand Journal of Family Therapy*, vol. 10, no. 2, pp. 77–83

Oden, S. 1988, 'Alternative perspectives on children's peer relationships', integrative processes and socialization: early to middle childhood, eds T.D. Yawkey & J.E. Johnson, Lawrence Erlbaum Associates, Hillsdale, New Jersey

Olympia, D.E., Sheridan, S.M., Jenson, W.R., and Andrews, D. 1994, 'Using student-managed interventions to increase homework completion and accuracy', *Journal of Applied Behavior Analysis*, vol. 27, no. 1, pp. 85–99

Orlick, T. 1982, *The second cooperative sports and games book*, Pantheon, New York

Pepler, D., Craig, W., Ziegler, S. and Charach, A. 1993, 'A school-based anti-bullying intervention: preliminary evaluation', *Understanding and managing bullying*, ed D. Tattum, Heinemann Educational, Oxford

Perry, D. and Bussey, K. 1984, *Social development*, Prentice Hall, Englewood Cliffs, New Jersey

Perry, R. 1993, 'Empathy—still at the heart of therapy: the interplay of context and empathy', *Australian and New Zealand Journal of Family Therapy*, vol. 14, no. 2, pp. 63–74

Petersen, L. 1990, *Teaching your child social behaviour*, Peterson & Stop Think Do Pty Ltd, Aldgate, South Australia

Petersen, L. and Ganoni, A. 1989, *Teacher's manual for training social skills while managing student behaviour*, ACER, Melbourne

Peterson, G.W. and Leigh, G.K. 1990, 'The family and social competence in adolescence', *Developing social competency in adolescence*, eds T.P. Gullotta, G.R. Adams & R. Montemayor, Sage, Newbury Park, CA

Porteous, M.A. 1979, 'A survey of the problems of normal 15-year-olds', *Journal of Adolescence*, vol. 2, no. 4, pp. 307–323

Porter, L. 1996, *Children are people too*, 2nd edn, in press

Putallaz, M. and Wasserman, A. 1990, 'Children's entry behavior', *Peer rejection in childhood*, eds S.R. Asher & J.D. Coie, Cambridge University Press, Cambridge

Putnam, J.W. 1993, 'The process of cooperative learning,' *Cooperative learning and strategies for inclusion*, ed J.W. Putnam, Paul H. Brooks, Baltimore

Reder, P. 1983, 'Disorganised families and the helping professions: who's in charge of what?', *Journal of Family Therapy*, vol. 5, no. 1, pp. 23–6

Reid, R. and Harris, K.R. 1993, 'Self-monitoring of attention versus self-monitoring of performance: effects on attention and academic performance', *Exceptional Children*, vol. 60, no. 1, pp. 29–40

Rekers, G.A. 1984, 'Ethical issues in child behavioral assessment', *Child behavioral assessment*, eds T.H. Ollendick & M. Hersen, Pergamon, New York

Rigby, K. 1993, 'Countering bullying in schools', *CAFHS Forum*, vol. 1, no. 2, pp. 19–22

Rigby, K. and Slee, P. 1992, *Bullying in schools: a video with instructional manual*, Institute of Social Research, University of South Australia, Adelaide

——1993, 'Children's attitudes towards victims', *Understanding and managing bullying*, ed D. Tattum, Heinemann Educational, Oxford

Robinson, M. 1980, 'Systems theory for the beginning therapist', *Australian Journal of Family Therapy*, vol. 1, no. 4, pp. 183–94

Rogers, C.R. 1951, *Client-centred therapy*, Constable, London

——1978, *On personal power*, Constable, London

——1983, *Freedom to learn for the 80s*, Merrill, Columbus, Ohio

Rogers, W.A. 1989, *Making a discipline plan: developing classroom management skills*, Nelson, Melbourne

——1990, *'You know the fair rule'*, ACER, Melbourne

——1991, 'Decisive discipline', *Classroom discipline*, eds M.N. Lovegrove & R. Lewis, Longman Cheshire, Melbourne

——1994, *Behaviour recovery*, ACER, Melbourne

Roland, E. 1993, 'Bullying: a developing tradition of research and management', *Understanding and managing bullying*, ed D. Tattum, Heinemann Educational, Oxford

Rolider, A., Cummings, A. and Van Houten, R. 1991, 'Side effects of therapeutic punishment on academic performance and eye contact', *Journal of Applied Behavior Analysis*, vol. 24, no. 4, pp. 763–73

Rose, S.R. 1983, 'Promoting social competence in children: a classroom approach to social and cognitive skill training', *Social skills training for children and youth*, ed C.W. LeCroy, Haworth Press, New York

Rosenshine, B. and Stevens, R. 1986, 'Teaching functions', *Handbook of research on teaching*, 3rd edn, ed M.C. Wittrock, Macmillan, New York

Rubin, Z. 1980, *Children's friendships*, Harvard University Press, Massachusetts

Sapon-Shevin, M. 1986, 'Teaching cooperation', *Teaching social skills to children: innovative approaches*, 2nd edn, eds G. Cartledge & J.F. Milburn, Pergamon, New York

Sayger, T.V., Horne, A.M. and Glaser, B.A. 1993, 'Marital satisfaction and social learning family therapy for child conduct problems: generalisation of treatment effects', *Journal of Marital and Family Therapy*, vol. 19, no. 4, pp. 393–402

Schmuck, R.A. and Schmuck, P.A. 1988, *Group processes in the classroom*, 5th edn, William C. Brown, Iowa

Schneider, B.H. 1989, 'Between developmental wisdom and children's social skills training', *Social competence in developmental perspective*, eds B.H. Schneider, G. Attili, J. Nadel & R.P. Weissberg, Kluwer Academic Publishers, Dordrecht

Schunk, D.H. 1989, 'Social cognitive theory and self-regulated learning', *Self-regulated learning and academic achievement: theory, research, and practice*, eds B.J. Zimmerman & D.H. Schunk, Springer-Verlag, New York

Seligman, M. 1975, *Helplessness: on depression, development and death*, W.H. Freeman & Co, San Francisco

Seymour, F.W. and Epston, C. 1989, 'An approach to childhood stealing with evaluation of 45 cases', *Australian and New Zealand Journal of Family Therapy*, vol. 10, no. 3, pp. 137–43

Shapiro, E.S. 1984, 'Self-monitoring procedures', *Child behavioral assessment*, eds T.H. Ollendick & M. Hersen, Pergamon, New York

Sharp, S. and Cowie, H. 1994, 'Empowering pupils to take positive action against bullying', *School bullying: insights and perspectives*, eds P.K. Smith & S. Sharp, Routledge, London

Sharp, S. and Smith, P.K. eds, 1994, *Tackling bullying in your school: a practical handbook for teachers*, Routledge, London

Sharp, S. and Thompson, D. 1994, 'The role of whole-school policies in tackling bullying behaviour in schools', *School bullying: insights and perspectives*, eds P.K. Smith & S. Sharp, Routledge, London

Simpson, R.L. 1990, *Conferencing parents of exceptional children*, 2nd edn, Pro-Ed, Austin, Texas

Skinner, B.F. 1989, *Recent issues in the analysis of behavior*, Merrill, Columbus, Ohio

Slee, P.T. 1994a, 'Life at school used to be good: victimisation and health concerns of secondary school students', *Young Studies Australia*, Dec 1994, pp. 20–3

——1994b, 'Situational and interpersonal correlates of anxiety associated with peer victimisation', *Journal of Child Psychiatry and Human Development*, vol. 25, no. 2, pp. 97–107

——1995a, 'Peer victimisation and its relationship to depression among Australian primary school students', *Journal of Personality and Individual Differences*, vol. 18, no. 1, pp. 57–62

——1995b, 'Description of peer victimisation among junior primary students and of a primary school programme to reduce bullying', in press

Slee, P.T. and Rigby, K. 1994, 'Peer victimisation at school', *Australian Journal of Early Childhood*, vol. 19, no. 1, pp. 3–10

Smith, J., Osman, C. and Goding, M. 1990, 'Reclaiming the emotional aspects of the therapist-family system', *Australian and New Zealand Journal of Family Therapy*, vol. 11, no. 3, pp. 140–46

Smith, P.K., Cowie, H. and Sharp, S. 1994, 'Working directly with pupils involved in bullying situations', *School bullying: insights and perspectives*, eds P.K. Smith & S. Sharp, Routledge, London

Smith, P.K. and Sharp, S. 1994, 'The problem of school bullying', *School bullying: insights and perspectives*, eds P.K. Smith & S. Sharp, Routledge, London

Smyrnios, K.X. and Kirkby, R.J. 1989, 'A review of brief, child-oriented family therapy outcome research: descriptive reports and single group studies', *Australian and New Zealand Journal of Family Therapy*, vol. 10, no. 3, pp. 151–9

——1992, 'Brief family therapies: a comparison of theoretical and technical issues', *Australian and New Zealand Journal of Family Therapy*, vol. 13, no. 3, pp. 119–27

Smyrnios, K.X., Kirkby, R.J. and Smyrnios, S.M. 1988, 'Brief family therapy: a critique of Kinston and Bentovim', *Australian and New Zealand Journal of Family Therapy*, vol. 9, no. 3, pp. 139–42

Stark, K.D., Best, L.R. and Sellstrom, E.A. 1989, 'A cognitive-behavioral approach to the treatment of childhood depression', *Cognitive-behavioral psychology in the schools*, eds J.N. Hughes & R.J. Hall, Guilford, New York

Stark, K.D., Rouse, L.W. and Livingston, R. 1991, 'Treatment of depression during childhood and adolescence: cognitive-behavioral procedures for individual and family', *Child and adolescent therapy: Cognitive-behavioral procedures*, ed P. Kendall, Guilford, New York

Strohl, T. 1989, 'Symptoms: The price we pay to control', *Control theory in the practice of reality therapy*, ed N. Glasser, Harper & Row, New York

Swetnam, L., Peterson, C.R. and Clark, H.B. 1983, Social skills development in young children: preventive and therapeutic approaches, *Social skills training for children and youth*, ed C.W. LeCroy, Haworth Press, New York

Tattum, D. 1993a, 'What is bullying?', *Understanding and managing bullying*, ed D. Tattum, Heinemann Educational, Oxford

——1993b, 'Short, medium and long-term management strategies', *Understanding and managing bullying*, ed D. Tattum, Heinemann Educational, Oxford

——1993c, 'Child, school and family', *Understanding and managing bullying*, ed D. Tattum, Heinemann Educational, Oxford

Tauber, R. 1990, *Classroom management from A to Z*, Holt Rinehart and Winston, Texas

Thompson, C.L. and Rudolph, L.B. 1992, *Counselling children*, 3rd edn, Brooks/Cole, Pacific Grove, CA

Tollefson, N., Melvin, J. and Thippavajjala, C. 1990, 'Teachers' attributions for students' low achievement: a validation of Cooper and Good's attributional categories', *Psychology in the Schools*, vol. 27, no. 1, pp. 75–83

Topping, K. 1988, *The peer tutoring handbook: promoting co-operative learning*, Croom Helm, London

Towns, A. and Seymour, F. 1990, 'What about the family in family therapy research?', *Australian and New Zealand Journal of Family Therapy*, vol. 11, no. 4, pp. 222–8

Turnbull, A.P. and Turnbull, H.R. 1990, *Families, professionals and exceptionality: a special partnership*, 2nd edn, Merrill, Columbus, Ohio

Vollmer, T.R., Iwata, B.A., Zarcone, J.R., Smith, R.G. and Mazaleski, J.L. 1993, 'The role of attention in the treatment of attention-maintained self-injurious behavior: noncontingent reinforcement and differential reinforcement of other behaviour', *Journal of Applied Behavior Analysis*, vol. 26, no. 1, pp. 9–21

Walker, J.E. and Shea, T.M. 1995, *Behavior management: a practical approach for educators*, 6th edn, Prentice Hall, Englewood Cliffs, NJ

Watzlawick, P., Weakland, J. and Fisch, R. 1974, *Change: principles of problem formation and problem resolution*, W.W. Norton and Co, New York

Weissberg, R.P. 1989, 'Challenges inherent in translating theory and basic research into effective social competence promotion programs', *Social competence in developmental perspective*, eds B.H. Schneider, G. Attili, J. Nadel & R.P. Weissberg, Kluwer Academic Publishers, Dordrecht

Westwood, P. 1993, *Commonsense methods for children with special needs*, 2nd edn, Routledge, London

Wheldall, K. and Merrett, F. 1984, *Positive teaching: the behavioural approach*, Allen & Unwin, London

Whitman, T.L., Scherzinger, M.L., and Sommer, K.S. 1991, 'Cognitive instruction and mental retardation', *Child and adolescent therapy: cognitive-behavioral procedures*, ed P. Kendall, Guilford, New York

Whitney, I., Rivers, I, Smith, P.K. and Sharp, S. 1994, 'The Sheffield project: methodology and findings', *School bullying: insights and perspectives*, eds P.K. Smith & S. Sharp, Routledge, London

Whitney, I., Smith, P.K. and Thompson, D. 1994, 'Bullying and children with special educational needs', *School bullying: insights and perspectives*, eds P.K. Smith & S. Sharp, Routledge, London

Williams, B.F., Williams, R.L. and McLaughlin, T.F. 1989, 'The use of token economies with individuals who have developmental disabilities', *The treatment of severe behavior disorders: behavior analysis approaches*, ed E. Cipani, The American Association on Mental Retardation, Washington, DC

Wolery, M., Bailey, D.B., and Sugai, G.M. 1988, *Effective teaching: principles and procedures of applied behavior analysis with exceptional students*, Allyn & Bacon, Boston

Wragg, J. 1989, *Talk sense to yourself: a program for children and adolescents*, ACER, Melbourne

Young, M.E. 1992, *Counseling methods and techniques: an eclectic approach*, Merrill, New York

Zarcone, J.R., Iwata, B.A., Mazaleski, J.L. and Smith, R.G. 1994, 'Momentum and extinction effects on self-injurious escape behavior and noncompliance', *Journal of Applied Behavior Analysis*, vol. 27, no. 4, pp. 649–58

Zentall, S.S. 1989, 'Self-control training with hyperactive and impulsive children', *Cognitive-behavioral psychology in the schools*, eds J.N. Hughes & R.J. Hall, Guilford, New York

Zirpoli, T.J. and Melloy, K.J. 1993, *Behavior management: applications for teachers and parents*, Macmillan, New York

INDEX